XR
FORDS

IN · COLOUR

Escort · Fiesta · Sierra

EDITOR   *DENNIS FOY*

WINDROW & GREENE

Published in Great Britain by
Windrow & Greene Ltd
5 Gerrard Street
London W1V 7LJ

A C.I.P. catalogue record for this book
is available from the British Library.

ISBN 1 872004 33 4

When he isn't hurtling around the country in one
high-performance Ford or another, **Dennis Foy** sits
down at his desk and writes about the cars he has
driven. He has been doing this since the later part of
the seventies, which was when he managed to
convince an unsuspecting magazine editor or two that
he was capable of joined-up writing, as well as of
aiming a box brownie camera with a degree of
success.

His life prior to that initial period of freelance work is
something of a mystery, but when pressed he will
hark further back to his happy childhood as the
youngest son, and sixth of eight children, of his
parents in Warrington, Cheshire. When asked about
education he normally suggests that it is a good thing
and will own up to having had one in his home town.

He worked in London for some five years as Features
Editor of *Hot Car* magazine (a title which has since
disappeared, a phenomenon for which he will accept
no responsibility) and returned to his native county in
1982 to resume a freelance work ethic. In 1987, his
wife and he created *Performance Ford*, a monthly
magazine which covers everything connected with the
blue oval and which has gone on to become the
biggest one-marque title on the British market.

There have been five books prior to this one: *Escort
Performance; Automotive Glassfibre; Ford Escort — A
World Celebration; RS Fords In Colour;* and, in
collaboration with Terry West, *Classics In Colour:
Ford Sierra Cosworth*. He also harbours an ambition
to write a cookery book.

When not out and about, he lives as quietly as can be
expected in Cheshire (nearby where it meets the
Peak District) with his wife Pat and son Ben, along
with their collection of cats. He drives the family
XR4x4 as often as he can get his hands on it...

Additional design and production:
ghk DESIGN, Chiswick, London

Printed in Singapore

CONTENTS

Acknowledgements

This collection of features — all of which first appeared in the pages of Performance Ford — *didn't just happen. Their production involved a lot of teamwork. I would therefore like formally to thank my colleagues at* Performance Ford *for their ongoing help in ensuring that everything happens when it is supposed to!*

I would also like to thank the owners of various private examples of XR cars which appear in these pages, who have given their time to our staff, our contributors and myself to ensure that we managed to get both photographs and information just as we wanted.

Then there are the teams at Sarah Curl Phototypesetting and at Denton Repro, who have regularly gone beyond the line of duty in handling their specific roles within our monthly production schedules. Without their enthusiasm and unstinting help, life would be appreciably more difficult each month.

Finally, I would like to single out for their help and encouragement the two people who are closest to me: my son, Ben, and my wife, Pat. Ben shows incredible patience when I am working and tolerates being fed late because 'I'm just in the middle of doing something... Can you wait a few minutes until I'm finished'. Pat shows unbelievable patience too — she'll say that she needs to, living with me — but more importantly she is the reason why I am still able to enjoy doing the same job after so long. Without her love, encouragement and the many other things she gives to me, I wouldn't have been able to sustain such a working life.

Thanks, all of you.

Dennis Foy,   July 1992

INTRODUCTION

XR. I wish I had a pound for every time I have been asked
what those ubiquitous initials stand for. A look under 'X'
in the Oxford English Dictionary provides no suggestions at all; nor
are there any clues to be found in such places as Ford dealerships.
In fact, you have to ascend the ladder (or more accurately the lift) at
Ford of Europe's headquarters in Warley, Essex, to find the truthful
answer to that question.

And the truthful answer, of course, is that the letters actually mean
nothing at all: they simply have a rather nice ring to them.

The XR designation was originally found on a Ford product back in
1967, as a sporting tag to the American Cougar: that car was an XR-7

The first British XR Ford: the XR3 of 1981.

The XR2 of 1982 created a new niche market.

(note the hyphen) and was a derivative of the Mustang series of performance coupes. Then, as now, while the Mustang enjoyed a Ford badge, the Cougar was badged as a Mercury product.

Distinctly sporting in nature — at least by American standards — the XR-7 came with either 289ci (4.7-litre) or 390ci (6.4-litre) engines. There was also an XR-7G variant which made use of tuning ace Bob Gurney's name (if not his considerable tuning knowledge) to give enhanced appointments such as gold-plated trim features.

That the first XR was suffixed by the number 7 was a demonstration that strict chronological sequencing was not a Ford priority. As it happened, the debutante XR model in Britain was the XR3 of 1981. This was the first sporting variant of the recently-introduced MkIII Escort series — the first Escort to have a front-wheel-drive format, rather than the familiar front engine driving out through the rear wheels.

In XR3 form the 1600cc carburated Escort gained a power advantage of 17 horsepower over its less sporting stablemates, with a nett 96 brake horsepower. It came with a four-speed transaxle which shared its ratios with the rest of the 1.6-litre Escorts, but had the lower 3.84:1 final drive ratio of the 1300cc saloon — this was a move toward sharper acceleration and a bid to optimise the performance available from the engine. Offered only with the three-door bodyshell, the XR3 (which actually went into production late in 1980, at Ford's Halewood plant) had wide aluminium alloy wheels with low-profile tyres, and accordingly needed special 'spats' to ensure that they remained within the confines of the bodywork.

As well as those spats, there was a substantial spoiler attached to the bustleback of the rear hatch 'door' and a pair of over-riders on either end of the car; the front pair could, on payment of £78.90, be converted to house headlamp washer jets. As was so often the case with sporting Fords, there was a restricted colour range available — initially white, red, black or silver, but later blue as well — and there were also dedicated graphics on the rearmost edge of the tailgate. Inside, there was a pair of sports seats which offered an increased level of lateral support, and which also encroached upon rear seat space. Laterally-striped Laser trim was a feature of the car, as was also the use of high-grade instrumentation: this meant that the driver gained a tachometer and a 140mph speedometer. The final touch was a smaller, thicker-rimmed two-spoke steering wheel than that found on the rest of the Escort range.

Once launched, the XR3 was immediately perceived by some sections of the motoring press as the destined replacement for the RS2000 — a car which had ceased production a year and a half before. Such a comparison was a shade unfair — the XR3 was giving away 14 horsepower, for a start — but the car met with a reasonably warm response, anyway. Its road grip was much-praised, as was its overall driveability. Matters improved still further when the five-speed gearbox was introduced in February 1982; and got better still in September that year with the addition of a little 'i' to the car's nameplate.

The suffix indicated that the car had gained electronic fuel injection, and in the process put on a further nine brake horsepower, raising the stakes to 105bhp, with 101lb/ft of torque. As well as the Bosch K-Jetronic injection system (which gave improved driveability — the additional power came from detail changes to the engine specification, including revised camshaft and exhaust system), the XR3i also gained revised rear suspension geometry and a plusher level of trim. Although much of the interior detailing was as the previous carburated model, there was a new three-spoke steering wheel.

Whereas the original XR3 had been a mainstream development car, the ultimate mechanical specification of the XR3i had been entrusted to the fledgling Special Vehicle Engineering division This huge R & D facility was based at Dunton, just far enough away from Southend-on-Sea for comfort. Headed by Rod Mansfield and staffed by some of Ford's best engineers, SVE was a forty-strong team of serious car nuts, and their enthusiasm showed in the new car. It was lively, sharp, quick, and altogether just about as good as it was possible to be, given the development restraints under which the team was working. Once again the car received a favourable reception, going on to achieve a 14 percent slice of the Escort's substantial British market share.

Injection and five speeds came with the XR3i.

SVE was also responsible for the second Ford of Europe car to bear the XR legend: the XR2.

Born out of a desire by the resident hooligans at Ford Motorsport to see what would happen when the 1600cc Federal (American-market) block was tuned and then shoehorned into an unsuspecting Fiesta 1300S bodyshell, the entire XR2 programme was blessed almost from the beginning by a high level of committment from the Top Floor at Warley. The specific office which was offering such encouragement was that of Sam Toy, possibly the last of the great car-orientated directors of Ford in Britain. In time to come, Sam would send away the chauffeur-driven Granada which came with his job as God, FoB, and instead drive himself to work in an XR2.

As with so many other Ford sporting saloon programmes, there was a healthy amount of bin-raiding involved in the XR2 programme: the engine came from the American Fiesta range, the tuning equipment was straight from earlier Escort GT models, the suspension was simply upgraded Fiesta S hardware, and so on and so forth. Yet, once again, Ford had found themselves a winner.

Of course, the market position of the XR2 had already been established — the Supersport version of the 1300S (which amounted to nothing more than a cosmetic package on the existing model) had blazed the trail. Pre-launch examples of the XR2 were selectively released to members of the press; the writer tried one at the time, when working on the now-defunct magazine, *Hot Car*, and was seduced, as everyone else was, by its blend of cheekiness and performance. Just as the XR3 had done with the Escort, the XR2 was soon enjoying a good-sized slice of the lucrative Fiesta market.

Capri meets Sierra — the XR4i of 1983.

Then came the XR4i. This was intended to be quite a different package from that of the earlier XRs, in that it was a long-legged cross-country machine rather than an around-town 'hot hatch'. In effect, the XR4i was the mechanical package of the 2.8i Capri slotted into a specially-modified variant of the Sierra bodyshell, and it gave the best of both: it had a smooth and torquey V8 engine of 2800cc, but with a suspension layout several generations on from the fairly agricultural underpinnings of the Capri. Unfortunately it never caught on quite as rapidly as was anticipated, and in sales terms was the least successful of the XR models sold in Europe.

The XR4ti was an American-market variation on the theme, built in Germany by Wilhelm Karmann. It used the engine and transmission of the underwhelmingly-successful Mustang Turbo (hence the 't' in XR4ti) in the six-lite XR4i body, again with Sierra suspension and brakes. This again was only moderate successful, but those who bought the car considered themselves elite and there is still a considerable following for the model in the USA.

It was 1986 when the next major development on the XR front appeared, this being the arrival of the facelifted (or so it first appeared) version of the XR2. In truth, there was appreciably more to the new Fiesta than met the eye, with a redesigned nose section — more curvaceous, in keeping with corporate styling dictums — concealing a new engine. Or at least a new engine as far as the XR2 was concerned: in reality it was the old 96bhp warhorse which had been found in the XR3 of 1980! This was teamed with the five-speed transmission of the XR3i and ran a final drive ratio of 3.58:1 — changed later (in July 1986) to 3.82:1. The suspension layout was essentially unaltered, although there had been some fine-tuning to compensate for the different engine weight, and there was some work done to try and improve high-speed braking action.

Inside, there was a new fascia (in common with the rest of the Fiesta range) and there were fresh trim fabrics. None of these various changes blunted the character of the car, and it maintained its high level of popularity throughout its lifetime.

The next generation moved further still from what was perceived as the concept of the XR range (to wit, inexpensive, fun, high-performance cars based on more mundane stablemates) and led to the car which is the writer's personal favourite Ford — the XR4x4.

Mention was made earlier of Sam Toy, and another Ford man who fell into much the same category as Sam was the American, Bob Lutz. It was Lutz (now at Chrysler USA, but then effectively running Ford of Europe) who was the catalyst for the XR4x4, but it was once again early experiments at Motorsport which were called upon for inspiration. Throughout the sixties and seventies, there had been a number of flirtations with the concept of four-wheel drive, most notably the Capris which had been used in rallycross by such drivers as Roger Clark and Rod Chapman. An out and out car-crazy character, Bob Lutz wanted desperately to match the technical prowess of Audi, who in 1981 had proven the concept by dominating the international rallying scene with their awesome quattro.

Four-wheel drive for the masses — the XR4x4.

As Ford already had the hardware — at least in prototype form, thanks to input by the likes of Ferguson Engineering — then it was inevitable that Bob would fire up the enthusiasm of the team at SVE. He wanted — and got — a running showcar with permanent four-wheel drive in time for the 1982 Frankfurt Show. As it happened the car never appeared, but not because it wasn't ready; instead, it was because the concept had moved from being a statement of what Ford could do — which is what the showcar would have been — to a full-blown, serious production model.

Working closely with Ferguson, and also with mainstream engineers at Dunton's sister facility in Merkenich, Germany, the SVE team beavered away on the XR4x4, despite the fact that Bob Lutz had already moved on to greener pastures with his old boss, Lee Iacocca. The completed car made its bow at the Geneva Salon in March 1985 and went on sale a short time afterwards. The driveline differed from that of the Audi in several vital respects, most notably that the V6, 2.8-litre engine was mounted inline (rather than transverse) with 63 percent of the power reaching the road via the rear wheels; on the Audi, power was split 50/50 front to rear. A five-speed transmission was standard, as were limited-slip viscous couplings in the central differential and the final rear final drive cluster. There was never a need to have a limited-slip facility on the front wheels.

The final generation of Erike XR3i, 1989.

Although the car cost some 12 percent more than the XR4i which it succeeded into the showrooms, and despite the general motoring public being unaware of the benefits of four-wheel drive in road cars (until the 1980s, 4x4 vehicles were almost invariably off-road, Land Rover-type devices), the XR4x4 picked up nicely where the XR4i left off: the vast majority of those who have ever driven four-wheel-drive Sierras never want to return to two-wheel-drive cars. In common with the writer's own experience, they become used to the security, poise and balance which sets a 4x4 Sierra apart from the rest of the herd, especially when surfaces are loose or slippery.

Eighteen months after the XR4x4 first appeared the next generation of XR3i was put on show and, as with the Fiesta before it, seemed to be nothing more than a cosmetic exercise. However, this was not the case. For a start there was a revised engine which made use of the lean burn technology favoured by Ford's Director of Engineering, Clive Ennos, as a means of improving exhaust emissions. Although power was not increased, there was a marked improvement in economy. Then there was the SCS anti-lock braking system, which was an optional extra...

Developed in conjunction with Lucas-Girling, the SCS (Stop Control System) was an inexpensive mechanical means of avoiding brake lock-up and its adoption by Ford for the Escort range was a minor revolution: previously, anti-lock braking had been very much a big-car feature. To go along with the mechanical and panelwork changes was a revised interior, and such detail touches as a pair of electrically-adjusted mirrors, and the availability of electrically-heated windscreen and mirror lenses.

The XR3i was steadily refined over the next four years, gaining a fresh management system for its engine, among other details. The XR4x4 also gained from a reworking in 1989, the engine growing from 2.8 to 2.9 litres and the interior trim of the Ghia Sierra being used — although the excellent sports seats were retained.

1989, with snow still on the ground, saw the next major revision to the hot Fiesta, with the arrival of the XR2i. Once again, this was an example of Ford's often-underestimated ability to raid the parts bins and come up with an impressive package. By using the latest version of the CVH engine with a fresh fuel injection system (which was carried over to the XR3i at much the same time), Ford endowed their three-door variant of Fiesta with a large and substantial heart — 110bhp in a package weighing comfortably less than a tonne was not to be sneered at — and matched it to a lively SVE-developed chassis.

Aborted attempt to retrieve XR4i, 1990.

Interior appointments were very much more sporting than those in the rest of the Fiesta range and, as with the XR3i, there was the option of SCS braking insurance, by now into a second and more responsive generation. Despite a gap of some months between the laying to rest of the old XR2 and the arrival of the injected MkIII car, the newcomer immediately carried on where the old one had left off and continued to sell well.

There was an ill-conceived (rare for Ford) attempt to revitalise the XR4i badge in early 1990, by appending it to a reworked five-door DOHC two-litre-powered rear-drive saloon, which had in turn derived from the 2.0iGLS. Available only with a bright blue stripe around its tum, and featuring the sports suspension of the GLS augmented by a rear anti-roll bar, the car was over-expensive and failed to sell. It was withdrawn in 1991 and, because of its low production total, will perhaps become a collector's item.

Simultaneously with the re-introduction of the XR4i, a two-litre XR4x4 was made available. It used the same two-litre twin-cam eight-valve engine as the 4i, with an identical 125bhp power output. This has persevered and is likely to remain in production until the entire Sierra range is replaced by CDW27 in April 1993. Despite its continued appearance within the range, the car lacks the awesome torque and thus the driveability of the V6 version. Had Ford been able to fit the sixteen-valve head from the RS2000 to either of these two-litre XR4s, one would probably have felt appreciably more enthusiastic about them.

The latest chapters of the XR story have only just been written. It was spring 1992 when the new Escort XR3i finally appeared, some eighteen months later than the rest of the redesigned Escort range. For the first time in the 12-year history of the XR Escorts there was a choice of engine sizes, the standard 130bhp sixteen-valve twin-camshaft unit being joined by a similar capacity, detuned 105 horsepower unit. The explanation given was that this was an attempt to find a way around the excessive insurance premiums the XR models have attracted during the late '80s and early '90s, though whether the insurance companies will deem it sufficient reason to reduce their charges for providing adequate cover remains to be seen...

The XR2i also gained the same engine within a matter of months — although only the 105bhp version; the Fiesta with the 130 horse unit became known as the RS1800, which puts it into a different branch of the family! In 105 Zeta form, the XR2i is a lively and thoroughly enjoyable little performer — the engine is what the car ought to have had from new. Let down only by horrendous insurance premiums and over-heavy steering at parking speeds (due to be cured by the adoption of power steering early in 1993), the XR2i-16v continues the tradition set by the very first XR Fiesta, of being affordable, fun, and giving the impression of being furiously fast even if the hard figures show that the car is not the rocket it appears to be!

So what of the missing numbers? Two, three, four and seven are already accounted for — and there are plenty of features in this book which cover them — but are there any other numbers not yet mentioned?

In a word, yes.

XR1 has never been used by Ford, and neither has XR5. But XR6 and XR8 are both in circulation — in both cases on Ford South Africa-built cars. XR6 was a three-litre V6-powered Cortina MkV which was simply a high-torque cross-country machine with a suspension system beefed up to deal with the poorly surfaced roads of its homeland, and the XR8 was a similar package produced to supplant it in 1983. This latter car came with a five-litre American-built Cleveland V8 engine beneath the bonnet of a Sierra five-door. Perhaps indicating a more logical approach than their European counterparts, the staff at FSA were able to take the name-tags of these two models from the number of cylinders in their respective engines.

New Fiesta of 1990 in XR2i form.

XR8 also appeared in Australia, but this time as an appendage to the Falcon S. Known as Ford Falcon S XR8, the car arrived with a five-litre V8 beneath its bonnet, a lump of Detroit muscle able to deliver 225 brake horsepower (with a stomping 290lb/ft of torque) which was delivered to the ground via a five-speed Borg Warner gearbox and limited slip differential. Uprated suspension and disc brakes on each corner ensured that the 1991-debuted car was able to corner and stop as effectively as it went, thus making the XR8 variant of the Falcon a true contender in the muscle-saloon stakes. Unlike the European-market XR models, it was also possible to specify automatic transmission on the Australian car, this being electronically controlled and featuring a sports/economy switching facility to suit driving whims.

Nobody at Ford of Europe has satisfactorily explained why they used the numbers they did for Escort, Fiesta and Sierra. But, whatever the case, the fact remains that the 'XR' tag has been a highly successful marketing tool for the Ford Motor Company — and, as far as anyone can foresee, it will remain so for some time to come.

EXTRA XR

THE COMBINATION OF THE XR2
AND A TURBO TECHNICS
TURBOCHARGER
SYSTEM MAKES
FOR AN
EXCITING CAR
AS
DENNIS FOY
HAS BEEN
FINDING
OUT

EXTRA XR

horsepower CVH engine of its superceded stablemate, the XR3.

The small hatchback sector of the market is fiercely contested, and at the cutting edge are such cars as the Peugeot 205, the Renault Five, the Metro, and the Nova. All of these cars offered high-performance derivatives, and for a while at least, the XR2 was able to hold its own against them. However, during the past couple of years there have been more and more radical "hot" models appearing in this class of car, not just from those makers already mentioned but also from the land of the rising sun. The result is that the XR2 is now often out-classed; on sheer standing-start acceleration, there is only the MG Metro Turbo which can be beaten by the XR2.

Ford's chassis engineers have done an excellent job of continuing development on the XR's suspension system, and the car is subsequently still able to out-handle many of its quicker and more powerful rivals. Where the car is letting itself down is in its relative lack of horsepower — and the blame for that lies squarely on the shoulders of the Marketing Department at Ford of Britain, who are unable to cope with the concept of the XR2 being able to out-perform, and more specifically out-run, its equivalent models from further up the model range scale. If the XR2 was to become the XR2i (a perfectly feasible

proposition, in fact several such development models are known to have been built) then it would blow away the XR3i, leaving that car struggling in the wake of the smaller model) — and that would never do. So, until such time as the XR3i receives the boost in power that it desperately lacks at present, the XR2 will be unable to progress further. This situation is further deadlocked by the fact that the Fiesta's replacement is in the advanced stages of readiness — and Research and Development resources are naturally being concentrated there, rather than on the existing range, which is fast approaching retirement age.

Enter Turbo Technics.

This company is well-known for its range of well-designed and executed turbocharger conversions of many makes of car, and Ford cars in particular. Turbo Technics already enjoyed a good working relationship with Ford of Britain, having joined forces with the manufacturer to produce the Capri 2.8 Turbo. What is more, Turbo Technics have been turbocharging XR3 Escorts since the early part of 1982, and their knowledge of forced induction on this engine is virtually unrivalled. It was therefore a totally logical development for the two companies to put their respective heads together and see what could be done about the XR2. The result is a turbocharged version of the car which endows it with enough power to once again meet the competition head-on — but without Ford having to have diverted the resources of their Research and Development Department. In simple terms, Geoff Kershaw and the team at TT have developed the installation, and Ford will market the cards. That way, everybody wins, including the customer who now has the option of a worthwhile

For all its contemporary looks, the XR2 is relatively old-fashioned in design terms; the first car to bear the tag appeared on our roads in the summer of 1981, but it was based upon a model range which had been initiated a decade earlier, and had already been on sale for some six years. Performance of those early XR2s was quite acceptable, if not exactly earth-shattering, the original 84 bhp crossflow engine being adequate to propel the car to a little over a hundred miles per hour, having passed the 60 m.p.h. benchmark at something like 9½ seconds after starting a full-power run. These figures improved a little in 1983 when, as part of the mid-life facelift to which the entire Fiesta range was treated, the XR2 was given the carburated 96

MEETING THE OPPOSITION

Acceleration 0-60

FORD FIESTA XR2 TURBO 7.8 secs	
FORD FIESTA XR2 9.3 secs	
PEUGEOT 205 GTi 1.9 7.8 secs	
RENAULT 5 TURBO 7.9 secs	

Maximum speeds

FORD FIESTA XR2 TURBO 122 m.p.h.	
FORD FIESTA XR2 110 m.p.h.	
PEUGEOT 205 GTi 1.9 127 m.p.h.	
RENAULT 5 TURBO 128 m.p.h.	

Prices

FORD FIESTA XR2 TURBO £8,583	
FORD FIESTA XR2 £7,208	
PEUGEOT 205 GTi 1.9 £9,285	
RENAULT 5 TURBO £7,990	

alternative to the 205 GTi, the Renault 5 Turbo, et al.

The heart of the conversion is the latest generation of Garrett AiResearch turbocharger, the T25. This is water cooled, and runs from a purpose-designed cast manifold made from high nickel content iron. Air is drawn into the inlet tract of the turbocharger via a foam air filter, and passes through an air-to-air intercooler on its way from the turbo to the carburettor. The standard XR2 carburettor is retained, although a number of modifications have to be made to ensure its compatibility and efficiency within the revised induction system. A high-pressure electrical fuel pump with pressure regulator is added to the fuel feed system, and the ignition timing is re mapped to suit the requirements of the turbocharger. New spark plugs are specified for the engine, and finally, the standard front suspension bushes are upgraded. In all other respects the car is standard — which says a lot for the quality of chassis engineering that has gone into the car in the first place.

There is often something of a gap between principle and practice on cars which have been turbocharged, brought about by the "on/off switch" characteristics of certain aftermarket conversions; what happens is that there is little power developed below, say, 3000 r.p.m., and then the turbo starts to develop positive boost and suddenly there is a massive amount of muscle kicking through the driveline. Such cars are only fun to drive on open, sweeping-curve roads or on motorways, and in town traffic conditions can vary from the uncomfortable to the downright dangerous. Yet read the specifications on these conversions and could be forgiven for believing that you are learning about

"If the theory of this car is smooth, surging power, then the practice is also smooth, surging power."

cars which offer smooth, surging power at all engine speeds. I am pleased to report that this car very definitely does not fall into that category; if the theory of this car is smooth, surging power, then the practice is also smooth, surging power.

Talking recently to Geoff Kershaw about this car (some two or three weeks before I had the opportunity to drive it, due to certain over-zealous colleagues from other magazines having done damage to the

transmission in the pursuit of bettering seven seconds for the 0-60 time during the SMMT Test Days at Donington) he recounted a conversation with a Ford Main Dealer principal who had come down to try out the car. He had driven down to Northampton in a Granada Scorpio 4×4, and had test-driven the XR2 Turbo soon after arriving. Discussing the car with Geoff, the dealer reported that "It didn't feel any different to an ordinary car. There's nothing much to choose from between it and the Scorpio...". As the Granada's 2.9 V6 delivers torque by the bucketful throughout its revolution range, that is some eulogy.

Having since driven the car, I can only agree with the dealer; Had I not already been aware of what lay beneath the Fiesta's diminutive bonnet, I could have been easily convinced that there was a two-litre twin-cam sitting in the engine bay. Easing out the clutch and feeding in the throttle, the car accelerates smoothly right through to its 6000 r.p.m. redline with a total absence of sudden "power punch" as the engine makes the transition from vacuum to positive boost. Yet for all of that tractability, the car is no slouch — in fact, it is downright fast, with a time for the sprint to sixty of less than eight seconds — one and a half seconds faster than the standard XR2, and a full second faster than the RS Turbo Escort. Holding the power in will eventually see

the speedo needle pointing to a spot just past the 120 m.p.h. marker, again not a bad achievement for a little 1600.

During our week with the car, it was driven in just about every type of situation imaginable, from runs through the countryside along deserted open roads through to London's Park Lane in the rush hour, taking in a half-dozen motorways en route, and at no time did the car give any cause for alarm — it simple did as requested, as efficiently as a standard XR2 would have done under the same circumstances. The main difference was that where a standard XR would start to sound a little strained, and subsequently run out of steam, the turbocharged version didn't — it simply kept delivering more and more power, right through to its 125 brake horsepower peak.

On bendy roads, the XR2's most comfortable habitat, the turbo version of the car displayed no unfortunate tendencies, the extra power on hand serving to make a good car even more fun to drive. The XR2 is a notoriously difficult car to unstick from bends (its wheels and tyres continue to grip long after many drivers would have decided that the car is being pushed quite hard enough already, thank you...) and the additional power does not appear to upset this balance; to lose this car would call for some suitably ▷

EXTRA XR

the perfect machine for wreaking sweet revenge on the more agressive of London and Manchester's Black Cab drivers.

Yet for all of my obvious enthusiasm for the car, I must express a couple of reservations. The first and foremost of these is that this is an extremely powerful car (its power-to-weight ratio puts it on a par with cars such as the Audi Quattro, BMW 325i and Lotus Excel) and is thus to be treated with the respect it deserves. For that reason, it really only ought to be entrusted to drivers capable of handling it;

foolish exploit, such as going into a bend far too quickly (which would lead to terminal understeer) or lifting off the power suddenly in mid-bend at high speed, which would lead immediately to the back end of the car overtaking the front. In either case it would be a case of driver error, rather than any fault within the chassis design of the car.

On motorways, the car is stable even in quite high crosswinds, and the turbocharger supplies adequate bursts of power to deal with overtaking situations without having to shift down a gear. In traffic, the combination of punchy acceleration and compact dimensions make the car virtually unbeatable; I found myself aiming the little machine through ever-decreasing gaps in the traffic. This is

"The additional power does not appear to upset the balance of the car."

someone getting behind the wheel of this car who is not used to cars of this calibre could so easily be fooled into thinking that they are not progressing as quickly as they actually are — and by the time that they realise they have overstepped the mark, it is too late to do anything about it. The car is deceptively quick, especially in the middle of its stride (the 50-70 time for the standard XR2 is in the region of 9 seconds — a time which the turbo version halves) and an inexperienced driver could

very easily come to grief. I would most strongly recommend that anybody intending to make the transition from ordinary XR2 to one of these Turbo specials takes one of the better high performance driving courses.

The other reservation is that this car does not come available with any form of anti-lock braking system. Turbo Technics are entirely blameless in this respect, as the Fiesta is the one car on Ford's fleet which doesn't have such a fitment available (Perhaps they intend to fit the Stop Control System to the next generation of Fiesta?) but all the same, I would feel happier driving the car quickly if I knew that the chances of locking up the brakes were minimised. As it is, the standard brakes of the XR2 are perfectly adequate for the Turbo version, and pull the car up to a halt quickly and efficiently, even in the wet.

However, having got those reservations out of the way, we are left with a stunningly effective little car, one which suits ideally British roads and driving conditions — and one which can achieve what it has set out to do, which is to once again give a hard time to the equivalent products from rival manufacturers such as Peugeot and Renault. The car is as easy to drive slowly as any standard Fiesta, and can produce a very rapid turn of speed whenever called upon to do so. Perhaps the greatest praise that I can heap upon the car is that it doesn't feel like a conversion; it feels like a more powerful version of the XR2, one that has been developed from scratch to achieve the required performance levels by installing a larger, high-output engine.

To obtain an XR2 Turbo calls for nothing more than a visit to your local Ford dealership, who will be happy to oblige you — in return for the premium of £1,375 plus VAT over the basic cost of the XR2, which is £7,208. And in case it has been bothering you, the conversion does not

"Perhaps the greatest praise that I can heap upon the car is that it does not feel like a conversion."

affect the warranty of the car: Ford will only baulk at a claim which can be directly attributed to the turbocharger installation, and such contingencies are catered for by the provision of an additional Car Care Plan scheme, which is included in the purchase price of the conversion.

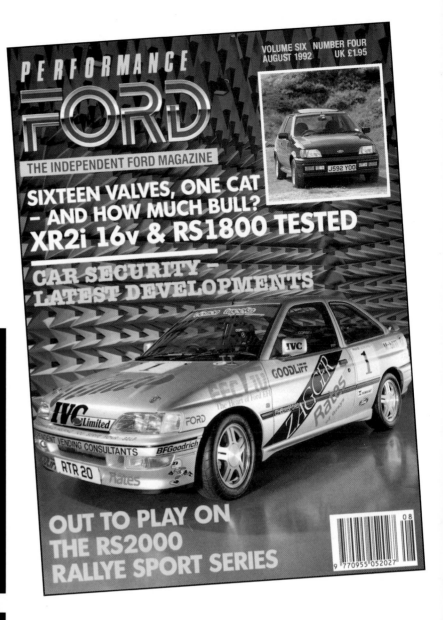

RED ROCKET

A 300 B.H.P. XR4i
BY IAN KUAH

When the XR4i was introduced in 1983, its radical aerodynamic aids drew comments from everybody who saw the car; people either loved it or hated it. The first Sierra to use the 2.8i Cologne V6 engine, the car was the subject of much speculation — mostly centred around the car being a replacement for the Capri. However, the two cars were very different concepts, the Capri a 2+2 coupé and the XR4i a high-performance tourer with plenty of space for four or five people, plus useable luggage space. If you like, the relationship between these two cars can most easily be likened to that of the Porsche 911 and 928.

The XR4i was short-lived (the last car being sold in 1985), as Ford re-defined the high performance saloon to mean the XR4x4, a car which arguably comes much closer to being all things to all men. In its short life, however, the XR4i developed a strong following, and most present owners (many of whom have bought their XRs secondhand) have very definite views on how the car should have appeared when it originally came from the factory. One particular illustration of this is the way in which very few examples have not been subsequently colour-coded, to eliminate ▷

IAN KUAH

RED ROCKET

◁ the somewhat tacky appearance of the grey plastic lower panelwork.

One such owner is Robin Bullock, who acquired the ex-demonstrator car that is the subject of this feature when it had 8,700 miles registered on its odometer. Being a dyed-in-the-wool enthusiast, Robin had been studying various illustrations of the XR4i that had appeared in magazine articles, and had been particularly taken with the all-white Janspeed turbocharged car that had been given much editorial exposure. Starting with the visual appearance of his red car, Robin had a front spoiler fitted, and the bottom half of the car colour-coded to match the rest of the car. A set of alloy wheels with BFGoodrich Comp T/A tyres were also added.

The car was turbocharged by Turbo Torque using a Janspeed system, and a Sachs heavy-duty clutch was added to help the drivetrain cope with the 210 b.h.p. that the car was now developing. Before too long the gearbox's layshaft did its party trick of stripping its teeth. Rather than simply swapping it for a new one under warranty, Robin had Rovercraft modify the box by installing stronger bearings and layshaft.

The blower was installed at 19,500 miles, and the engine performed well until 47,000 miles. At that point, however, various engine oil leaks suggested that it was time to carry out some serious work on the engine, and so Swaymar Engineering stripped and blueprinted the engine, before rebuilding it in their usual meticulous manner. 4,000 miles later, a larger Rotomaster T04 turbocharger was installed in place of the original item.

The Karl Schmidt pistons began to give problems, when ring wear allowed excessive bore wash — the result of which was oil finding its way into the intercooler. Obtaining new rings for these 0.030" overbore items was difficult, and after several involved telephone conversations to Germany, the decision was made to forget about that make, and to instead fit Mahle pistons with an overbore of 0.040". Putting the car on the dyno showed a power reading of 220 b.h.p. — which equates to some 300 b.h.p. at the flywheel. At the same time the car was fitted with a Sachs Sporting suspension kit, which consists of a complete set of matched springs and uprated dampers which lower the ride height of the car by an inch, and offer vastly-improved control without destroying the ride quality. To the casual observer, the bonnet louvres and grille moulding may smack of the owner having jumped onto the "Cosworth imitation" bandwagon. However, such addenda are an essential part of dealing with a large turbocharger.

When the turbo installation was being

"The rush of power is progressive and smooth, and astonishing progress can be made."

revised, the extra fuel injector from the original turbo installation was removed, and a boost-sensitive warm-up regulator fitted in its place. This has improved driveability, and led to more power lower down in the rev range. This is due to the fuel being regulated at each individual injector, rather than outside the plenum. As soon as the turbo starts to produce positive boost, the warm-up regulator supplies fuel to the injectors. Two switches are mounted to the side of the plenum, which control the ignition retardation and overboost controls. Finally, the camshaft used in this installation is a Holbay Tornado VT240, designed to give maximum torque at

3500 r.p.m., with strong power starting to develop at 2000 r.p.m.

The characteristics of the camshaft and the way in which Gary at Turbo Torque has calibrated the engine means that on the road the car does not feel like it has 300 b.h.p., that only becomes apparent when the speedometer is read. That there is a strong push in the back when the car comes "on cam" is beyond dispute, but the rush of power is progressive and smooth. Astonishing progress can be achieved without undue drama, and planned modulation of the "loud" pedal can blast the driver down A and B roads very quickly, safe overtaking being a particular strength of the turbocharged 2.8i engine.

Effective slowing and stopping power is taken care of by a set of Tar-Ox slotted and ventilated discs, fitted by Turbo Torque. These have substantially improved pedal feel and bite from the pads is similarly improved.

If the engine, suspension and brakes on Robin's XR4i are impressive, then the steering, unfortunately, is not. The geometry of the system had been set up by somebody who had best remain nameless, and in the opinion of this tester had been given far too much castor action, which resulted in a massive area devoid of feel about the straight-ahead position, with a lack of reaction to initial turn-in input. If anything, the car gave the driver the opinion that it had let go in terminal understeer. By the time that you read this, the car will have been to the premises of Beatrix Racing in Brighton, who will have reset the steering geometry properly. As Beatrix have campaigned Capri race cars for several seasons (this year, they are preparing the Honda for Smith Brothers of Hampshire, but we will have to forgive them that ...), they are eminently qualified to sort out the XR4i's steering gear. ●

The man behind Turbo Torque, Gary Passingham, has the youthful good looks of the boy next door who went off in those dreadful Cliff Richard films of the early '60s, and became a pop star. However, the tunes that Gary plays are on a Clayton rolling road, a machine which is the lynchpin of his tuning business in Burgess Hill.

Experience with tuning came as a result of an early interest in this field, but this was strengthened when he went to work for a garage with a rolling road facility. His interest in turbocharging was sparked by a request from a customer one day to turbocharge an otherwise-standard Renault 5, and the spark was fanned into a flame by his boss purchasing an Escort RS1600i which was pronounced to be underpowered — and turbocharging was seen as the logical solution. Initially an Allard system was fitted to the car, but this proved problematic despite the 130 b.h.p. that the car was producing at the front wheels. The car was eventually taken over to Janspeed, who took one look at it and decided that starting again from scratch would be the only sensible solution. It was suggested that Gary become seriously involved at this stage, and so he spent time at Janspeed learning the ropes. The upshot was the formation of Turbo Torque, with the RS1600i gracing Janspeed's stand at the Motor Show.

The bulk of Turbo Torque's work is rolling road tuning of road cars, along with the major servicing which often accompanies such a tune-up. Increases in power output beyond the normal levels can be undertaken by either conventional methods or by turbocharging — the latter being carried out under the banner of an official Janspeed distributor. For customers who wish to progress beyond the "bolt on" stage, specialised engine machining and blueprinting is carried out in-house by Peter Frazier.

Beyond engine tuning, the company extend their service to include suspension and brake systems. This allows the company to offer a comprehensive service to their customers. By keeping the show small and personal, Turbo Torque have established a high level of customer loyalty, and they feel able to offer an extra edge to the finishing of customers' cars that may be missing from the service of some competitors with a higher turnover. "It would be nice to expand and take on some more bookings," says Gary, looking at a schedule showing three weeks' advance bookings, "but we feel that technical developments are more important right now than expansion, so the expansion will have to wait." ●

OPEN SEASON

NEW CAR TEST: FORD ESCORT XR3i CABRIOLET

BY DENNIS FOY

February, with its lashing rain, howling, galeforce winds and temperatures hovering at about five degrees Centigrade, is hardly the ideal time of year to be able to make the most of Ford's only true convertible, the Escort XR3i Cabriolet. But on the other hand, the conditions were perfect for us to be able to evaluate the real practicality of the car.

This was not the first Cabriolet that we have ever tested; we had one for a week about nine months ago, when the weather was sufficiently dry and bright for us to be able to spend most of our time with the car in its open state. However, with that first example, our enthusiasms were quite literally dampened when the skies clouded over and began to issue bucketsful of late-spring rain. The roof proved itself to be poorly sealed against the elements, and within a matter of minutes a neatly-synchronised

DENNIS FOY

pair of drips had started to the right and left thighs of the driver and front passenger respectively.

Fortunately, the latest version of the car proved itself to be perfectly sealed against the elements, all occupants remaining dry and comfortable even in the wildest and most foul of weather conditions.

The Cabriolet is a handsome machine from all angles. Built by Karmann in West Germany alongside its only real rival the Golf CTi, the Cabriolet starts life as a two-door Escort Estate bodyshell. The roof is removed and the windscreen header rail rebuilt, a pair of massive longitudinal strengthener beams are added inboard of each sill, and the bulkhead is strategically stiffened and strengthened. An anti-roll bar is installed level

with the trailing edge of the door shuts, and new panels are added which endow the car with its distinctive rear hip kick-ups.

The hood is a superb piece of Germanic fabrication. Double-skinned, it displays none of its framework as everything is concealed within the slim, padded fabric of the hood. New for 1988 is power operation (a £500 option), which enables the entire assembly to be raised or lowered at the touch of a button mounted to the centre console adjacent to the gearshift. A heavy-duty servo motor is mounted neatly within the capacious boot, and this is both quick and quiet in operation. To avoid any problems with wind resistance damaging the hood assembly during the raising or lowering process, it is impossible to carry out the operation with the engine running; the ignition key has to be turned back one click from the "live" position before the motor can be used. To lower the roof it is necessary to unclip it from the windscreen header rail, by depressing a lock-out trigger and then pulling down the grab-handle on each side of the hood's frontal extremity.

The button is then depressed, and held until the entire roof has folded down astern of the rear seats. The whole operation takes approximately fifteen seconds. Once folded, a stud-fastening cover clips neatly into place over the hood, which serves to tidy everything up nicely. Closing the hood again is a simple reversal of the process, and the time involved is about the same.

In all mechanical respects, the Cabriolet is identical to the XR3i hardtop. Power comes from the tried-and-tested 1600cc fuel injected engine, and this endows the car with 105 b.h.p.; enough to see the benchmark 0-60 spring taken care of in less than ten seconds, and adequate to give the car a maximum speed of almost 115 m.p.h. Backing up the engine is a five-speed transaxle with both fourth and fifth gears over-driven, and the final drive ratio is the same 4.27:1 which is unique to the XR3i range.

The Cabriolet shares the sports suspension system of the XR3i, which differs from that of lesser Escorts by the provision of a greater diameter (24mm) anti-roll bar and suitably revised dampers and spring rates. Rather surprisingly, whereas the XR3i has the excellent Stop Control System of anti-lock brakes as standard unless specified otherwise, the open version of the car does not; they are still listed as an extra-cost option. The system was fitted to our test car, and we would strongly recommend its installation on any model of new Escort; the asking price of £354 is a small amount to pay for the great degree of safety and reassurance that this particular option brings with it.

The trim specification of the Cabriolet is only reasonable. It is furnished in the standard XR3i Daytona fabric trim, with co-ordinating deep-pile carpeting. Central locking, as well as tinted glass, a high-specification stereo, and remote control door mirrors are all standard features. There is the overhead clock (which has recently lost the calendar/stop watch facilities which featured on earlier examples of the Mk IV Escort) and a sports steering wheel which serves to set the car apart from lesser variants of Escort. ▷

"The engine delivers its power freely — though the noise levels at high engine speeds can become unacceptable."

OPEN SEASON

into the top 1000 r.p.m. band of the engine's rev range pays a penalty in the form of barely acceptable noise levels; the din can become quite unbearable if sustained for any longer than a couple of seconds. Clutch action is light and precise, and the gearbox too is clean in its shifting action — a marked improvement on earlier examples of the Mk IV Escort, and proof that Ford do make continual alterations to their specification without letting on to anybody but their dealership service personnel. According to a contact of ours who heads the service department at a major dealership, Ford have altered both the gear linkage and the clutch cable pedal cam recently. It shows.

◁ Out on the road, the Cabriolet proved itself fun to drive. Our impressions of the first Cabriolet that we tested highlighted something of a problem with "scuttle shake", a phenomenon which led to the impression that the two ends of the car were acting quite independently of each other. Ford do not admit to having made any major modifications to the car, but the particular example shown on these pages felt far more of one piece than the earlier car, with far less twisting and shaking evident when running hard through a series of bends.

The engine delivers its power willingly, and revs freely to its 6250 redline — although the driver making regular incursions

Interior of basic XR3i Cabriolet is reasonable, but fuel computer, ECU stereo, etc. are options at extra cost.▼

PRICE GUIDES

Basic Price	£10,983.03
Stop Control System	£354.15
Power Operated Hood	£500.00
Electric Mirrors	£75.48
Fuel Computer	£127.06
ECU2 Sound System	£166.29
Heated Windscreen	£108.89
Black Paint	£114.18
Alloy Wheels	£250.57
Power Windows	£228.40

The relationship between the two remaining pedals leaves a little to be desired when running fast, and wishing to make "heel and toe" changes, as the relative heights of the brake pedal and throttle pedal are some two inches apart, which makes such a change difficult. The Escort's real Achilles' heel, though, is its steering. This is quite heavy at parking speeds, and has, by modern standards, a quite appalling turning circle; a Granada has greater manoeuvrability at low speeds than an Escort!

In fairness to the makers, the XR3i Cabriolet is more than competent on winding roads, and the feedback from the steering when making rapid progress is very good indeed. This is an easy car to drive quickly, with no hidden treachery emerging from its suspension system. If driven with a light touch and a degree of mechanical sympathy, the car rewards with a safe and predictable, but never boring, set of road manners.

Likewise, the Cabriolet proved itself a comfortable machine for eating up the miles on a motorway run. Our first full weekend with the car saw us heading south from Cheshire to Plymouth, with weather conditions varying from dry and sunny to lashing rain driven by 50 m.p.h. winds. At no point during our four hour journey did the car feel anything other than stable and foursquare on the road, and it proved itself unaffected by even quite stiff crosswinds. If anything, the car is actually better than the hardtop model of XR3i when encountering such weather conditions.

PERFORMANCE

0-60	9.6 seconds
30-50 in Fourth	7.7 seconds
¼ Mile	17.6 seconds @ 77 m.p.h.
Maximum Speed	115 m.p.h.

It is also a surprisingly economical device. On a motorway run, it averaged almost 34 m.p.g., and our average for the entire 2,250 miles which we covered in the car was 30.9 miles to each gallon of four star. To put this into perspective, our own Mk IV Escort 1600 Ghia averages 30.5 m.p.g., and on a motorway run will turn in about 33 miles to the gallon.

The double-skinned, insulated hood of the Cabriolet acquitted itself very well indeed, with no apparent drumming even at speeds close to three figures. With the roof up and the windows closed, the occupants would be hard-pressed to distinguish between this and a car with a fixed roof. A substantial aid to the civility of the car is the rear screen, which is glass and which contains a heater element. This is a vast improvement on the traditional approach with a convertible of installing a perspex rear light, and Ford and Karmann have proven that a glass window can successfully be installed in a folding roof without penalties. The only price that has to be paid is that the car does not have the usual integrated radio aerial within the screen heater element; this has been impossible, because the rear screen is folded away below the line of the bodywork when the car is in its open mode, and this would neatly cancel any chances of the antenna picking up radio signals. On the Cabriolet, therefore, there is a separate electrically-operated aerial mounted on the rear wing of the car.

In the course of our two weeks living with the Cabriolet, the weather was nice enough on a couple of occasions to lower the roof, and catch a few rays of sunshine. With the heater turned up full and the windows left in their raised positions, the car remained quite snug and warm, even for rear-seat passengers. When the weather suddenly turned, we were able to return to closed-top motoring before the first drops of rain fell, without leaving the car; rear seat occupant Ben unclipped the roof cover, and I pressed the button and fastened the front clips. Neatness itself.

You will therefore gather that the Cabriolet has proven itself a versatile and practical car. It seats four in comfort and five at a bit of a squeeze, and has enough load-carrying capacity to deal with most needs; the boot will carry a couple of large suitcases and a variety of smaller bags, and there is adequate stowage within the car for odds and sods. There is a lock on the glove compartment (although for some reason, presumably that of cost, it has a pre-Chubb lock), and there is even provision for storing a handful of cassette tapes.

Being a press demonstrator, our particular car was loaded with all of the options, such as anti-lock braking, a fuel computer, and a heated front screen. Were I to buy a new Cabriolet I would specify all of these options, as all proved themselves useful or

worthwhile in one way or another. They do, however, all add to the cost of the car, and increase it from its base price of £10,983 to more than £12,300. Add another £250 for a set of alloy wheels and it becomes one very expensive motor car — a total bill of about £13,000 on the road is the harsh reality of it all. Fortunately, the car does seem to hold its price well, and

Motive power comes from tried-and-tested 105 b.h.p. version of CVH engine.▼

depreciation is slow. The cars are also rare — accounting for about 2½% of all new Escort sales in Britain — and so this could be a decisive factor in ordering one. Finally, the Escort Cabriolet is still substantially cheaper than a similarly-equipped example of its only real competitor, the Golf CTi from Volkswagen. As the old saying goes: "You pays your money and you takes your choice ..."   ●

SPECIFICATIONS
FORD ESCORT XR3i CABRIOLET

ENGINE TYPE	Transverse four cylinder SOHC	WEIGHT	2125 lbs
BORE x STROKE	80mm x 79mm	POWER/WEIGHT RATIO	109 b.h.p./ton
SIZE	1597cc	WHEELBASE	94.5"
BHP @ RPM	105 @ 6000	LENGTH	158"
TORQUE LB/FT @ RPM	102 @ 4800	WIDTH	72"
FUEL SYSTEM	Bosch K-Jetronic electronic injection	HEIGHT	55"
DRIVEN WHEELS	Front	TEST MILEAGE	2,254 miles
TRANSMISSION	5-speed manual	MANUFACTURER'S MPG	27.7
SUSPENSION: FRONT	MacPherson struts, anti-roll bar	TEST MPG	30.9
REAR	Independent, transverse arms, coil springs, separate dampers	PRICE AS TESTED	£12,680
		INSURANCE GROUP	5
BRAKING SYSTEM	Front discs, rear drums, servo assisted. Optional Stop Control System anti-lock mechanism		

MANUFACTURER: Ford Motor Company, Dagenham, Essex, England.

THE POWER & THE GLORY

ON TEST: POWER ENGINEERING'S SPRINTEX-SUPERCHARGED XR4x4

DENNIS FOY

The first time that I drove Ford's Sierra XR4x4, I realised that I was in a car which had tremendous reserves of handling and roadholding, a car which was capable of dealing with much more power than the 150 b.h.p. being developed by the Cologne V6 engine. Subsequent experiences, both with this car and with Ford's other four-wheel-drive machine, the Granada 4x4, have reinforced that original opinion, almost to the point of frustration. Whenever the car has felt less-than-precise it has

been because there has not been enough muscle to haul it onto a tighter line through the curves. If that extra power was available, I knew instinctively that the car would be able to corner at substantially higher speeds.

A flirtation with a turbocharged XR4x4 showed that form of tuning to be only a partial "cure" for the "problem", due to the characteristics of an engine thus-equipped; the turbocharger

starts to deliver its goods from perhaps 3000 or 3500 r.p.m., and with certain installations, there is a very pronounced crossover point, from low to very high power output. If this transition occurs midway through a bend, the sudden surge of extra power can upset the chassis, creating a twitchiness which I find unnerving.

Where turbocharged cars have proven particularly difficult to drive is in two areas — tight bends and long sweeping curves. On tight bends, there is a danger of the "lag" between punching the throttle and the turbocharger actually starting to work causing a momentary delay in the feed of power; instead of being able to feed the power in once the exit of the bend is in sight, the real power doesn't make it through to the road for a second or two — and that can mean the difference between a progressive and smooth exit from a bend, and a departure which turns into a scrap between driver and wheel to avoid piling the car.

On long sweeping curves (motorway slip roads are the prime example), it can be necessary to maintain a constant feed of steady power to balance the car on its line, with no acceleration or deceleration until the end of the curve is again in sight. If this happens to mean that the car is running at the crossover point between normal aspiration and turbo boost, the slightest addition of pressure on the throttle pedal can be enough to produce a substantial chunk of extra power which again can upset the balance of the car.

I am not for a moment suggesting that all turbocharged engines display such tendencies — I have driven several turbo-equipped cars lately which have been smooth and progressive throughout their rev ranges, thanks to the careful matching of components and electronic management systems; the Turbo Technics Fiesta and the Cosworth RS500 typify the breed.

Even conventional tuning methods may not be the answer to such power shortages as the four-wheel-drive Fords suffer. To gain horsepower normally involves the installation of a camshaft which enables the engine to develop its power quite high up its speed range, and this again can lead to a sudden surge in the middle of the acceleration process. What the XR4x4 and Granada need are not engines which produce masses of horsepower in the higher reaches of the speed range, but engines capable of delivering a solid wave of real, useable torque from right down at low revs — and to keep delivering that torque right up to the red line.

A couple of months ago, we tried out a Sprintex supercharged Capri V6, and were amazed by the engine's ability to produce something like double the normal amount of torque at

2000 r.p.m., and to keep on producing it right through to 6000 r.p.m. Then Power Engineering showed us their next project, an XR4x4 which was being given the same engine treatment. This, thought I, could be the answer: the very engine for which the chassis was crying out.

On the Capri, the supercharger unit was situated in the top of the vee, but such an installation on the Sierra would have called for a power bulge in the bonnet which would have been unsightly. Because of the nature of the system the actual location of the compressor is not crucial, and so Power Engineering have mounted it to the offside of the block. Drive comes straight to it from the crankshaft via a specially-developed grooved belt which operates more quietly than the more normal toothed item. An adjuster mounted on the front flange of the compressor carrier ensures that tension on the belt is maintained.

Air is drawn into the rear of the Sprintex compressor, and out into the intake plenum via specially-manufactured castings. The electronic fuel injection and ignition system's management chips are re-mapped to ensure that they match the revised needs of the engine. As part of the installation programme, Power carry out an inspection of the customer's engine (advising of any problem areas before carrying out necessary remedial work) and ▷

THE POWER & THE GLORY

The supercharger, a Sprintex 1024, sits neatly on the engine's nearside. All pipework is cast alloy, plastic coated for durability. ▼

◁ then carry out a full service of the engine to ensure that all is well. Once the installation is completed, the car is thoroughly road-tested and safety-checked before being handed over.

In addition to the engine conversion, Power Engineering are also able to offer a range of other services as part of the plan. These include a complete uprating of the brake system (new, anti-fade friction materials, braided steel flexible hoses to remove all tendency to expansion, and the substitution of Extreme High Temperature brake fluid), two standards of suspension conversions, a free-flow exhaust system, a full body styling conversion, a complete electronic alarm system, and a set of burr walnut interior cappings, along with a leather trimmed steering wheel. Naturally, the customer can specify as much or as little as desired in each area. A full price list is available from Power Engineering, which sets out in detail the various options and their costs.

The demonstrator that Power Engineering have produced is, for my tastes, a superb balance. It looks dramatic, thanks to the KAT Designs body kit which comprises a set of side mouldings, new front and rear combined bumper and valance panels, a new grille panel, rear spoiler arrangement, and strategic colour coding. The foot-high SPRINTEX lettering down each side in silver is a shade over the top, but these are very definitely there purely because it is Power's own demo car, and not a part of the regular package.

The car sits lower than a standard XR4x4, due to Power Engineering's uprated system, which replaces the standard springs with a lowered and stiffer set. The anti-roll bar bushes are replaced with stiffer items, but the standard-specification damper units are retained. Should the customer prefer, the ride height of the car can be left standard, with uprated springs, or the entire suspension system can be overhauled by installing the stiffer springs, a set of fully-adjustable damper units which are substantially uprated from the standard, and the stiffer bushings. Again, the ride height can be either standard or lowered.

Inside the car, the already-substantial interior has been subtly added to by the inclusion of a set of burr walnut cappings to each door, to the fascia insert, to the console switch panel, and to the rear ashtrays. An American walnut gear knob and leather rimmed Personal steering wheel complete the interior package.

But so much for the way in which the car appears. What really matters with a device such as this is exactly how it performs; when stationary it is a piece of sculpture, and only becomes a car when in motion. And what motion it goes into! What matters with this car is not so much the amount of power that it delivers, but the way in which it delivers it. Yes, the figures are impressive; 240 brake horsepower at 5250 r.p.m. is not to be sneezed at. But the main thing is that the car has an amount of torque that is nothing short of stunning; at 2500 r.p.m. it is pumping out 180 lb/ft, and by 3000 r.p.m. that figure has risen to almost 300 lb/ft. To put this into perspective, a standard 2.8i engine has 133 lb/ft and 144 lb/ft at the same engine speeds.

This amount of pure, instantly accessible muscle is enough to punch the car from standstill to sixty in a mere 6½ seconds without really trying :– a few tenths could actually be shaved from that figure, but there is no point in punishing the driveline for the sake of such an academic gain. The point of this engine is that rolling acceleration is equally quick; 30 to 50 m.p.h. in 6.7 seconds, 50 to 70 in 6.1 seconds, 70 to 90 in 6.7 seconds, and 90 to 110 in 6.4 seconds. And those figures were all taken in **fifth** gear! In fourth gear the car manages 30 to 50 in 4.5 seconds (against 7.5 for the standard car) and the same sprint in second gear can be accomplished in less than 3 seconds.

SPECIFICATIONS
SPRINTEX SUPERCHARGED XR4x4

ENGINE TYPE	Pushrod V6	BRAKING SYSTEM	Front discs, rear drums, anti-fade friction materials, electronic anti-lock braking
BORE x STROKE	93mm x 68.5mm		
SIZE	2792cc		
BHP @ RPM	240 @ 5250	WEIGHT	2800 lbs
TORQUE LB/FT @ RPM	2951 @ 3000	POWER/WEIGHT RATIO	192 b.h.p./ton
FUEL SYSTEM	Bosch K-Jetronic electronic injection Sprintex S1024 Supercharger	WHEELBASE	102.7"
		LENGTH	175"
DRIVEN WHEELS	All	HEIGHT	52"
TRANSMISSION	5 speed manual, viscous coupled final drive, split torque 34% front, 66% rear	WIDTH	67"
		TEST MILEAGE	See text
		MANUFACTURER'S MPG	See text
SUSPENSION: FRONT	McPherson struts, stiffened and lowered springs, gas-filled dampers, anti-roll bar	PRICE AS TESTED	See separate panel
		INSURANCE	Special quotation
SUSPENSION: REAR	Semi-trailing arms, stiffened and lowered springs, gas-filled dampers		

MANUFACTURER: Power Engineering, Unit 9, Wyvern Way, Uxbridge, Middlesex UB8 2XN.

Given an open road the car will achieve about 145 m.p.h., and this means that cruising along the motorway at the legal limit is an easy and effortless process. Should it ever prove necessary to overtake other vehicles, a quick burst of speed is on hand,

without recourse to changing down. If the driver was to drop down from fifth to fourth, a burst from 70 to 80 m.p.h. would take a mere 2½ seconds.

There is much more to this car, though, than an almost unmatched ability on the motorway. Show this machine a bend, and it rockets effortlessly through it, encouraging an even faster run at the next curve. My intuitions about the chassis being able to handle, and being improved by, more power, were substantiated the moment I pushed the car into the first of a series of tight twists in Derbyshire's Peak District; such is the power available that a depression of the throttle was adequate to tighten the car nicely on its line. At the same point the standard car would be running out of steam, and starting towards understeer. It is a simple process to run this car very quickly indeed, without every deviating from the correct side of the road. The lowered and stiffened springs certainly contribute to the driveability and control of the car, but the major advantage comes from beneath that bright red bonnet.

In fact, I would go so far as to say that the car could even be driven badly without it being a danger to other road users, as there is sufficient power on tap to compensate for the driver who has entered a bend in too high a gear; there is adequate muscle available to ensure an ample feed of balancing torque through into the chassis. And because there is no sudden input of extra power in the mid-range, the car's attitude always remains as poised and well balanced as the driver would like it to be, regardless of engine speed.

As much of the car is standard, there are no penalties paid by the driver in the form of excessively-heavy controls. The clutch and throttle are perfectly balanced against each other in weights and responsiveness, and the gearshift is as clean as any Ford five-speed box will ever be. The steering is immediate and precise on bends, and again perfectly weighted. The uprated brake system improves pedal feel without increasing the pressures needed to operate them, and proved to endow the car with precise feedback from the hubs. This car has Ford's excellent ABS system and this proved useful when braking hard on loose surfaces, and would also be a most worthwhile back-up in wet, icy or snowy weather. As an aside, I would state that I question the intelligence of anybody who purchases a new XR4x4, intending to have it Sprintex supercharged by Power Engineering, without they specify ABS on their initial order for the car from their dealership.

What Power Engineering have accomplished with this car is to make a good machine great, by equipping the chassis with the engine it deserved in the first place.

Every aspect of the car is right, from its effortless ability on the motorway to its bend-eating blasts through winding country roads. The standard XR4x4 pales into insignificance when put alongside, being exposed for the underpowered machine that it is, and the turbocharged car that I tried now appears positively crude by comparison.

What is more, those usual two bugbears of economy and reliability seem to be non-existent with the Sprintex-equipped car. Power Engineering have painstakingly logged every mile that the car has covered since it was completed, and the worst figure that it has achieved was with yours truly behind the wheel, when it returned 22.3 m.p.g. Prior to this the car has averaged closer to 25 m.p.g., and on a series of high-speed motorway runs gives closer to 30 m.p.g. The official Ford figures for their Simulated Urban Driving consumption test is 18.5 m.p.g. With a turbocharged 2.8i Capri that I tested recently, I managed a best tankful average of 19 to the gallon.

Regarding the reliability, there are a number of factors which ought to reassure. Should the belt drive ever fail (and that is a rare occurence in its own right), the car will remain driveable, albeit much down on power. Power have stripped and checked their various development engines regularly, and have found that there is no perceptible additional wear brought about by the Sprintex supercharger. The wide torque spread means that there are no sudden shock-loads to the transmission. And finally, the supercharger itself is engineered to outlast most cars.

The XR4x4 is, in its own right, a sensible package for the enthusiast driver, combining comfort and superb handling in an attractive, low-profile package. All that was hitherto missing was the extra power to enable it to perform as well as Ford's chassis engineers have intended. Were I to order a new XR4x4, there is no way that I could live with the machine until it had been treated to a Sprintex supercharger at Power Engineering. But until that time comes along, I'll have to content myself with the memory of a very fast run, a totally exhilarating run, along the Cat and Fiddle pass in Derbyshire. It will be a long time before such a rewarding car comes along again, I'm sure. ●

PRICES
SPRINTEX SUPERCHARGED XR4x4

In addition to the basic price of the car
the prices for the conversion options are:-

Engine conversion	£2,975
Supplement for A/C cars	£75
Uprated brakes	£175
Uprated suspension	£275 to £475
Freeflow exhaust	£278
Body styling kit	£1,087
Leather steering wheel	£85
Electronic alarm system	£441
Burr walnut interior trim	£300

All prices plus V.A.T.

FURIOUS FIESTA

Ian Kuah track-testing a rather special Fiesta

IAN KUAH

You've heard it all before, racing improves the breed and other such adages. In truth, many improvements in durability and design of components evolve through the hard battles fought on circuits and forest stages, but there are times when members of the public want to see competition cars that more closely resemble the cars that they themselves own.

More than that, even production saloon car racing has become very seriously embroiled in the world of big bucks sponsorship, and with the tab to run a potentially winning production saloon Cosworth Sierra for a season running well into the six figures league, a series like the Shell Oils Super Road Saloon Championship, where cars are allowed only basic modifications, is most welcome.

It was into this series that Gordon Luxford, owner of a firm specialising in heavy road haulage in the Horsham area, decided to pit his family shopping car, a late 1985 Fiesta XR2. "This was my first racing car and my first go at racing," said Gordon, "and as I did not want to get involved with the big spenders at what must be regarded as a trial stage of the game, the Shell Oils Super Road Saloons Championship seemed a good starting point." Underlining the roadgoing side of the series, all cars must be driven to and from the circuit and have valid current road fund licence, MoT and insurance to be eligible, and must be totally road legal. Naturally, a roll cage and a racing harness are necessary, and you can have a racing seat for the driver, but the rest of the interior trim must remain standard.

On the mechanical side, carburettors, cylinder head and exhaust are free to be modified and you can change the tyre type, but not size. Suspension springs and dampers are also free, but must remain of the same configuration as the car's standard equipment.

Thus, Gordon's XR2 sits on lowered, uprated coil springs, Leda 20-point adjustable struts and Yokohama A001 185/60HR13 tyres on stock XR2 alloys. The cars takes on a wider and more aggressive appearance in this form, and looks instantly different when you see it in your mirror on the road. Living seven miles from Gordon, I have seen it more than once on the A24 Horsham bypass and can attest to the fact that the little car looks menacing as it closes in from behind.

Although the actual building of the engine was done by Gordon and a friend, both self-taught engineers, the bottom end of the CVH engine was lightened and balanced by Chris Tyrell Racing of Leatherhead, and the full race cylinder head was done by Dave Martin of Swaymar Engineering, also in Leatherhead.

Swaymar's experience of the CVH engine goes back to 1983. They now offer two stages of head work for this engine. The "fast road" version has polished and reshaped chambers, reshaped valves which are set up via a shaping stone to get the right stem and head profile. The rally head, which is used on Gordon's car, has more radical chamber work, with a high-flow area in the chambers. The porting is taken out reasonably larger than standard and while the valves diameters remain standard, their shape is altered dramatically with the stems necked down to the point where they may look fragile but are actually still very strong. Valve springs are full race items. The intake manifold for the twin downdraught Weber 44DCNF carbs needed quite a lot of work to match the cylinder head ports. As a Janspeed exhaust system and manifold was being used, the exhaust ports were machined out to match this. The compression ratio was raised very slightly, Mahle pistons were used internally, and a Kent CVH 25 Full Race camshaft was the final touch.

Even for a road-going series, you are perhaps looking at £10,000 to £15,000 to run a car properly for a season, and so sponsorship is always welcome. Gordon has been lucky enough to gain sponsorship from J.K. Leech Fuels of Coolham, West Sussex, who distribute and supply all sorts of fuel oils and lubricants in the area. They follow the car's progress at race meetings (as well as putting up the money) and are very enthusiastic, especially as Gordon is doing well. In 1986, he did four rounds of the series for experience, never having raced before, and had a best fourth place. Those rounds were really used to set the car up properly and also get used to the techniques and close tussle of serious competition.

1987 found Gordon contesting seven out of the eleven races in the series, the loss of the other three being due to two engine blow-ups and a crash. Four second places, two wins and a fourth (ending as a tenth after time penalties for a rolling start) resulted in Gordon finishing third overall in the 1987 Championship.

Right now, Gordon would like to contest the 1988 Ford Credit Fiesta Challenge, and is actively seeking further sponsorship for this exciting series. In the meantime, the current car is being

"Once the oil had warmed through, it was time for a few fast laps."

offered for sale at £8,500, and Gordon will also build racing Fiestas for other people.

Performance Ford recently booked a session at Goodwood to try the racing XR2 in its element. With a dreary summer leading into a very wet and foggy autumn, we were lucky to get a sunny and dry day to exploit the XR2's potential. With my "bone-dome" in place, I strapped myself into the little silver racer and fired up. The Janspeed exhaust boomed much louder than a standard system but the well-tuned engine that had just been rolling road tuned at Hailsham, showing 116 b.h.p. at the front wheels, was as sharp as a new pin.

Exiting the pits and changing up at 4000 r.p.m. until the engine oil warmed through, I did a couple of slow laps to get used to the car. Goodwood is a bumpy circuit, and first impressions were of a ride stiffness unknown to Fiesta drivers. ▷

▲ The engine of the Fiesta features a Swaymar head, twin downdraught Webers, Janspeed exhaust – and puts out 145 b.h.p.

FURIOUS FIESTA

▲Owner Gordon Luxford with his Leech Fuels-sponsored Fiesta XR2.

◁Jonathan Palmer once said: "If you're not hard on the throttle or hard on the brakes, then you're wasting time." With such a sharp throttle response and this clear an exhaust note, it is easy to tell whether or note you are going around a circuit quickly in this car. Once the oil had warmed through, it was time for a few fast laps.

Down the pit straight, and towards Madewick — a bumpy, off-cambered right-hand sweeper with a double apex. Move over to the left two feet from the grass, and get the ideal line for the bend, having braked in a straight line. Turning in towards the first apex, and letting the car's understeering characteristic carry it wide is the way to go, feeding in the power progressively as we sweep past the second apex. The exhaust note is crisp and strident, with the engine on full song. With the throttle buried into the floor we approach Fordwater, a right kink which is taken flat out. Once again, the car's momentum is allowed to drift it out towards the left of the track on exiting the kink. Aproaching the next bend we turn in early, and let the car adopt a controlled four-wheel drift, again picking up the ideal line for the curve.

So it goes around the track: picking the line, braking with the wheels facing straight ahead, and letting the understeer drift us out of the bends. The brakes, with their Tar-Ox discs and Mintex M171 competition pads at the front and original drums at the rear, hold up well, and show no tendency to fade even after several hard and fast laps.

The only aspect of the car which disappoints is the five-speed gearbox. The engine pulls very nicely up to 6500 r.p.m., and it feels that there is more to come from it; a later conversation with owner Gordon establishes that when racing, he runs it to 7000 r.p.m. Yet such is the "hole" between third and fourth that an upshift gives the impression of the engine "falling off the cam" — which accounts for a top speed along the straight which could be equalled by a Golf GTi. A closer-ratio box would make all the difference to the driveability of the car on the circuit. The situation is saved somewhat by the engine, which revs sweetly right through to its redline — a characteristic that the standard CVH engine is not exactly known for.

The handling of the car is totally different from that of a standard XR2. Whereas a production XR2 is rather nervous — and on occasion twitchy — on a circuit, this particular car feels stable and relatively neutral. It portrays none of the untidy understeer and dramatic oversteer of the showroom car, being easy to place and hold under power, without any scrabbling in the lower gears.

For a team which has not been in the game long, Gordon and his crew have built up a very credible and user-friendly car which has proven itself as a potential race-winner. With a close-ratio box, it ought to have no problems winning next year's championship. ●

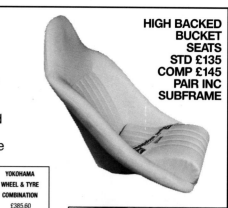

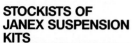

THE DEFINITIVE XR3i

Power Engineering have installed their new System Two Litre engine into an XR3i, making it into the car which Ford ought to be building — but aren't. Dennis Foy has been testing it.

This is the XR3i which Ford ought to be building. It is no fire-breathing monster which calls for a driver with nerves of steel and the strength of a Russian shot-putter to control it, yet it is easily capable of out-running most other "hot hatch" cars. The car will soar with the eagles for as long as circumstances will allow, yet is equally content to handle the stop-start-stop driving routine which typifies city driving in Britain.

The mercury grey XR3i is the handiwork of Power Engineering of Uxbridge, a company already familiar to many **Performance Ford** readers because of their highly-successful supercharger conversions on the XR4x4. Being specialists in forced induction, Power's initial thoughts were to consider supercharging the

DENNIS FOY

Escort, but cost factors made this an impractical solution to the problem of inadequate performance from the 1600 injection engine; the Sprintex blower which forms the basis of the XR4x4 conversion is a very expensive piece of precision hardware, and the amounts of money involved would be unacceptable on a car costing ten thousand pounds or less. Back to the drawing board.

Power's desire was to produce a high torque engine for the XR3i, and they felt that the key to success would lie in increasing the capacity of the CVH engine, ideally by using a crankshaft which would give a deeper piston travel. Their gambit was to try out a kit being marketed by a Dutch company which took the engine out to 1851cc, and gave a power output in the region of 120 to 125 b.h.p. We sampled this car earlier in the year (a report

appeared in our August 1988 issue), and were very impressed by the power gains, but had some reservations concerning the increased engine noise levels.

We attributed the extra noise to the excessive bore clearances required by the unbraced aluminium pistons used in the Dutch kit, and were quite correct in our assumptions: the expansion rate of the pistons meant that cold clearances of four thousandths of an inch were required, a figure substantially in excess of what is normally considered acceptable. The noise was being caused by the pistons slapping against their respective bores when not heated through, and a strip-down of the engine after it had covered a couple of thousand miles showed that wear points were already in evidence on the sides of all four pistons.

Power Engineering then entered into another phase of development. Their resident engine-building ace, Ian Swinyard, started by looking at the dimensions of every piston available on the market, but found that none gave the required combination of dimension and compression ratios. At the same time, he experimented with a number of Escort 1.6 cylinder blocks, in an attempt to discover the safe limit of overboring of the cylinders. This research proved two things: the first was that no suitable piston was generally available, and the second was that 1600 CVH cylinder blocks are inconsistent in their cylinder wall thickness. To overcome these hitches, Ian Swinyard commissioned sets of pistons which are to Power's own design, made from forged aluminium and with integral steel bracing to minimise expansion. He also decided that all blocks would have to be fitted with cylinder liners. By combining these new moves ▶

THE DEFINITIVE XR3i

◄ The car is fitted with an uprated suspension system to complement the two-litre engine. Roadholding and stability are much improved

with a long-throw crankshaft, Ian has been able to take the displacement of the block out to two litres, and is able to build in a clearance of only one thousandth of an inch on the piston-bore clearance — a better figure even than Ford's own, and a vast improvement on that specified for the Dutch kit.

The new engine is very deep-breathing, and because the original valve sizes are retained, gas velocities are very high — which means that the amount of torque developed by the engine is nothing sort of phenomenal. There is nothing "peaky" about the way in which the power develops; it starts on its torque curve at the very bottom of the engine's rev range, and is still feeding through massive amounts even as the engine reaches its redline.

This translates on the road into a car which is very user-friendly. There is a great deal more power being fed through the driving wheels than there ever has been on any standard XR3i, but it feeds through as a steady shove which is directly relative to the amount of pressure on the throttle pedal. There are no sudden "shock" inputs of power which might unnerve the chassis, and in consequence the driver is not having to battle with torque steer or skittish behaviour from the front wheels.

The car is therefore extraordinarily good for "point and squirt" driving. It is at all times safe and predictable yet never, ever, boring. To deal with possible handling problems, Power Engineering took the precaution of installing a newly-developed handling kit which features lower springs with revised rates, and a set of adjustable gas-filled dampers. These combine to endow the car with a degree of sharpness and precision that is lacking on the standard car, without making the ride quality suffer. In feel, the car is akin to a well-sorted, tuned Mk II RS 2000 — although the XR3i is appreciably quicker in this form than all but the most radical of RS 2000s would be.

From a standing start, it is possible to unstick the front tyres quite easily if too much weight is applied to the accelerator pedal, but our track tests proved that there is nothing to be gained by being heavy-footed with the car — our best times were

GEAR RATIO COMPARISONS

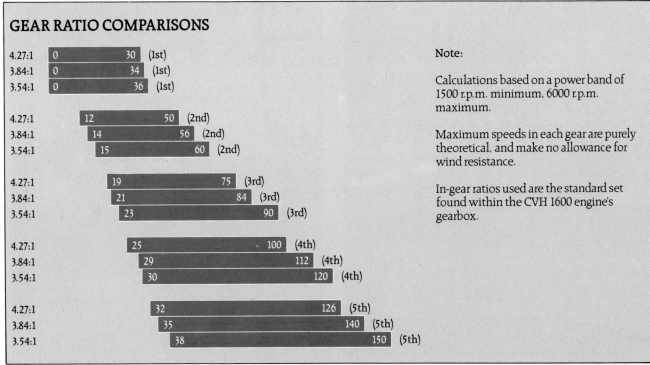

4.27:1	0 — 30	(1st)
3.84:1	0 — 34	(1st)
3.54:1	0 — 36	(1st)
4.27:1	12 — 50	(2nd)
3.84:1	14 — 56	(2nd)
3.54:1	15 — 60	(2nd)
4.27:1	19 — 75	(3rd)
3.84:1	21 — 84	(3rd)
3.54:1	23 — 90	(3rd)
4.27:1	25 — 100	(4th)
3.84:1	29 — 112	(4th)
3.54:1	30 — 120	(4th)
4.27:1	32 — 126	(5th)
3.84:1	35 — 140	(5th)
3.54:1	38 — 150	(5th)

Note:

Calculations based on a power band of 1500 r.p.m. minimum, 6000 r.p.m. maximum.

Maximum speeds in each gear are purely theoretical, and make no allowance for wind resistance.

In-gear ratios used are the standard set found within the CVH 1600 engine's gearbox.

gained by being reasonablys gentle away from the line, and then putting the throttle pedal to the floor once the car was moving. As is usual with front wheel drive Escorts, the gearshift doesn't respond too enthusiastically to fast shifting, tending to baulk particularly badly whenever anything nearing a powershift is approached. This hurt the 0-60 times whenever we went in search of them — a more precise shift mechanism would have clipped another half-second from the already-impressive 7.8 second optimum time that we achieved.

But the gearbox is not Power's problem, rather it is a characteristic of the original car. The same applies to the final drive ratio. In an effort to get the best intermediate acceleration times from the relatively underpowered standard XR3i, Ford decided to install a set of 4.27:1 gears as the last link in their transmission chain. They were successful in their quest, and production models display a reasonably nippy turn of heel.

However, add another bucketful of torque in the way that Power Engineering have, and that final drive ratio becomes a liability: first gear runs out at 30 m.p.h. — almost before the driver can blink — and it is necessary to make the second-to-third upshift at fifty miles per hour, some six seconds after leaving the start line. Other models within the Escort range have taller sets of final drive gears, and the use of these in conjunction with the new engine would not affect in-gear acceleration times in the slightest, but would make for far more relaxed cruising. We have compiled a chart which shows the relative speed ranges of the three commonly-available gear sets as a sidebar to this feature, which might prove useful to potential customers of Power Engineering.

As it stands, the System Two Litre XR3i, as it is known, is stunningly effective at covering ground quickly. Virtually regardless of the gear selected, acceleration is brisk — overtaking can easily become a matter of "stick it in anything and let the torque do the rest ...". Punching through a series of tight and twisting turns on a fast run through Derbyshire's Peak District gave the distinct impression that there can be very few cars

indeed capable of keeping up with this one. This car can out-gun the Golf GTi 16V, and both out-run and out-handle an Astra GTE/16. Ford's own RS Turbo Escort wouldn't even get a look in on the action.

Getting the braking over with the car still heading in a straight line, let the nose start to drift a little as you approach the apex of the bend, and then roll on as much power as you like, and the four wheels will track through exactly where you intend them to go. Over-enthusiastic use of the loud pedal will see the inside front wheel start to spin on a particularly tight bend, but even there the handling is so forgiving that a slight easing of power will regain traction without upsetting the balance of the car. On wider roads with more gradual curves, this machine is faultless

"A fast run gave the impression that there can be few cars indeed capable of keeping up with this one."

in its behaviour, displaying a voracious appetite for eating up the miles.

Straight line stability at higher motorway speeds was never a strong point of the standard XR3i, but thanks to the lower stance and increased power of this car only the strongest of crosswinds present any kind of problem — and by the time that wind speeds reach that point, the prudent driver will already have backed off anyway. The motorway also highlights the usefulness of all of the additional power in overtaking situations, as it is no longer necessary to make a downshift from fifth to get past slower traffic briskly. This car makes a standard XR3i appear to be on a constant course of Valium.   ▶

The pistons used in the Two Litre are steel braced to ensure minimum expansion — note absence of any bracing whatsoever on original Dutch-sourced pistons used in Power's first approach to bigger engine for XR3i.

THE DEFINITIVE XR3i

The principle of System Two Litre is that it is just what its name alludes to – a system. The heart of the conversion is a complete package of cylinder block, crankshaft, connecting rods (as with the pistons, these have to be specially made for Power Engineering), and pistons, all ready-assembled and supplied in a transit case complete with all necessary gaskets; even a new oil filter. These are supplied on an exchange basis (a deposit is pre-paid with the order for the new block, and this is refunded upon Power's receipt of your old cylinder block assembly).

In addition to the basic engine conversion, Power are also in the process of testing for approval a number of other components such as camshafts, exhaust systems, and so forth – the aim is to offer an entire package of complementary engine tuning pieces which will fit not just the Escort XR3i, but also every other car which comes from the factory with a 1.6 litre CVH engine under the bonnet. The list includes the Fiesta XR2, Orion and Escort saloons, even the Reliant SS1-1600 Scimitar and the Morgan 4/4 models. In the XR3i the power gain is in the order of 30%, and there is every reason to expect similar gains from carburated engines; enough to comfortably out-perform any of those cars' existing rivals.

In typical fashion, Power Engineering have come up with several different ways of making the conversion available. The first of these is to have Power themselves carry out the work. Then there is an expanding network of official Power System Two Litre dealerships around the country, who can carry out the work on Power's behalf. The third option is to approach your local specialist engine building company – Power have a "trade package" available which will enable them to put an engine together using the basic block assembly from Power along with whatever other tuning parts your local company suggest to suit your needs. The final option is to buy in a complete package from Power, and to carry out the work yourself. As the old cliché has it, you pays your money and you takes your choice ...

Speaking of money brings us neatly to the bottom line – just

how much it costs to take your 1600 CVH engine out to a two litre. This depends upon the way in which the job is undertaken; naturally, there are savings to be made by doing all of the spanner work yourself, but assuming that you take the most expensive option and take your car to either Power Engineering

PERFORMANCE

	System Two Litre	Power 1850*	RS Turbo Escort	Escort XR3i
0-30	3.2 secs	3.4 secs	3.1 secs	3.4 secs
0-50	6.0 secs	6.3 secs	6.1 secs	6.9 secs
0-60	7.8 secs	7.9 secs	9.2 secs	9.7 secs
0-70	10.0 secs	10.3 secs	11.5 secs	12.4 secs
0-90	18.6 secs	19.2 secs	19.3 secs	22.7 secs
30-50 (2nd)	2.6 secs	2.9 secs	2.7 secs	3.1 secs
30-50 (3rd)	3.6 secs	3.9 secs	4.4 secs	6.9 secs
30-50 (4th)	5.3 secs	5.7 secs	6.3 secs	7.7 secs
50-70 (3rd)	4.0 secs	4.6 secs	4.3 secs	7.1 secs
50-70 (4th)	5.5 secs	5.9 secs	6.1 secs	8.9 secs
50-70 (5th)	8.2 secs	9.4 secs	8.4 secs	14.0 secs
70-90 (4th)	6.6 secs	6.8 secs	7.1 secs	13.2 secs
70-90 (5th)	9.7 secs	10.9 secs	10.1 secs	21.1 secs
Standing ¼ Mile	16.3 secs @ 89 mph	16.7 secs @ 87 mph	16.8 secs @ 85 mph	18.1 secs @ 71 mph
Maximum Speed	127 mph	125 mph	124 mph	115 mph
Average Fuel Consumption	28.2 mpg	26.7 mpg	29.0 mpg	26.8 mpg

*Whilst the figures taken for System Two Litre are not substantially quicker than those for the earlier 1850cc XR3i tested (August 1988 issue), the cars feels far more substantial, and indications are that the engine will hold together for far longer than the earlier example would have done.

SECOND OPINION

In 1983, after reading various reports on what was billed then as the "replacement RS 2000", I purchased a white five speed XR3 Escort. That was my first mistake. My second mistake was to hope that the 96 b.h.p. CVH engine could provide as much "get up and go" as my previous RS 2000.

The car's build quality was faultless, as was the economy, but the car lacked any kind of get up and go — this was brought into sharp perspective by its rivals, all of which had fuel injection, 1.8 litres, and masses of torque. Even after S.V.E. had revised the suspension and added fuel injection, it was still necessary to work hard with the gearbox in order to extract any kind of meaningful performance.

Still disappointed, I went on to test such cars as the Astra GTE, Fiat Abarth 130T/C, Peugeot 205 GTI (both 1.6 and 1.9), but failed to find anything to fit the bill.

Late in August this year, our Editor asked me if I would pop down to Uxbridge and pick up a test car. I arrived shortly after lunchtime (following the usual dismal brawl with the M6/M1/M25 motorway network) to be met by David Power, who outlined the specification of the car before handing it over to me. Feeling disinclined to return on the route I had taken to Uxbridge, I instead opted to head back for home via the M40 and A-roads, through Oxford, Banbury, Warwick before picking up the M6 at Birmingham. Despite the sheer volume of Friday afternoon traffic on the M40, it soon became apparent that the car was blessed with a torque curve nothing short of fantastic, and that the acceleration in fourth and fifth gear was unbelievable when compared with a standard XR3i.

After the busy motorway, it was great to be on the open road, and anybody who knows the A423 will doubtless agree that it is a fantastic road for flying. With this car, overtaking a line of traffic could be a simple matter of flooring the throttle in fifth and shooting past the cars in question. Only a hooligan would really need to drop down to fourth or third before hitting the throttle.

This car is the best point-to-point car that I have **ever** driven across country, the suspension complementing perfectly the excellent work carried out (to a quality of which Rolls-Royce would be proud) by David Power and his team to the engine. In some respects it reminded me of my last 2.8i Special Capri, especially its third gear, which seems to go on forever. It also is happy to pull away from as low as 30 m.p.h. in fifth without any complaints. Try that in a standard XR3i and you would shake loose any dentures you happen to possess ...

There was only one car which out-paced me on the journey, and that cost appreciably more — it was a late-model Testarossa finished in the almost-obligatory red.

The CVH has been criticised for its roughness beyond 5000 r.p.m., but not this little baby — it ran as sweetly as any BMW six-cylinder engine. This is the car which Ford ought to be building — had they done so, they would have cornered the "hot hatch" market. Anybody looking for a new car in that class ought to try out the System Two Litre. There are no trick bits beneath the bonnet, just a superb piece of solid, no-nonsense engineering. Long live the new RS 2000.

Phil Newton.

themselves or to one of their official agencies, the total bill ought to work out at something in the region of £1,600 for the conversion as we have tested it — obviously such further changes as a revised camshaft, trick cylinder head, uprated exhaust system or whatever will add to the cost — but then, the same would apply with any engine. Interestingly, in addition to supplying an entire package of parts in the basic price, Power are also happy to fit a new clutch assembly should you request it, without incurring any additional labour charges — you would pay only for the components used.

There is one aspect of the conversion which is at present untouched by this feature, and that is the normally thorny issue of fuel economy; so often, such a great increase in power is to be traded off against a worsening of the number of miles which can be achieved per gallon of fuel. In this car's case, we are happy to report that our overall average, based upon more than a thousand miles of motoring on all types of road (including our track tests, which never fail to hurt the m.p.g. figures) were an improvement on those gained in a standard example of XR3i. Not by a lot, true — the actual figure was 28.2 miles per gallon for the System Two Litre versus 26.8 m.p.g. for the standard XR3i — but it is nonetheless an improvement, and an owner who drives

less, um, heavy-footed than we do would achieve a better improvement still.

The final issue harks back to the matter of longevity — just how long can a converted CVH engine be expected to last? It is obviously too early to say for certain, but given that the System Two Litre is built to closer tolerances than a standard XR3i's engine, it in consequence runs more smoothly and quietly. What is more, Power stripped down their development engine after ten thousand miles, and there was no discernible wear on pistons or bores. It is therefore a reasonable assumption to predict that the two-litre ought to outlast a standard CVH engine, given similar maintenance and driving methods.

It is not very often that we really miss a test car after it has gone back to its rightful owners, but we have all missed this one. We have missed its sheer musclepower, and the way in which the car has become a wolf in wolf's clothing. We have missed it so much that we are in the process of getting one of these engines installed into our Escort Ghia ... ●

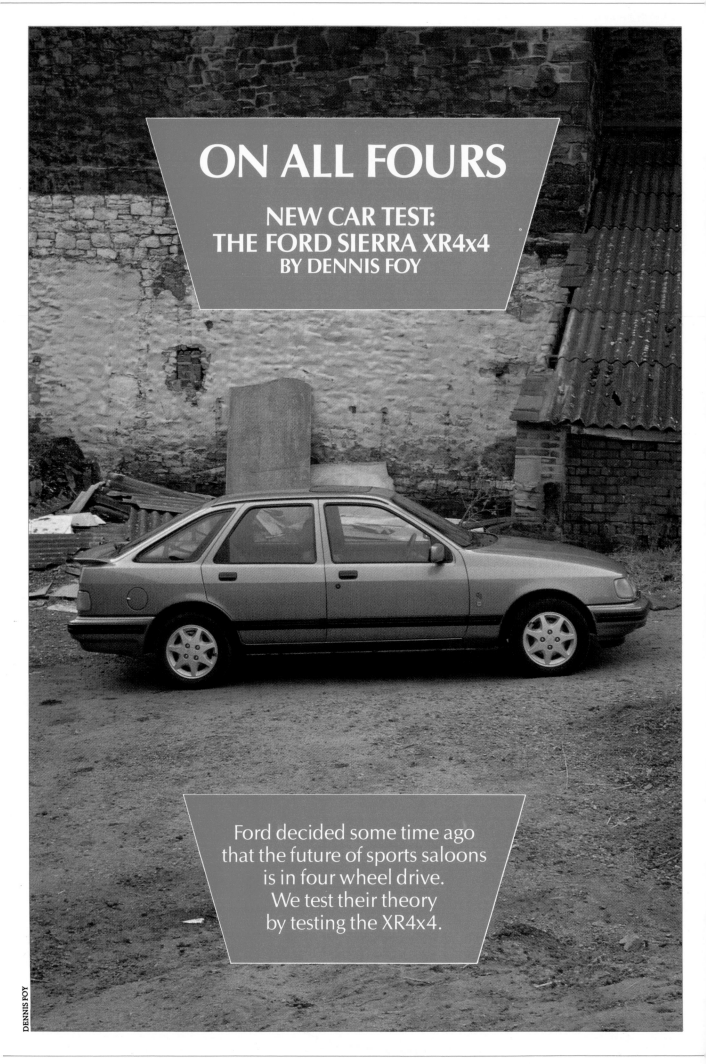

ON ALL FOURS

NEW CAR TEST:
THE FORD SIERRA XR4x4
BY DENNIS FOY

Ford decided some time ago
that the future of sports saloons
is in four wheel drive.
We test their theory
by testing the XR4x4.

DENNIS FOY

I read an article recently in one of the quality Sunday newspapers, a piece written by an "automotive engineering expert" which supposedly cut a swathe through the various descriptions of technical features which abound on new cars. At one point in his diatribe, the writer made mention of four wheel drive, and stated, quite categorically, that such a system in no way assists any improvement in roadholding. If he believes that he will also believe that the earth is flat, and that the moon is made of green cheese.

We have just spent a week, a fairly typical 800-mile week, with an XR4x4 Sierra, and the degrees of grip that the car achieves is nothing short of phenomenal. The car's predecessor was the XR4i, a car not exactly renowned for its high levels of grip through the bends. The XR4x4 uses the same engine as its predecessor, but instead of putting all of the power through the rear wheels, divides it between all four; the result is a chassis which both pushes and pulls through a curve, rather than just pushing. And because of this, bends can be negotiated at much greater velocities than could ever be attempted in the earlier XR4i.

The XR4x4 is a complex piece of machinery, because in addition to dividing the power 66% to the rear, 34% to the front wheels, it also has a pair of limited-slip viscous couplings, one which controls the relative drives to front and rear axles, and the other which controls the rear differential. This means that wheelspin is non-existent on the car; put the throttle down, and the power instantly feeds straight onto the tarmac. Where this facility immediately comes in very useful indeed is punching the car out from a side road into a stream of traffic; whereas a rear-wheel drive car would exit such a junction under full throttle with its inside rear wheel spinning – and quite possibly with its tail end hanging out – an XR4x4 doesn't. It simply launches out, in a drama-free manner.

Another major contributor to the effectiveness with which the car can be used is the steering. This is power-assisted, but the

ON ALL FOURS

◁assistance is variable. What actually happens is that at parking speeds the steering is light and easy to turn, whereas at higher speeds, whilst the steering weight never actually becomes heavy, there is a feedback and precision from the wheel which would have been totally alien to a power-assisted car of even a couple of years ago.

The suspension of the car is independent, with MacPherson struts (gas-filled) and coil springs at the front, tied by a rearwards-facing anti-roll bar, and semi-trailing arms with gas-filled dampers and rising-rate springs at the rear. Braking is comprehensive, with ventilated discs at the front, solid discs at the rear, servo assistance — and this particular car was fitted with that most worthwhile of options, anti-lock control.

Under the bonnet is the familiar Ford V6 in 2.8 litre, 150 b.h.p. form. This revs freely, delivers adequate amounts of torque, and manages to return about seventeen to the gallon when driven hard — pussyfooting around can get the mileage up to a little over twenty to the gallon. The gearbox is another familiar item, the Ford five speed manual. The change on this particular car was typical of the breed, being baulky and obstructive. When the new transmission finally puts in an appearance towards the end of 1988, will Ford finally admit that the present unit is a disaster?

The bodyshell of the Sierra is familiar to us all — there have been hundreds of thousands of them built since its introduction — yet to the credit of Ford's design team, the detail changes that appear on the XR version serve well to set the car apart from its lesser brethren. At the front, a pair of driving lamps have been let into the spoiler assembly, and at the rear, a purpose-designed spoiler is attached to the tailgate. These don't sound much, but by the time that they (along with the rest of the below-the-hip panels and door mirrors) have been painted in the same colour as the rest of the bodywork, the effect is most impressive. A full set of rubbing strakes, and a set of RS alloy wheels and low-profile tyres complete the exterior.

Inside the car is roomy and spacious, with the front occupants being given a pair of semi-bucket seats. These are fully reclining, and have adjustable lumbar support, with the driver having the additional facility of being able to adjust the height of the seat. The rear seat, the back of which folds forward in two unequal parts, offers adequate room for three passengers. Instrumentation is comprehensive (although I would like to see the addition of an oil pressure gauge to complement the speedo, tachometer, temperature and fuel level gauges), and all instruments are clearly visible through the sports steering wheel of the car. The switchgear is classic early '80s Ford, with the trafficators and dip beam controlled by the left-hand stalk, wipers (with variable intermittent sweep) by the closer of the two right-hand stalks. Lights are controlled by the rearward right-hand stalk. Rear and (optional) front screen heaters are controlled by switches fascia-mounted to the right-hand side of the driver, alongside the switches for the high-intensity rear lamps, and the front auxiliary lamps. Our test car was equipped with optional air conditioning but, as with most Fords, there was no provision to have warmth to both upper and lower parts of the car at the same time.

The radio-cassette unit that is fitted to the XR4x4 as standard is of a high specification, having sixteen presets for the radio, local/distance switching, noise reduction circuitry, and separate bass and treble controls. It also has automatic switching to the other side of the tape when the first side has finished playing. A separate amplifier (giving 4 x 13.5 watts per channel) feeds the six speakers, and radio reception is provided via an aerial integrated with the rear screen heater element. A graphic equaliser is offered as an option to this latter item.

As with most cars on the Ford Press Demonstration Fleet, our car was loaded with options. In addition to the standard fitments already mentioned, central locking and a sunroof are provided as part of the basic package, which is listed at £13,990. However, our car also had the anti-lock braking system, which ought to be specified by anybody ordering a car, which adds another £977.48 to the price, plus air conditioning (£751.82), headlamp wash and wipe (£151.25), metallic paint (£160.94), and a heated front screen (£108.99). This brings the total for the car to £16,131.23 — although keeping the options to A.B.S. and the heated windscreen would bring that price down to a more acceptable £15,007.

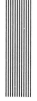 "Put the throttle down, and the power instantly feeds to the tarmac."

What you get for your money is a car which rarely fails to delight, albeit in a very subtle way; this is no street racer, nor is it a poor relation to the Cosworth. It is a car which is both quick enough and fast enough for most tastes and requirements, being capable of the benchmark 0-60 sprint in 8.3 seconds, and can achieve almost 130 m.p.h. whenever circumstances allow. It is quiet and civilised, the ample sound-proofing managing to suppress all but the worst of the 2.8's noises — as the redline approaches there is something of a din from beneath the bonnet, a barrage of sound that is beyond the insulating capabilities of most known materials.

Ride quality is exceptionally high, even when the car is being pushed hard through a series of bends. It is extremely difficult to upset the car's balance provided the power is kept on, and there is no skittishness when a mid-curve pothole is encountered. The comfortable seats effectively cancel any suspension bumps which manage to get through the excellently balanced suspension system, and there is enough support from the side bolsters of the front seats to ensure that driver and passenger remain in place. It is very much a driver's car, but not at the expense of passenger comfort.

A long run in the car on empty winding roads highlights the sheer pleasure that a driver can gain from the car — and also draws out the car's two deficiencies. It is a car which is light and easy to drive even at high speeds, and can be set up for a series of fast curves with consumate ease; it takes a bad driver to be able to bottom out the suspension of this car. The steering is light, and the pedals are ideally weighted and balanced in their relationship to each other. At the edge the car adopts a gentle, controllable understeer, and this is directly attributable to a lack of power when compared with the awesome levels of grip that the car can attain — this point was proven in our recent (November 1987 issue) test of the Power Engineering XR4x4, which has 240 b.h.p. on tap. This car simply kept gripping, and

maintained a tidy line regardless of speed. The other problem area with the car is the gearbox; the amount of effort needed to change gear was at odds with the lightness and sensitivity of the rest of the controls.

High speed cruising on an autobahn brings out one other negative aspect of the car, namely a susceptibility to crosswinds whenever more than three figures are displayed on the speedometer. This is not a serious fault, but a good degree of attention is called for if the car's straight line attitude is to be maintained. In high winds, it would be inadvisable to proceed at much above 80 or 90 m.p.h. This characteristic is a trait of the Sierra bodyshell (though not of the Sapphire model) and the only solution would be to fit a Cosworth-style spoiler to the rear of the car, to improve airflow, and thus directional stability. Such a move would negate the subtlety of the XR4x4, and would serve to draw far more attention to the car. Fitting a rear wing of

that type would enable the driver to make substantially more rapid straight-line progress in crosswinds — but would do nothing to ensure that other vehicles would not be blown into the path of the high-speed Sierra ...

Ford will neither confirm nor deny that a 4x4 version of the Sapphire is planned; whether or not the market is big enough to justify the development costs would determine the eventual appearance (or non-appearance) of such a car. Ford will also not say whether they intend to market an XR4x4 with the 204 b.h.p.

Cosworth twin-cam engine — though such a car would be stunning. The likelihood of the Cosworth 4x4 is high, particularly as the days of the 2.8 V6 are numbered — it will be ceasing production in eighteen months or so, according to sources within the company. The one remaining option for the future is a tuned version of the forthcoming 1-4 twin-cam, the two-litre replacement for the Pinto engine which is about to go into production.

Even as it stands, the car is superb. Reasonably good value for money, comfortable, quick off the mark and quietly understated, it is a worthy flagship to the Sierra range. ●

SPECIFICATIONS
FORD SIERRA XR4x4

ENGINE TYPE	Pushrod V6	BRAKING SYSTEM	Front discs, rear discs, anti-fade friction materials, electronic anti-lock braking
BORE x STROKE	93mm x 68.5mm		
SIZE	2792cc		
BHP @ RPM	150 @ 5700	WEIGHT	2700 lbs
TORQUE LB/FT @ RPM	216 @ 3800	POWER/WEIGHT RATIO	128 b.h.p./ton
FUEL SYSTEM	Bosch K-Jetronic electronic injection	WHEELBASE	102.7"
DRIVEN WHEELS	All	LENGTH	175"
TRANSMISSION	5 speed manual, viscous coupled final drive, split torque 34% front, 66% rear	HEIGHT	53.5"
		WIDTH	67"
		TEST MILEAGE	812 miles
SUSPENSION: FRONT	McPherson struts, gas-filled dampers, anti-roll bar	TEST MPG	17.3
		MANUFACTURER'S MPG	18.5
SUSPENSION: REAR	Semi-trailing arms, rising rate springs, gas-filled dampers	PRICE AS TESTED	£16,141
		INSURANCE	Group 6

MANUFACTURER: Ford Motor Company, Dagenham, Essex, England.

XR2

*with added sauce

IAN KUAH

It doesn't seem that long ago when a lot of us were spending the weekend under the bonnet of early Escorts and Cortinas fitting a high-lift camshaft, four-branch free-flow exhaust manifold and twin Webers. We would then spend more time setting up the carbs and running up and down the local bypass making sure that all the settings were right to give us optimum performance and reasonably smooth running across the board.

Remember also the bad cold starter, lumpy tickover and poor tractability around town? But the glorious noises that those four induction throats and the strong push in the back made it all worthwhile. Then the civilised and more subtle "hot hatchback" came on the scene in the form of the Golf GTi and Ford XR3. The latest XR3i with its Bosch fuel-injection starts first time in the morning in all weathers, is perfectly mannered from cold, and returns the sort of fuel consumption that tuned cars of the old school can only dream about. But today there is something missing from the equation; in this rush for development, the modern car with its computer-designed engineering edict has lost the important ingredient that separates cars; that makes a machine more than just a means of getting from A to B. We are of course talking about this elusive quality called character.

Early Escorts, BMWs and VW GTis had heaps of it. Their current variants have become sanitised in that respect and are better cars overall but less inspiring. Even modern Ferraris with their Bosch injection and four-valves-per-cylinder heads have lost that lovely carburettor induction noise that made them sound so glorious.

Enthusiasm was thus the feeling in the air as I beat a familiar path to Mike Spence Motorsport's premises in Shinfield near Reading. Director, Richard Thorne, and I had recently been having a chat about lack of character in modern cars, and he mentioned that a couple of XR2s had been breathed upon by the old school of thought as an experiment to see how the car would respond to this route and also to compare it with a supercharger installation they had previously done. This latter tweak had achieved a remarkable improvement in torque and power across the band and also had the added benefit of making the car quieter through its muffling of the induction system. Choking the car for decent cold starting and running was a big problem with the factory twin-choke carburettor though, and Richard explained that a fuel-injection set-up would have been the ideal combination — but at a price.

To cope with the extra power liberated by the supercharger, the little car had been given a thorough going over in the chassis department. XR2s are known for being rather bouncy and nervous at speed, so the shell was first stiffened by a front strut brace which attached to the top of the MacPherson strut towers to the bulkhead. Koni dampers were used as inserts with the standard springs and it was decided that more rubber would have to take the extra power to the road. 50-Series tyres were in order, so the alloy wheels had to follow the Plus One route and went up to 6J x 14 inch wearing 185/50VR14 Dunlop D4s which were the only tyres available in this odd size. The Dunlops fortunately happened to be very effective at reducing tramlining and the tendency to follow every pebble on the road, a normal problem with ultra low profile rubber. In terms of suspension geometry, the track was set to parallel, something that Mike Spence Motorsport does to all its modified cars. This is said to reduce "nervousness" when going quickly.

With these modifications already in place, the conversion from supercharger to natural aspiration and conventional tuning was straightforward. It is a known fact that the CVH engine does not respond to conventional tuning as well as the old Kent pushrod unit. The design of the combustion chambers is such that the engine only really comes to life with turbo or supercharging when the gas velocities are much higher and literally blast their way through the swirl areas. Some careful thought was given to the cylinder head by M.S.M.'s Technical Director, Gerd Van Aaken, who carefully shaped and equalised the combustion chambers and gas-flowed the head. A Janspeed inlet manifold was used to hang the twin 40 Dellorto carburettors and a Kent cam of 279° duration fitted. This had to be of a special design as the standard engine

uses hydraulic lifters, and the cam comes with solid lifters to prevent valve bounce.

The opposite end of the cylinder head of this crossflow engine was then treated to a Janspeed four-branch manifold and complete Janspeed free-flow exhaust which is worth about 8 b.h.p., the complete conversion extracting 135 b.h.p. from the engine, for the reasonable cost of £732 plus V.A.T. and a £250 fitting charge. The wheels, tyres, Konis and strut brace will set you back a further £561.50 plus V.A.T. and a £50 fitting charge and you can have one of M.S.M.'s personal steering wheels as a finishing touch for £71.50 plus V.A.T. Starting the XR2 brings memories of tuned Escort Mexicos flooding back. A couple of prods cn the throttle are necessary to prime the carbs before you turn the key, and then the engine barks into life and you have to blip the throttle carefully as the power unit yawns and stretches in the light of day. Tickover with the wild cam is a touch lumpy, but nothing like as bad as some I have encountered, and once the engine is warm, it is quite civilised. Even driving the car gently while all the vital fluids are allowed tor each their proper operating temperatures, the XR2 sounds more purposeful than anything in current production at Dagenham. There is always a danger of over-choking a car when you use two large carbs, but M.S.M. have got this one spot on and there is good tractability around town with instant power on tap from fairly low revs.

Warmed through now as we reach the end of the first stretch of the A33 heading for Hartley Witney, we can give the car its head. Full bore acceleration is exhilarating as the car pulls towards 6500 r.p.m. in the gears. The shove in the

back is progressive and strong, the sounds and sensations an instant throwback in time ... Heeling and toeing and blipping the throttle to take third from fourth as we sweep towards a corner brings back memories of fabulous drives in a similarly modified RS 2000 nearly a decade ago. But the difference is that the XR2 is front-driven so there is little chance of exiting the corner with a touch of opposite lock. For all that, the M.S.M. XR2 with its sorted suspension feels much more stable in fast sweepers than the stock item which can feel a touch tail-happy, nervous even as it turns in. The ride with the Konis is also surprisingly comfortable. Make no mistake, this car is taut, but you never reach the stage where you feel as if the inside of the roof is awfully close! The improvement in handling alone is quite dramatic though, and I would recommend these alterations for owners of standard XR2s who drive hard.

So how do the modifications to the engine stack up against turbocharging, supercharging or fuel injection in this day and age? Firstly, if you are after a totally civilised car that starts first touch of the button and purrs like a contented cat from cold, forget it. Microchip technology or even straightforward carbs with automatic chokes win hands down here. It is on a twisty road with the engine on full song that the excitement starts, and as the red mist descends, you want to keep on driving and driving, and here the other ugly spectre of poorer fuel consumption rears its ugly head. In hard driving on A and B roads, our test car's fuel gauge was seen to fall quite rapidly and the car must be down to the low 20s with this sort of treatment. The fun factor is undeniable too; if some bright spark came up with a device for providing twin carb induction noise on fuel-injected cars — he might make a lot of money. ●

COSTS

Engine: Cylinder head modifications by M.S.M., new Kent camshaft, Janspeed inlet and exhaust manifolds, Janspeed silencing system, twin Dellorto sidedraught 40mm carburettors. **£732+£250 fitting charge**

Suspension: Strut brace, Koni dampers, wheels and tyres. **£561+£50 fitting charge**

Prices exclude V.A.T.

PERFORMANCE – DYNO FIGURES

MIKE SPENCE MOTORSPORT XR2

RPM	BHP	(std XR2)
2000	45	—
3000	72	—
4200	102	—
5000	108	—
6000	120	96
6300*	125	
6700	135	

*max revs on standard car

Torque: 141 lb/ft @ 4800 r.p.m. (standard XR2 98 lb/ft @ 4000 r.p.m.)

ZULU WARRIOR

Take an XR4i, add an extra pair of cylinders and the result is an XR8. If the mathematics are somewhat suspect, the car itself certainly isn't.
By Ian Kuah.

Once upon a time America, land of the free, was the home of the muscle car. Unfettered by emission controls, the pre-1968 Yank V8 could have anything up to 7½ litres under the bonnet, enough to give several hundred horsepower and sufficient torque to see off any piece of Italian exotica. Until the first corner, anyway ... The Shelby Mustang, Pontiac GTO, Firebird 455HO and Dodge Challenger immediately spring to mind as cars which were capable of laying down sub-fourteen second quarter-mile times all day long. ▷

ZULU WARRIOR

◁ It all changed after the environmentalists achieved their ambitions, and stifled the power outputs of such machinery by ensuring the installation of catalytic convertors and suchlike. Much the same situation was mirrored on the other side of the globe, where revised Australian Design Rules took a similar toll on the more musclebound Holdens and Chargers. But whilst the rest of the world either came to terms with emasculation or started to develop more efficient and powerful small machines,

> "There are subtle clues dotted about the car which hint to it being something special."

one country blithely continued its crusade in the name of muscle cars.

South Africa has always produced interesting permutations of cars which were never considered in the homelands of those various machines (witness the Chevrolet V8 engined Firenza, the 5-litre Capri, and suchlike), and the XR8 is probably the ultimate example of their philosophy.

The fastest naturally-aspirated Sierra around, the XR8 was the brainchild of one Derek Morris, Ford South Africa's Director of Product Development. He envisaged a homologation special which could become a winner on the racetracks of his country, which accounts for the mass of competition-orientated parts that are found under the skin of the car.

The heart of the car is a V8 engine of 302 cubic inches (5.0 litres) which was originally developed in 1968 as an American unit class-legal for Nascar and Indy racing. Whilst a vast range of performance parts were available from the factory in the U.S.A. for this engine, the version as fitted to the XR8 is only very mildly tuned from baseline, producing 203 b.h.p. at a low 4800 r.p.m., and about 250 lb/ft of torque. However, the engine is fitted with a pair of neat 4/2/1 exhaust manifolds, and there is

also no power-sapping cooling fan on the engine; a pair of thermostatic electric fans mounted in front of the (British made) Serck radiator take care of that chore. The radiator itself is sealed into position to cancel any engine bay turbulence, and there is an oil cooler mounted immediately below it.

Sitting atop the engine, under the large pancake air cleaner, is a four-barrel Holley carburettor which is capable of passing up to 780 cubic feet of air each minute. The camshaft of the engine is of a fairly mild grind (to ensure good tractability and decent low-speed response), and this is partly responsible for the fact that this is no 7000+ r.p.m. screamer. On the other hand, this does not mean that the engine cannot spin freely and eagerly.

Compared with many cars, the transplant of the 302 into the Sierra was a piece of cake; the engine bay is so generous that it looks as though the car was designed specifically to take this engine. Barely five inches longer than a Cologne V6, the engine sits well back in the chassis (an aid to good weight distribution), and there is plenty of room around the engine for working on it. Yet for all of the visual similarity to a standard Sierra, the car is in fact lengthened in the nose by about 100 mm, in order to accommodate the larger-than-standard radiator.

Transmitting the substantial amount of torque back from the engine to the axle is a Mustang five-speed manual gearbox, which is endowed with a short, precise shift lever. At the rear of the car is a Granada-style differential unit which contains a 3.5:1 crown wheel and pinion, and either side of this are enlarged and strengthened Constant Velocity joints and halfshafts, connecting to redesigned hubs. The stopping arrangements are impressive, with 280 mm AP Racing ventilated discs (complete with four-pot calipers) at the front, and Teves 285 mm slotted, vented rear discs. The latter items have cast calipers, and these incorporate a handbrake mechanism. Footwear for a car of this performance is surprisingly modest, being 195/60 VR 15 tyres on Ford RS Ronal alloys.

Such a modified driveline from the designed Sierra system called for new crossmembers at both front and rear of the car. The front one lowers the engine by 10 mm and picks up the V8's engine mounts, whilst the rear one is redesigned to accommodate the final drive unit. Front springing is uprated by around 50% when compared with an XR4i, and the damping actions have been altered to match the revised springing. The spring pans and front anti-roll bar fouled on the new wheels, and so these were altered in shape to provide clearance. The diameter of the bar is identical to that of an XR4i. The alterations to the rear suspension system were more radical, with revised semi-trailing arms which lower the ride height. Whereas the XR4i has progressive-rate springs, the eight has linear-wound units significantly stiffer, matched to gas-filled damper units. These are of similar bounce characteristics to those of the XR4, but have increased rebound control to suit the new springs. These changes were adequate to endow the car with almost neutral handling; had an anti-roll bar been added to the rear, the car would have been prone to oversteering far too readily. As the car is, oversteering can only be brought about by powering on.

On first impressions, the XR8 could be visually mistaken for a five-door Sierra 2.0iS to which an XR4i biplane rear spoiler and set of alloy wheels have been added. However, there are subtle clues dotted about the car which hint to it being something special, such as the way in which the headlamps are moved forward in their mounts to be more flush with the surrounding panels, and the additional slotting to the grille which ensures an adequate supply of air to the radiator. Inside, the car is virtually identical to the standard XR4i, right down to the horn push buttons.

Anybody weaned on four-cylinder hot hatchbacks is in for a big surprise when they make the acquaintance of this car. Adjust the seats to suit, belt up, alter the mirrors, and twist the ignition key — and a brief churn of the starter motor is rewarded with a bark from the exhaust, then a solid-sounding burble as the V8

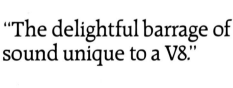

settles into its 700 r.p.m. tickover. Prodding the "loud" pedal is enough to bring on a snarl from the single fat tailpipe.

The competition clutch is heavy to release, but it is balanced in pressure to the firm, progressive throttle, and feeding out the clutch is surprisingly easy, thanks to its precise, well-cushioned feel. With 1500 r.p.m. on the tachometer, the car will surge away eagerly in first gear, with an unmistakeable eight-cylinder beat. Into second. The shift is precise if a shade heavy, and it is advisable to use fingertips to operate the lever; any manhandling will cause baulking, but treat it gently and it will not let you down. Upshifting at 4000 r.p.m. will see 100 m.p.h. effortlessly, as the muscle from the big, torquey engine makes contact with the ground. Washing off speed is just as easy, as firm and progressive pedal action relates perfectly to the retardation action. These brakes are good; better even than those of the RS Cosworth.

A straight emerges as we round a right-hand bend. Checking the mirrors and finding all clear, we position out to the right in what the High Performance Club describe as a "Mobile Parking Space", and check thoroughly for oncoming cars, and junctions from which a car might emerge. All is clear, the throttle is depressed, and a surge of firm acceleration sets in, that gorgeous V8 bark building. A firm and progressive push in the back accompanies us past three, four, five cars, and neatly back onto the left-hand side of the road, following a neat triangle throughout the manoeuvre.

This car is good for 135 m.p.h., and can reach the yardstick sixty from standstill in 7.2 seconds. Whilst this is slower than the RS Cosworth, the XR8's big V8 is achieving the figures effortlessly — and without the aid of electronic "life support systems". And all the time, there is the delightful barrage of sound unique to a V8. So what of the handling? The XR8 feels nice and taut immediately, with pretty good ride comfort, and a good turn-in. The feel from the unassisted steering is fine, and its weight only becomes annoying when trying to park the machine in a tight

"The delightful barrage of sound unique to a V8."

space. When you consider that the car was developed in 1984 from what amounts to off-the-shelf parts, and when it is compared with our then-sporty Sierra the XR4i, the great job that Ford S.A. have done comes into sharp perspective. The XR4i feels underpowered, but that, of course, is understandable as the V8 of the South African car is almost twice the capacity of the British car. The chassis comparison is night and day. The XR8 is taut and precise, whereas that of the XR4i feels like a wet sponge. The XR4i was given to strong understeer, much wallowing and pitching, and then terminal oversteer. In contrast, the XR8 has a controllable oversteer which enables the car to be steered and balanced on the throttle, always safely and never a terminal proposition.

And this is what a muscle car is all about; an abundance of torque on tap at all times, with no peakiness or turbocharger lag to worry about. When coupled to a sharp-handling chassis, the recipe is one for pure, unadulterated fun. When new in 1984, the XR8 would cost under £14,000 — about the same as a fully-equipped Granada Ghia. The car in our photographs was brought back to the U.K. by businessman John Critchley. "I usually keep my cars for two or three years, until I get bored with them," he told us, "but I'm having so much fun with this one that when it wears out, I'll have it rebuilt." ●

SHOOTOUT

Tested back-to-back, the Fiesta XR2 and the Peugeot 205 GTi. Which one wins? By Dennis Foy.

The hot hatchback is an eminently sensible way of having fun on four wheels; it is the sports car of our time. There will, of course, always be a place for the traditional sports car, a close-coupled two seater which often has a stowable roof. Unfortunately, such rarely have enough space or practicality for everyday use and are usually bought as second, or even third, cars. In contrast the hot hatch is a four, and sometimes five-seater, and is usually capable of dealing with not only everyday driving, but also with accommodating an entire family or group of friends for longer-distance outings.

What is more, the typical hot hatch, with its sub-ten second 0-60 sprintability and a maximum speed on the far side of a hundred miles an hour, is often quicker than a traditional sports car. They are usually fun to drive, yet are at the same time practical and economical to run. It is no wonder that they are to be seen on our roads in such numbers.

One of the most popular examples of the genre to be found is the Fiesta XR2, which combines lively performance and small car practicality in equal amounts. The French manufacturer Peugeot came up with an equivalent model to the XR2 shortly after that car's arrival on the scene, with an uprated version of their little shopping car, the 205. Known as the GTi, that model was initially available only in 1.6 litre form (a 1900cc model is now also offered), and since its introduction it too has made quite a few friends. So how do they compare?

Both cars are equipped with 1600cc overhead cam engines, the XR2's being a carburated version of the CVH which was originally designed for the Escort range. In the XR2 it develops 95 brake horsepower at 5750 r.p.m. The 205 GTi is supplied with its fuel by electronic injection, and this is the principle reason why the power that it produces is higher. ▷

"Unlike many front wheel drive cars, when there is a break in traction the Fiesta doesn't slide sideways."

SHOOTOUT

at 115 b.h.p. Both cars have five-speed transmissions as standard, and both are front wheel drive. Both cars feature independent front suspension, both have ventilated front disc brakes with drums at the rear, and both are three door, four seater cars. But there the similarities end.

Although rounded off by the facelift of a couple of years ago, the XR2 is still quite angular in its appearance. Accommodation for four adults is quite reasonable, and the driver is presented with a fascia which is reasonably comprehensive. A small soft-feel steering wheel is employed, behind which are the controls for lights, wipers and trafficators. To the right of the binnacle which contains the speedo, tachometer, water temperature and fuel gauges are three "piano key" switches which control the heat rear window switch, the rear wash/wipe, and the high-intensity rear lights. To the left are the stereo and the heater controls, as well as the ashtray and cigarette lighter. Face level vents are to be found at each end of the dashboard and also in the centre. A small glovebox ahead of the front seat passenger, a pair of door pockets and an oddments tray ahead of the gear lever provide homes for odds and ends.

Firing up the XR2 for the first time conveys immediately the nature of the car, as all of the right noises come through to the driver; even if it only produces 95 horses, it sounds sportier.

Clutch action is light, and the gear lever will engage the appropriate set of cogs without too much hassle — it couldn't, in all honesty, be described as clean and precise, but it is a vast improvement on earlier examples of the car, which were

downright baulky. Steering action at parking speeds is pleasantly light, and it says much for the development work which has gone into the design of the front suspension system that the wheel never becomes too light, even at higher speeds than are legally allowed in this country.

As the car reaches its correct operating temperature the quality of gearshift actually deteriorated on our test car, and

the same has happened on other examples of Fiesta and XR2 that we have known. This means that an extra degree of forethought is necessary when running the car quickly through a series of winding bends; the gearshift just isn't quick enough for changes which have not been anticipated. What saves the day is the engine. Once hot, it delivers its power willingly, and maximum torque is developed at 4000 r.p.m., which reduces the need for a number of gearchanges most effectively. Had there not been such a good spread of torque available, it would be necessary to make far more excursions through the available ratios.

As with most hot hatchbacks, the car is most enjoyable when running hard on

winding back roads. The free-revving engine picks up cleanly and quickly, and the brakes consistently scrub off speed in a manner which would put to shame many traditional sports cars; pedal action and slowing down are in direct proportion to each other, progress was always halted without any untoward wanderings of the road wheels, and there was no tendency to locking up, even on slippery, rain-soaked roads. Such is the feedback to the driver via the

SPECIFICATIONS
FORD FIESTA XR2

ENGINE TYPE	Transverse 4 cylinder SOHC	**BRAKING SYSTEM**	Dual circuit hydraulics, discs front, drums rear
BORE x STROKE	90mm x 79.52mm		
SIZE	1597cc	**WEIGHT**	1860 lbs
BHP @ RPM	95 @ 5750	**POWER/WEIGHT RATIO**	113 b.h.p./ton
TORQUE LB/FT @ RPM	98 @ 4000	**WHEELBASE**	90.1"
FUEL SYSTEM	Weber 32/34 DFT 4B carburettor	**LENGTH**	144"
DRIVEN WHEELS	Front	**WIDTH**	68"
TRANSMISSION	5-speed manual	**HEIGHT**	52"
SUSPENSION: FRONT	MacPherson struts, pressed tie bars	**TEST MILEAGE**	871 miles
REAR	Coil springs, beam dead axle, trailing arms, telescopic dampers, Panhard rod, anti-roll bar	**MANUFACTURER'S MPG**	33.2
		TEST MPG	34.3
		PRICE AS TESTED	£7,783
		INSURANCE GROUP	4

MANUFACTURER: Ford Motor Company, Dagenham, Essex, England.

brake pedal that it would take a particularly insensitive driver's heavy-footedness to lock up the front wheels.

Steering feedback too is of the highest order, the driver constantly being made aware of what is happening at the point of contact between tyres and tarmac. The front suspension system uses a pair of coil springs on strut-style dampers, but instead of the normal Ford practice of having the bottom links joined by the anti-roll bar, a pressed transverse link and tie bar is employed at the bottom end of each strut which acts almost as a lower wishbone link to the frame rails. This aids response tremendously, and acts most effectively to counter torque-steer; unlike many front wheel drive cars, when there is a break in traction the XR2 doesn't immediately slide sideways. At the rear of the car lives a simple dead beam axle suspended via short coil springs, a pair of vertical dampers, and aided by an anti-roll bar. There is also a Panhard rod link to aid lateral location.

Ford have managed to achieve a quite satisfactory compromise between ride and handling on the car. The amount of body roll is small, and the car manages to soak up most imperfections from the road surface before they get as far as the passenger compartment. Particularly bad potholes are felt with a crash and bang, but they don't put the car off its stride, the driver being able to continue regardless towards the next bend. Roadholding levels on the standard car are high, and compliance within the suspension system works well with the 185/60 Pirellis that were standard fitments on our test car. At the edge of its high cornering limits, the car starts to understeer, but for the most part handling is neutral.

The XR2 is also quite comfortable and happy when cruising on motorways and "A" roads. The various aerodynamic fitments of the car when compared with a standard Fiesta help high-speed stability, even in quite fierce crosswinds.

and the level of soundproofing material that has been installed in the car is enough to keep noise levels at an acceptable level; it will never be as quiet as a large saloon car, but then it was never meant to be.

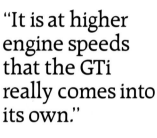

"It is at higher engine speeds that the GTi really comes into its own."

Being based on a design which was laid down in the early '70s, the car is now beginning to show its age a little, mainly in the area of standard and optional fitments. For instance, there is no provision for powered window lifters, no central locking, and no remote electric mirror adjustment; when the car was conceived such items were luxuries in all but expensive machinery. Today, however, they are available far more widely, and many drivers of XR2s would appreciate being able to order their car up with these features fitted from the factory.

The basic car, at £7,353, is quite reasonable value, given its performance, practicality and fun levels. However, to take it up to the standard of the car which we tested it is necessary to spend another £430 on the sunroof, alloy wheels, and tinted glass. A customer will be looking at a bill of about eight thousand pounds by the time the car is on the road.

The Peugeot 205, being a far more modern car than the Fiesta, is all curves; I doubt that there is a flat panel to be found on the car. The overall dimensions of the car are similar to those of the Fiesta (two inches longer, but six inches narrower than the Ford, the Peugeot has a wheelbase five inches longer), and the two cars weigh in at almost the same — which immediately gives an advantage, given its superior horsepower. Accommodation within the car is less good than the Fiesta, mainly because of the narrowness of the cabin; front and rear legroom is similar in both cars. Access to the rear seat of the 205 is made simple by a tilt and slide mechanism employed on the front seats, and once in, there is adequate room for a pair of adults. As with the XR2, a smaller steering wheel than those of the rest of the range is employed, and again, there is a separate binnacle housing the tach, speedo, water and fuel gauges. Switchgear follows the usual French logic of being a little scattered around the rest of the dashboard. Heater controls, for my tastes unnecessarily complicated in their use of graphics, are situated in the centre of the fascia, as is the stereo system. Stowage for odds and ends is less comprehensive; are the French a naturally tidier race?

The exhaust note of the GTi was sportier than I had expected it to be, and has an extra crispness to it which is most pleasing on the car. The gearshift on this car is an object lesson in such matters; this really is a front-driven car which has a gearchange as precise as the best machines with inline boxes. Snicking it ▷

SPECIFICATIONS
PEUGEOT 205 GTi

ENGINE TYPE	Transverse 4 cylinder SOHC	BRAKING SYSTEM	Dual circuit hydraulics, discs front, drums rear
BORE x STROKE	83mm x 73mm		
SIZE	1580cc	WEIGHT	1950 lbs
BHP @ RPM	115 @ 6250	POWER/WEIGHT RATIO	132 b.h.p./ton
TORQUE LB/FT @ RPM	98 @ 4000	WHEELBASE	95.3"
FUEL SYSTEM	Bosch L-Jetronic electronic fuel injection	LENGTH	146"
		WIDTH	62"
DRIVEN WHEELS	Front	HEIGHT	52"
TRANSMISSION	5-speed manual	MANUFACTURER'S MPG	33.7
SUSPENSION: FRONT	MacPherson struts, anti-roll bar	TEST MPG	34.2
REAR	Torsion bars, trailing arms, telescopic dampers, anti-roll bar	PRICE AS TESTED	£8,345
		INSURANCE GROUP	5

MANUFACTURER: Peugeot Talbot Motors Company, Ryton, Coventry, West Midlands, England.

SHOOTOUT

◁ into first and easing out the light clutch, it immediately becomes apparent why the 205 has been given the nickname of "the Pug", as it has the same get-up-and-at-em urge that typifies that breed of dog.

The engine revs freely, and even when cold gives the impression that it will spin on and on, ever faster. The torque figure for this engine is identical to that of the XR2, at 98 lb/ft, and again it delivers this at 4000 r.p.m. It is at higher engine speeds that the GTi really comes into its own, the extra horsepower coming through long after an XR2's engine would be getting breathless. The MacPherson strut front suspension system is as good as you will get, but the car suffers from excessive torque steer when punching out of a corner with high engine revs registering on the tachometer.

Running the car hard through tight bends is subsequently less of a pleasure

than the same series of manoeuvres in the Fiesta; where the car becomes its most enjoyable is on sweeping curves, where it adopts an attitude of gently-compliant four wheel drifts on a trailing throttle, which can be turned into sharp and responsive forward motion by the application of a little pressure to the accelerator pedal. This is the principle benefit of having that extra few inches in the wheelbase.

That same factor is also partly responsive for the better cruising stability of the 205, which has a smoother ride than that of its Ford counterpart. The rear suspension system of the French car is more sophisticated in its design, being torsion bar sprung with trailing arms, vertical dampers and an anti-roll bar, and this is able to provide the balance of ride quality and handling that is required of a small fast car as we near the end of the eighties. The beam axle of the XR2 is positively archaic by comparison.

In all other respects, the chassis of the Peugeot is more than adequate for the tasks demanded of it. The steering, whilst lacking that fine precision displayed by the Ford, is very good, and the driver is always aware of the attitude of the front wheels. The brakes, like those of the Fiesta, cannot be got with any kind of anti-lock mechanism (yet ...), but proved themselves to be fade-free, and resistant to locking up. When compared with the XR2 they are a little "dead" at the pedal end of the system, but they are nonetheless effective.

Just like the XR2, the basic price of the 205 GTi is indicative of reasonable value for money, at £8,026. Being a far more contemporary design, central locking and power windows are available as optional extras (at £325 for the two), and the factory sunroof that is offered for this car is a sliding one (£220) which tilts, whereas the Fiesta item can only be either tilted or removed entirely. This means that the car costs about £750 more than the Fiesta in basic form, and some £1,300 more if it is loaded with those extras mentioned.

Back-to-back tests such as this rarely draw a sharp conclusion, with one car beating another hands down — if that was the case we wouldn't have such a tremendous range of cars from different makers to choose from, as a single winner would soon have the rivals going out of business. Both cars have their merits, and both have their drawbacks; I would, for instance, like to put together a car which combines the front suspension of the Fiesta with the rear system from the Peugeot. The extra cost of the 205 GTi is justifiable when you consider that the car is both quicker and faster than the XR2, and its relative scarcity adds an additional cachet to the reasons for buying it. However, the XR2 is cheaper to run (servicing and insurance costs are lower), as well as to buy, and unless you are in the habit of permanently driving at ten-tenths of the car's abilities, the lesser performance of the Ford would not really be noticed very often.

What this exercise has shown, more than anything else, is just how much work has been cut out for the teams working on the Fiesta replacement, by cars such as the 205. The XR2 will have to be endowed with an engine which will give it a power-to-weight ratio of about 135 b.h.p./ton if it is to be a serious threat to its competition for the next phase of its life, and it will have to be equipped with a more sophisticated rear suspension system and a substantially improved transmission. If Ford get those factors right and can build on the car's existing good points, they will have a superb car on their hands. Until then, price differentials apart, the 205 GTi has to take the victor's mantle. ●

FOUR BY FOUR BY TURBO TECHNICS

DENNIS FOY

FULL TEST: The Turbo Technics 230 b.h.p. XR4x4

By Dennis Foy

After every drive of a Sierra XR4x4 I have drawn the same conclusion, that the car is very civilised as a form of transport, and that it has excellent road manners. It is, however, crying out for more power, as the basic engine hasn't enough muscle to be able to make the most of the chassis.

I am by no means alone in thinking that way, and there are a number of different ways of improving the engine's performance. One of the main proponents of uprating this particular model is the Northampton-based company Turbo Technics, who offer a range of turbocharger systems which take the power output of the engine up from its standard 150 b.h.p. to anything between two hundred and 280 b.h.p. One of their most popular installations is the mid-range 230 b.h.p., and it was an example of this model that we chose for test.

The heart of the conversion is a single Garrett AiResearch T3 turbocharger which sits neatly on the nearside of the engine block. This is mounted on a specially-designed cast iron manifold which contains a high nickel content, and which is designed to give pulse separation. Air is drawn via the original air cleaner element, passes through the turbocharger, and goes on through an air-to-air intercooler mounted ahead of the car's radiator before entering the standard 2.8i plenum chamber, which is turned through 180° in the interests of pipework routing.

The engine's compression ratio is lowered by machining the pistons, and the car's fuel system is modified electronically to ensure that an adequate mixture is maintained at all engine speeds and under all load conditions. The ignition is altered by incorporating a vacuum advance/pressure retard capsule, as well as an amended advance curve — failure to do this would result in excessive problems with detonation. Final changes to the ignition systems are the installation of wide heat-range plugs, and a different timing baseline.

In order to cope with the increased power output, the gearbox is stripped and rebuilt, with an improved layshaft alignment, more substantial bearings, ducted oil feed, and special oil. The standard clutch is retained, and the differentials are unchanged. Likewise, the braking system (this particular example is fitted with the optional anti-lock braking system, which should be considered as the No. 1 priority by anybody contemplating the purchase of an XR4x4) is standard, save for the fitment of a set of anti-fade pads on the front discs.

The TT230, as the car is known, comes standard with an uprated suspension system. This comprises a set of heavier springs which also lower the car very slightly (10mm to be precise), and stiffer mounting bushes for the rear semi-trailing arms. The standard XR4x4 dampers are retained on this package.

The engine fires readily from cold, and settles down immediately to a steady tickover. However, there is a marked reluctance for the engine to pull smoothly until a minute or two after it has fired up; attempts to pull away smoothly are ▷

FOUR BY FOUR BY TURBO TECHNICS

thwarted by the car doing a pretty good imitation of a kangaroo. The best way to overcome this is to start the engine, and then leave it idling for one or two minutes before moving off. The gearbox also is less than keen on the notion of co-operation when cold, being downright baulky and obstructive. Unfortunately it never really improves much as it warms up, which is a pity; whilst it never becomes so bad as to seriously impede the car's progress, it does detract from the overall pleasure of driving it. Second gear is the major offender, regardless of whether it is a shift up or down the ratios.

Whilst sitting waiting for a bit of heat to work its way through the induction system, there is time to ponder the inside of the car. Apart from the seats and steering wheel, there is little to distinguish the XR4x4 from any other reasonably-equipped Sierra. The driver is presented with the usual cluster of

"In the traffic light drag race, the car is all but unassailable; it would take something in the nature of a Porsche 911 or Cosworth RS 500 to beat the TT230."

instruments, being speedometer, tachometer, water temperature gauge, and fuel gauge, together with a battery of warning lamps. Primary lighting functions and wipers are stalk-controlled, and secondary switches are mounted to the fascia, as are the air-conditioning controls and suchlike. The level of trim that a purchaser gets with his or her new XR4x4 is reasonable, but lamentably short in certain areas. For instance, there are powered mirrors and front windows, but there are only manual window winders in the back of the car. Similarly, whilst there is the facility for the driver (and **only** the driver) to alter the height of his or her seat, such basic items as courtesy light switches on the rear doors are absent. And so the list goes on.

But that isn't the fault of Turbo Technics. Their involvement is purely and simply concerned with the performance aspects of the car, and they have handled that side of things extremely

competently. A primary advantage of four wheel drive on the XR is its ability to launch out of a side road and into flowing traffic without any fuss or drama. When the power output has been boosted by a shade over 50%, such a manoeuvre can be accomplished with consumate ease. For instance, if the intention is to leave a side road and join a line of traffic moving at perhaps 40 m.p.h., the move can be completed in a mere four seconds — rapidly enough to allow the car to slot into all but the tightest-packed line of traffic.

In the traffic light drag race, the car is all but unassailable: it would take something in the nature of a Porsche 911 or a Cosworth RS 500 to beat the TT230. We managed a best 0-60 sprint in 6.11 seconds, and it took only 14.9 seconds for the car to cover the distance needed for it to reach a hundred miles an hour from standstill.

SPECIFICATIONS
SIERRA XR4x4 TT230 TURBO

ENGINE TYPE	Pushrod V6	**BRAKING SYSTEM**	Front discs, rear discs, anti-fade pads, electronic anti-lock braking control
BORE x STROKE	93mm x 68.5mm		
SIZE	2792cc		
BHP @ RPM	230 @ 5000	**WEIGHT**	2715 lbs
TORQUE LB/FT @ RPM	275 @ 4000	**POWER/WEIGHT RATIO**	204 b.h.p./ton
FUEL SYSTEM	Bosch K-Jetronic electronic ignition with Turbo Technics modifications	**WHEELBASE**	102.7"
		LENGTH	175"
DRIVEN WHEELS	All	**WIDTH**	67"
TRANSMISSION	5-speed manual, viscous coupled final drive, torque split 34% front, 66% rear	**HEIGHT**	53"
		TEST MILEAGE	1,505 miles
		MANUFACTURER'S MPG	N/A
SUSPENSION: FRONT	MacPherson struts, gas-filled dampers, anti-roll bar	**TEST MPG**	16.8
		PRICE AS TESTED	£19,000 approx.
REAR	Semi-trailing arms, rising rate springs, gas-filled dampers	**INSURANCE GROUP**	Special Quotation

MANUFACTURER: Turbo Technics, 17 Galowhill Road, Brackmills, Northampton NN4 0EE.

As impressive as they are, the times for straight line sprints tell only part of the story. Where this car is most at home is on winding country roads. The engine's maximum torque of 275 lb/ft is delivered at 4000 r.p.m., and it starts a rapid climb towards that figure from about 2000 r.p.m. Provided the engine speed is kept above the 2000 mark on the tachometer, there is sufficient muscle on tap to punch the car neatly out of one bend, and send it whooshing towards the next. Only when a slip-up occurs (such as a mis-timed gearshift, or a lapse in anticipation) does the problem of turbo-lag rear its ugly head. What happens in such an event is that the car flounders a little around the apex of the bend, and then suddenly tightens on its line and heads in the intended direction as the engine climbs back onto the start of its torque curve.

Get it right, and the car can burn adrenalin almost at the same rate as it can burn petrol.

Our example of the TT230 Sierra came on the standard 14" alloy rims with 195/60 tyres — in this instance a set of very impressive Uniroyal Rallye 340 series which give excellent, progressive grip in the wet and in the dry. These seem to work very well with the revised suspension system, although I did on occasion feel that the car would benefit from slightly firmer damping; there was the odd tendency for the damping action to get a little way off from where it ought to have been whilst negotiating a particularly sharp series of bends along Derbyshire's Cat & Fiddle Pass. The car never became wayward, but did tend to understeer rather more than it ought to have done, a situation which would almost certainly be remedied by slightly firmer damping. Counterpoint to this, the ride quality of the car has not suffered in the slightest from the lowered and stiffened springs which have been fitted to the car, so I suppose it is a case of roundabouts and swings.

I gave the car a hard run on several occasions, and it proved very stimulating — and extremely rapid to boot. It was also quite hard work at times, primarily because the gearshift could prove so awkward when it came to getting it to engage second gear, a ratio used often on the very tight bends which feature prominently in the part of Derbyshire in which I tested the car. The combination of a powerful engine and ABS braking, compounded by very precise and responsive steering, were ideal for making very fast runs, as the ABS allows later-than-average braking, and the torque curve lets the car be pulled out of bends

in rapid fashion. All that spoils a perfect equation for fun is the manner in which the obstructive nature of the gearshift lost vital fractions of a second — and consequently vital engine revs. The Ford permanent four wheel drive system saved the day on a number of occasions, thanks to the extra chassis stability which it brings with it. Even when there is a momentary drop in the amount of power making its way through to the road the car never becomes too wayward, merely slipping towards a power-correctable understeer.

Out on a long motorway run, the car again proved itself more than capable of handling its tasks. The Turbo Technics system has quite a good amount of useable mid-range punch, which makes the overtaking of slower traffic a surprisingly rapid affair. Slotting the car down a gear or two has the car punching through the air past slower traffic unbelievably quickly, and even leaving the gearbox in a high gear still enables passing manoeuvres to be completed substantially more quickly than any normal XR4x4 could manage. To illustrate the point, a burst in third gear from fifty to seventy takes a mere 3.4 seconds. The same manoeuvre in fourth still only takes a shade over 4.3 seconds, and even leaving the car in fifth still has the run completed in 6.1 seconds. Those times are enough to show the driver that virtually any overtaking situation can be dealt with rapidly and effectively.

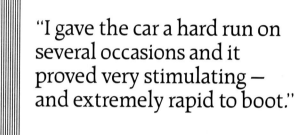

"I gave the car a hard run on several occasions and it proved very stimulating — and extremely rapid to boot."

It is a similar story around town. That vital burst from 30 to 50 can be dealt with in only 2.9 seconds with the car in second gear. Even being lazy and leaving the gearshift in its fourth slot it takes only five seconds or so to complete the run.

The turbocharger has a silencing effect on the engine's exhaust note, but even so, the XR4x4 would benefit from a little extra ▷

FOUR BY FOUR BY TURBO TECHNICS

◁ soundproofing – the engine's high-speed coarseness combined with excessive tyre roar can make high-speed progress more tiring than it ought to be. This again is a weakness of the car rather than the conversion, and could be remedied by spending £60 or thereabouts on as Acoustikit additional soundproofing system.

The car does, unfortunately, have one major shortcoming, and that is the amount of fuel which it is capable of consuming. Running the car quite hard it manages only to return a staggering 14 m.p.g., and even motorway cruising doesn't improve the picture by a great amount – we could achieve an average of only 18 m.p.g. there. Admittedly we weren't out on an economy drive when we tested the car, but even so, an average of 16.8 m.p.g. takes a bit of reconciling ... When we tested a standard XR4x4 back in our January 1988 issue, most of our runs were on cross-country roads, and that car managed an average of 17.3 miles per gallon – motorway cruising gave an average consumption of 22 m.p.g. But then, there was nothing like the same adrenalin burn from the standard car as could be got from the TT230.

On balance, the car is one which makes a good package. In the first place, the XR4x4 is a tidy combination of excellent handling, ample space for most needs, and a reasonable degree of comfort. When that basic formula is added to by incorporating the engine modifications carried out by Turbo Technics, then it becomes an affordable supercar; the total cost of the conversion work is in the region of £3,240+V.A.T., which covers the turbocharger installation, the suspension system uprating, and a full one-year warranty from the company. The price varies slightly, depending upon whether the car is equipped with air conditioning or not.

In terms of overall reliability, providing the engine is treated the way that any performance engine ought to be – never running it hard until it is warmed through, servicing it regularly, and so forth – there ought to be no fundamental differences between the longevity of this and any other high-output machine. The engine management system modifications see to it that detonation doesn't become a problem, and today's ultra-high performance synthetic oils will stay in grade even in a turbocharged engine to ensure that adequate lubrication for the duration of the time between services is a reality. And if the worst does happen and the turbocharger fails, Turbo Technics, through their Turbocare network, are able to ensure a speedy and economical replacement unit is available.

For further information, and details of their national network of dealers, contact Turbo Technics at Department P.F., 17 Galowhill Road, Brackmills, Northampton NN4 0EE. ●

A PAIR OF PLUS FOURS

BOTH THE SAME AND BOTH VERY DIFFERENT, WE LOOK AT THE POWER ENGINEERING SUPERCHARGED XR4x4 AND THE TURBO TECHNICS TT230 TURBOCHARGED XR4x4

BY DENNIS FOY

Whenever we have one or the other on test, there is always somebody sidles up and asks that most loaded of questions: "Which is best, supercharging or turbocharging?" And every time that it happens, we wish that there was a simple answer that we could trot out.

In an effort to come up with a definitive statement on the subject, we have taken two examples of Sierra XR4x4, one turbocharged and the other supercharged, and analysed them. We have laid out the similarities and the differences, the advantages and the disadvantages, and the relevant performance data for each car. For reasons which ought to have become clear by the other end of the feature we haven't come up with a definitive answer to the thorny question — but you will, hopefully, be able to determine for yourself what suits and what doesn't suit about them.

It's worth starting by giving an outline of the two systems, which explains the very different ways in which they achieve their common aim. Both are compressors, and increase the power of the engines to which they are attached by forcing a greater amount of air and fuel into the combustion chamber than it would ever draw in conventionally.

As its name implies, a turbocharger uses a pair of turbines as a means of compressing air. These are housed in the same casing, and share a common shaft drive, but they are totally insulated from each other. The first turbine's impeller is ducted from the exhaust ports via a specially-redesigned manifold, and when the engine is running the gases escaping from the combustion chambers act to spin the impeller blades. This in turn spins, via the shaft, the other impeller within the casing, which is ducted to the intake side of the engine. As there are no gears within the

turbocharger casing the two impeller sets spin at the same rate; for every full revolution of the exhaust impeller, the one for the induction side spins one turn. As engine speed increases, so does the rate at which gases pass through their manifold — and consequently the turbocharger spins ever faster. As it turns the induction impeller draws air in, it gradually changes from being at negative pressure to positive pressure — or what is more commonly referred to as "coming on boost".

Left to its own devices the turbocharger would keep on increasing the amount of pressurisation, right up until it ran out of exhaust power to turn it. However, every engine installation has a pre-determined limit, a point at which it is either inadvisable or potentially dangerous to allow boosting to continue. In the case of the subject of this feature, the boost pressure maximum has been set at 0.65 bar, which is governed by a device known as a wastegate. This, in simple terms, dumps the excess exhaust gases before they can spin the impeller for just as long as necessary to stabilise the pressures on the inlet tract.

A supercharger works by using a mechanical drive from the engine's crankshaft, which consists of two pulleys joined by a drive belt. The sizes of these two pulleys can be varied, and it is their ratio which determines the rate at which the supercharger spins. Within the casing of the supercharger are a pair of rotors, and like a turbocharger, it is these rotors which compress the air and force it through and into the engine's inlet tract. There are various types of rotor used within superchargers, and those in the Sprintex supercharger are generally accepted as being of the most efficient design, comprising a pair of screw-pattern metal devices which closely follow the contours of each other, and ▷

A PAIR OF PLUS FOURS

◁ which are separated from each other by the smallest of gaps. They are driven from a gear cluster at the front of the supercharger casing, and so revolve at a greater speed than the drive pulley.

Due to the design flexibility of the drive system, it is possible to have the supercharger running at a speed which is adequate to provide positive boost even at quite low engine speeds — and to then tailor the pulley sizes to ensure that the designated maximum boost setting is not overstepped when the engine is running at maximum speed. By judicious use of pulley sizes a supercharged engine can be made to produce a torque curve which starts at very low engine speeds, a characteristic which is difficult to achieve in turbocharged engines. In the case of our test car, the V6 starts to produce real, useable torque at 1400 r.p.m., and by 3000 r.p.m. is developing in the region of 275 lb/ft — a figure which it continues to produce right through to its 6250 r.p.m. redline. By comparison, the turbocharged V6 produces little useable power below 2500 r.p.m., and it is 4000 r.p.m. before it starts to hit the top of its torque curve.

Out on the road, there are marked differences in the behaviour of the two cars. With the turbocharged car little happens until 2500 r.p.m., but from there the power starts to develop in earnest, and the engine pulls and pulls, forever faster right through until the cut-out at 6250 r.p.m. screams enough. The effect is not dissimilar to a fairground ride, or the buzz that can be felt when an aircraft is hurtling along a runway, on take-off. The supercharged version of the XR4x4, on the other hand, feels far more like there is a substantially bigger engine under the bonnet. Instead of the sudden extra surge of power, there is a steady shove of muscle right from very low engine speeds, and right through. It may not burn as much adrenalin, but our figures prove that this version is, in fact, marginally quicker than the turbo car which actually gives the impression of being the more swift.

In terms of straight-line acceleration, the difference between the two cars is slight, and almost imperceptible; it is tenths of a second which separate them right through to 100 m.p.h. Both cars can hit the sprint to sixty from standstill in a shade over six seconds, and even at the end of a standing quarter mile there is only two-tenths of a second separating them; on a dragstrip it

would take only a slightly different shifting technique to allow a race to go either way.

It is in the mid-range that differences start to appear in the figures, with the supercharged car taking the advantage on every round, principally because of its superior low-end torque. Leaving the car in, say, fourth gear and making to increase speed from 50 m.p.h. to 70 m.p.h. the turbocharged car takes 4.94 seconds. The same exercise in the supercharged car takes 3.86 seconds. In fifth gear, the time for the same manoeuvre in the turbo car takes 6.13 seconds — but only 5.46 seconds in the supercharged version of the car. A similar pattern emerges for other in-gear times, as the separate table shows.

On the winding roads which are the natural habitat of the XR4x4, it is the supercharged version which is less demanding to drive, thanks mainly to the massive torque spread of the engine. In practical terms, the car can be driven quickly without ever having to anticipate quite when the power is going to arrive — floor the throttle, and there it is, as much as required. With the turbocharged version a degree of anticipation is required if the revs have been allowed to drop much below 3000 r.p.m. as it takes a moment for the power to climb back up to the level

ACCELERATION

	Turbocharged	Supercharged
0-30	2.7	2.8
0-50	5.2	5.3
0-60	6.1	6.2
0-70	8.5	8.6
30-50 (2nd)	2.4	2.4
30-50 (3rd)	4.2	3.7
30-50 (4th)	5.1	4.5
50-70 (3rd)	3.4	3.0
50-70 (4th)	4.9	3.8
50-70 (5th)	6.1	5.4
70-90 (4th)	5.8	5.4
70-90 (5th)	7.1	6.7
¼ mile e.t.	14.9/101 m.p.h.	15.0/100 m.p.h.
50-0	2.6	2.6
Maximum	140 m.p.h.	140 m.p.h.

required to make a rapid exit from the bend. The counterpoint to this is the way in which the turbocharged car seems to make the power climb more and more dramatically – which can, on occasion, give the driver the urge to pull the wheel back and fly the rest of the way home.

SPECIFICATIONS

	Turbocharged	Supercharged	Standard
BHP @ RPM	230 @ 5000	240 @ 5250	150 @ 5700
Torque lb/ft	275 @ 4000	295 @ 3000	216 @ 3800
Transmission	Uprated	Standard	Standard
Front Suspension	Uprated dampers	Uprated adjustable dampers, revised springs	Standard
Rear Suspension	Uprated dampers, stiffer bushes	Uprated adjustable dampers, lower springs	

CONTACTS

Both companies have regional dealers.
Contact them for details of your nearest.

Power Engineering
Unit 9
5a Wyvern Way
Uxbridge
Middlesex UB6 2XN

Turbo Technics
17 Galowhill Road
Brackmills
Northampton
Northants NN3 0EE

★Please mention **Performance Ford** when making enquiries★

And therein lies the fundamental difference between the two cars; the turbocharged version is ostentatious in its show of power; like Bluto in Popeye cartoons, it is ever willing to show off its rippling biceps by suddenly surging ahead once the engine comes onto boost. The supercharged version on the other hand, is quiet, subtle and understated in its manners. It delivers the same goods, but is never flashy about the way it does it, preferring to display a solid wave of serious power.

The one other vital difference between these two cars was highlighted at the petrol pumps; given that we did identical trips in both cars, taking in motorway work, town driving, and fast runs through open countryside on demanding roads, it was the turbocharged model which made the more frequent demands for fuel stops. This was good for the collection of Esso tokens, but not so good on the bank account. The bald facts were that over identical runs the turbocharged car returned an average 16.8 miles per gallon, whereas the supercharged version achieved an average of 21.7 m.p.g. – the latter being a substantial improvement on the 19 or so miles per gallon figure for a standard 150 b.h.p. XR4x4.

The initial cost for either conversion is similar, at over £3,000 plus the dreaded V.A.T. Both produce a similar nett power output, and both substantially improve what is already a good car. Both cars are extremely rewarding to drive, and both make light work of long distance trips, whether they are across country or down motorways. Neither conversion over-stresses the rest of the XR4x4's drivetrain by an undue amount – although Turbo Technics play safe by uprating the gearbox, a move which Power consider less essential, because there are no sudden power surges from their supercharger installation.

The eventual choice between the two conversions is very much a matter of personal preference; if you want a car which feels dramatically fast, then the turbocharged version is the one to go for, whereas if you prefer to make a steady, surging progress, then go for the supercharged version. The best idea, really, is to try out both versions, and decide which one you feel best at the wheel of. ●

RED HOT AND ROLLING

TURBO TECHNICS HAVE DEVELOPED A NEW SUSPENSION SYSTEM FOR THEIR TURBOCHARGED ESCORT XR3i DENNIS FOY HAS BEEN TESTING IT

I have driven more front-wheel-drive Escorts than I sometimes care to remember. Besides abundant "shopping" models, there have been quite a few examples which have been tuned to high heaven, from naturally-aspirated, cammed, carbed and exhaust-tuned little 'uns right through to turbocharged fire-breathers producing close to two hundred brake horsepower at the flywheel. With one or two notable exceptions, the drive has often been a battle of wills between myself and the car as I fought to overcome the difficulties of trying to put immense amounts of power through a driveline and suspension system which was clearly never designed to take it.

Torque steer is the name of the problem; as the engine hits its optimum torque delivery point, it makes the front end of the car

DENNIS FOY

dart from side to side. Much of the problem is directly attributable to a lack of positive location in the area of the front struts' bottom mounts. As the problem is at its most severe on cars which have turbocharged engines — the standard RS Turbo is a prime culprit — it is unsurprising to learn that Turbo Technics have been devoting much time, energy and cash to the problem in a bid to negate it. This car is proof that they have succeeded in their quest.

The starting point of the suspension system's reworking is a new alloy casting which replaces the original pressed steel item. Based on that which was developed by Ford Motorsport and subsequently used on the RS 1600i and the first model of RS Turbo, this offers substantially improved inboard location for the track control arms. Heavy-duty bushes are then used on all appropriate points, and a heavier anti-roll bar is used — this dramatically reduces the twisting and shimmying out-of-alignment which causes the car to change direction under load.

Having tightened up the front end of the car to a suitable pitch, it would do horrible things to the handling if the rear was left in its original state, and so that end of the car is also revised. Once again heavy-duty bushings are used throughout, and uprated coil springs are implanted to replace the originals. Finally a rear ▶

RED HOT AND ROLLING

anti-roll bar is installed. The result of the package is a car which handles very neutrally indeed — it drifts out on all fours when the edge of traction is reached, rather than the usual nose-first dive towards the outside of the bend which heralds the edge of a hot Escort's adhesion limits.

And this particular car is as hot as its colour suggests, for lurking beneath the bonnet is one of Turbo Technics' excellent 160 brake horsepower turbocharged XR3i engines. As is usual with their conversions, there is far more to turbocharging the CVH than simply bolting a Garrett T25 onto the front of the cylinder head. For a start, the exhaust manifold on which the turbo is mounted is specially designed, and cast-to-order in a high nickel content iron which is durable enough to withstand the tremendous variations in head which the engine's exhaust gases bring with them. Then the compression ratio is lowered by machining off the top of the pistons until the desired 7.9:1 level is reached. An intercooler is installed to bring the temperature of incoming air down to manageable levels, and then a Kenlowe fan is mounted close by the standard XR3i radiator to ensure that engine coolant is not allowed to reach boiling point. Fuel and ignition curves are reset to be certain that timing and quantities are always just right, and the oil system is revised to ensure constant lubrication for the turbocharger.

This particular car was Bristol Street Motors' demonstration vehicle, and in the interests of cutting a high profile it had been equipped with a Ford RS set of styling panels, colour-keyed to the red of the original paintwork. The inside of the car was virtually untouched, though, and were it not for the little toggle switch tucked just the other side of the lighting master switch, the unaware could easily feel that he or she was driving a stock, standard XR3i.

Until the ignition key was turned.

The XR3i has a distinctive rasp to its exhaust note, and a trained ear can tell one from half a block away. However, with the turbocharger interspersed 'twixt manifold and tailpipe, the note becomes more a deep burble which is most pleasant on the ear. The note never really rises much in pitch as engine speed

increases, nor does it get much louder thanks to the silencing effect of the turbo rotor blades. The only other giveaway to the fact that this car is anything different from a stock XR3i whilst stationary is that the uprated clutch necessary to deal with the power increase makes for a much heavier pedal action.

As it was raining when I collected the car from Bristol Street's Powerhouse, I decided that it would be prudent to get to know the car on reduced terms, and so flicked the toggle switch I mentioned earlier to a maximum boost level of 0.45 bar (about 6½ lbs), which translates in power terms to something in the region of 130 b.h.p. As hoped, torque steer was virtually non-existent even though traction was poor thanks to the amount of water which was standing at Birmingham's road junctions.

> "The most fun-per-minute is extracted from the car when the motorways are left behind and it is out on winding country roads."

Heavy rain dogged me all the way back to Cheshire, and it was the following morning before road conditions were dry and clear enough to allow me to try out the car's potential.

I have fond memories of test-driving a jet-engined dragster at Santa Pod under the tutelage of the late, and much-missed "Bootsie" Herridge. I can still remember well the surge of forward thrust as the machine's afterburner was switched into life, and was immediately reminded of that sensation when I flicked the Escort's boost control switch over to its high position in the middle of an acceleration run, and the car leapt forward like a racehorse on the final furlong when its nostrils are filled

PERFORMANCE TURBO TECHNICS TT160 TURBO XR3i	
0-30	3.17 seconds
0-50	5.39 seconds
0-60	7.19 seconds
0-70	9.53 seconds
30-50 (2nd gear)	5.83 seconds
30-50 (3rd gear)	5.87 seconds
30-50 (4th gear)	5.99 seconds
50-70 (3rd gear)	3.74 seconds
50-70 (4th gear)	5.63 seconds
50-70 (5th gear)	6.53 seconds
70-90 (4th gear)	4.61 seconds
70-90 (5th gear)	5.21 seconds
¼ Mile	15.94 @ 88 m.p.h.
Maximum Speed	131 m.p.h.
70-0 Braking	4.90 seconds

with the sweet scent of success.

Standing start runs with the boost switch on high, and a hundred and sixty brake horsepower leaving the flywheel, can induce a degree of torque steer. However, this is totally controllable and never anything like as acute as that felt in a standard Mk II RS Turbo. Feedback through the steering wheel is excellent, thanks to the very limited degree of absorption offered by the uprated bushings, and although Bristol Street Motors were unable to confirm it, I gained the impression that the front suspension angles had been altered slightly from the factory settings, which gave a more precise self-centering action to the road wheels.

The car is an ideal motorway machine, thanks to the considerable amount of power available which makes light work of overtaking, and the substantially improved stability which is brought about by a combination of the suspension system revisions and the bodykit. In a standard XR3i, you would need to allocate some twenty seconds to make a fifth-gear climb from seventy to ninety miles per hour; in this car, a mere five and a quarter seconds would suffice for the same manoeuvre. So it goes across the range of in-gear times, the turbocharged car cutting a swathe through the equivalent times from a stock example of the XR3i.

The car also proved itself extraordinarily well-behaved on motorway sliproads. Experience has shown that most of these are negotiated most comfortably at engine speeds between three and four thousand revs per minute. However, with turbocharged cars, this can prove problematic as the engine tends to come on and off boost within that range – which can upset the driveline of the car. Thanks to the quality of the suspension arrangement on this particular car there are no dramatic moments when this happens, the car maintaining a neutral stance. If only the current model of RS Turbo was equally well-behaved ...

The most fun-per-minute is extracted from this car when the motorways are left behind, and it is out on winding country roads. Running hard with the boost control switch (a device

which is described by American colleagues as the "granny switch" because you flick it onto its lower position when your grandma is borrowing the car) on low is exciting enough, but when it is switched over to its higher setting the Escort becomes positively scintillating to drive. The absence of a limited slip differential will see the inside wheel scrambling and scrabbling for traction, but the one on the other side of the front axle keeps hauling the car forward on its intended line until such time as the car is facing dead ahead again – and all of the time, the driver is aware of what is happening at ground level by a never-ending stream of information coming through to the steering wheel.

Long sweeping curves elicit no such traction problems, and highlight the balance that has been achieved between front and rear of the car; entering a curve on a trailing throttle the car will start to drift wide, all four wheels drifting in unison. A progressive application of throttle will then tighten the car on its line and have it lunging forward in direct response to the amount of pressure applied to the pedal. If ever there was a pocket-sized Cosworth, then this car is surely it. ▶

THE POWERHOUSE

Being astute enough to realise that owners of non-standard Ford cars appreciate being treated a little differently from Mr. & Mrs. Average with their Escort Popular, Bristol Street Motors have built a specialist performance centre at the Birmingham headquarters. Known as the Powerhouse, the centre caters for RS car owners and also those who have had Turbo Technics conversions on their cars – Bristol Street are TT's Midlands Approved Distributor.

Clients are greeted in a special reception area, and the service manager works hard to develop a rapport with each and every customer, understanding their peculiar needs and wishes. The client is able to meet the technician who will be working on their car, and is able to see directly into the workshop area via a glazed wall from the reception lounge. Fixed priced "menu" servicing is available for all of the RS range, and the TT converted cars.

In addition to servicing, clients of the Powerhouse can also purchase and have fitted any of the range of Ford RS aftermarket accessories, body kits and wheels, as well as improved sound systems, car telephones, and suspension systems.

The Powerhouse is situated at Bristol Street, Birmingham. Telephone: 021-666 6000.

RED HOT AND ROLLING

The usual bane of turbocharged smaller engines is lag, that awful moment whilst the driver waits for the power to start arriving in force when the turbo begins to do its stuff. I am pleased to report that Turbo Technics have all but eradicated the problem with this particular installation. Certainly there is a marked difference once all ten or so pounds of positive intake pressure is being forced into the engine, but even at low engine speeds when the manifold is running on vacuum pressure there is adequate power making its way from the flywheel. Having said that, the best is gained from the engine when the revs are kept towards the middle of the tachometer range if you are intending to do some serious running.

What Turbo Technics have done with the XR3i is to produce a conversion which doesn't feel like a conversion — it feels like a factory-produced car. In fact, I will stick my neck out and, at the risk of offending quite a few people to whom the letters RS are both old and new testaments combined, state that in my opinion this particular car feels more like a Rallye Sport car than the current model of Escort RS Turbo. It is quicker, faster, and feels far more "together" than the official Ford-produced turbocharged Escort. I get the sneaky feeling that this is the car which Rod Mansfield and the team would like to produce, were

they not hampered by the constraints imposed by the Marketing Department.

The only down side to the car is its cost; not having the benefit of Ford's resources or buying power, Turbo Technics have no option but to charge what they do for their conversions. In the instance of the XR3i, the starting point is £2,170 for the 160 b.h.p. turbocharging system (the lower option of 130 b.h.p. costs £1,645), plus £680 for the high-performance handling package. Then there is another £45 for uprating the front brake pads, and a further £725 for Powerhouse to add the bodykit, inclusive of painting. When these amounts are added to the showroom cost of a new XR3i, which stands at present at about £10,400 when the SCS anti-lock braking system option is specified, then the total bill comes to close on £14,000 — a lot of money by anybody's standards, and appreciably more than the £12,000 or so which is asked for a new RS Turbo. All that I can say is that the TT160 is a lot more of a car than the RS Turbo in its latest form.

You pays your money and you takes your choice. ●

Turbo Technics are at Department P.F., 17 Galowhill Road, Brackmills, Northampton NN4 0EE.

Bodykit is from RS catalogue, colour keyed after fitting by Bristol Street's Powerhouse.

CVH engine is able to produce 160 b.h.p. with aid of Garrett turbocharger.

SPECIFICATIONS
TURBO TECHNICS TT160 TURBO XR3i

ENGINE TYPE	4 cylinder SOHC	SUSPENSION: REAR	Swinging arms, revised spring rates, anti-rollbar, HD bushes
BORE x STROKE	80mm x 79.52mm		
SIZE	1597cc	BRAKING SYSTEM	Front discs, rear drums, Ford-Lucas Girling SCS anti-lock mechanism
BHP @ RPM	160 @ 6000		
TORQUE LB/FT @ RPM	170 @ 4000		
FUEL SYSTEM	Garrett AiResearch T25 water-cooled turbocharger, intercooled. Integral wastegate, max. 0.65 bar pressure. Bosch electronic injection, revised metering head	WEIGHT	2145 lbs
		POWER/WEIGHT RATIO	165 b.h.p./ton
		WHEELBASE	94.5"
		LENGTH	159"
		WIDTH	72"
DRIVEN WHEELS	Front	HEIGHT	54"
TRANSMISSION	5-speed manual	TEST MILEAGE	871 miles
SUSPENSION: FRONT	MacPherson struts, alloy crossmember, HD anti-roll bar, HD bushes	MANUFACTURER'S MPG	N/A
		TEST MPG	23.7
		PRICE AS TESTED	See text
		INSURANCE GROUP	Special quotation

MANUFACTURER: Ford Motor Company, Dagenham, Essex, England.
Modifications carried out by Turbo Technics, Northampton.
Car supplied by Bristol Street Motors, Birmingham.

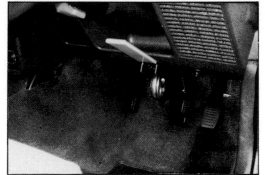

BUYER'S GUIDE

IN THE SECOND OF OUR
SERIES, WE SURVEY THE
MK I FIESTA XR2 SCENE

BY DENNIS FOY

DENNIS FOY

I remember well my first encounter with the XR2. I was amongst a party of a dozen or so journalists in Belgium, trying out the then-unannounced revisions to the range of Mk II Granadas, and we had stopped for lunch and the usual post prandial delights of a presentation which would tell us everything that we ever wanted to know about the car — and quite a few things which we were less than concerned with too. Part way through the "lecture" a member of the engineering staff was busy explaining the details about the grubby bits of the range, when I felt a tug at my elbow. I turned to find the Chairman of Ford of Britain at my side, and was promptly spirited away from the main party to be shown, in another building, the car which he considered to be the most interesting new car on the premises.

What Sam Toy (for it was he) led me to was a bright red transformation of the ordinary, boring little Fiesta which had been on sale for some four years or more. For a start, the car had wide alloy wheels with low-profile tyres, and these were shrouded with neatly-moulded arch extensions to ensure that the car fell within the requirements of the law on such matters. There were spoilers front and rear, the rectangular headlamps had been replaced by big round ones (supplemented by a pair of driving lamps), and there were decals on either side which created the illusion of the entire wing sides being flared out in the style of a Zakspeed RS Capri.

On the inside were a pair of bucket-style front seats trimmed in a fabric which co-ordinated with the body colour, a sports-style steering wheel, more substantial instrumentation, and so forth — right down to a red keyline around the leading edge of the binnacle housing the clocks. What Ford had done was to produce a GTi-style version of their basic compact car, and to back up its looks it was given an engine able to take it to more than 100 m.p.h.

▶

◀ Very little changed from that prototype which I first looked at in the early spring of 1981 to the cars which eventually went on sale through dealerships in December of the same year. As so often happens with Ford products, there was little new or revolutionary to be seen on or in the XR2; what set it apart from the herd was the way in which a wide selection of parts-bin pieces had been neatly woven by the team at Special Vehicle Engineering into the fabric of a characterful car.

It was character that the car was all about. Nippy and zippy, the XR2 proved embarrassing to quite a few owners of XR3 Escorts, as it could outrun and outhandle the latter car through a series of twists and turns. It was also more pleasurable to drive quickly, having a vastly-superior suspension arrangement and an engine which delivered its torque in a more businesslike manner.

Mechanically, the original XR2 was a simple device. The engine was the venerable old Kent crossflow 1600, with Mk I Escort Mexico-specification cylinder head and camshaft. The Weber

> "There was little new or revolutionary about the XR2 — the parts had been neatly woven by Special Vehicle Engineering into a characterful car."

DFT-A carburettor of the XR3 was used to supply fuel, and the only built-to-order bits on the engine were the intake and exhaust manifolds. On peak form an XR2 engine could develop 84 b.h.p., enough to see the car make the benchmark 0-60 spring in a touch over nine seconds, and the top speed some 106 m.p.h.

The car's transmission was originally designed for the XR3 Escort, and was a four speed item with low final drive gearing to enhance the acceleration times of either car. Suspension was pure Fiesta, with MacPherson struts at the front end (no anti-roll bar as standard ...) and a "dead" beam axle at the rear. Spring rates, damper settings and suspension geometry were all carefully chosen for the XR2 by Ford's S.V.E. team, and the result was a car which gave a feedback to the driver not unlike that experienced by drivers of RS cars.

Quite a few cars (more than twenty thousand examples) were built during the short lifespan of the first XR2 — the car ceased production some eighteen months after it first went on sale, thanks to the arrival of the Mk II version of the Fiesta which was already in the advanced stages of development when the first XR2 arrived on the scene. For this reason, although ownership of the car is considered desirable, prices are surprisingly reasonable at present, holding at about £3,000 for a clean, tidy and low-mileage example — as the car was in production for such a short length of time, the age of the car matters much less than the condition.

The immaculate Sunburst Red example which is featured on these pages is the sort of car which anybody looking for a Mk I XR2 would find impossible to improve on. Owned from new in October 1972 by Keith Snelson, the car is totally original with the exception of a new silencing system which was fitted recently, and the RS leather-rimmed steering wheel. The car has only covered 16,000 miles from new and is absolutely spotless inside and out.

Never used during the winter, the car has been entered in concours competition at several XR Owners Club events, winning a number of awards including the coveted "Best Car of the Day" trophy at the club's annual National Day. Like so many owners of Mk I examples, Keith feels that his car is far closer to the ideal of the XR car than the Mk II model which superseded it at the end of 1983.

The car was treated to a full tune-up session (recalibrating the carburettor, resetting the ignition system and so forth) at Geoff Goodliff's G.R.V. workshops in Littleborough shortly after Keith purchased the car, and since then the servicing schedule has been adhered to precisely. The only problem which has arisen with the car concerned the new exhaust system — Keith found that the systems being sold by his local Ford dealership were not as well made as the system originally fitted to the car. Eventually, after some detective work, he discovered that T.I. Bainbridge were able to supply a new system which was identical to the original, and was fully stove enamelled — that offered by his dealership was simply spray-painted, which is a far less durable finish than stoving.

Keith professes to being very happy indeed with his car, and has no immediate intention of parting with it — although he might be persuaded if it would lead him to owning an RS 1600i Escort, another favourite machine of his. He is contemplating fitting the revised valvetrain assembly mentioned in the main text as a means of doing away with the only aspect of his car with which he is less than happy — the excessive noise from the top end of the Kent engine. That apart, there are no other changes which Keith would like to make to the XR2 — he likes it just the way it is ...

The only other major problem areas (as in they may cost a lot of money to put right) are the front brake discs and the suspension system. The quality of metal which has been used in producing the brake discs has varied tremendously, depending upon the country in which they were sourced, inferior ones soon making their presence known by an increasing amount of shudder coming back through the pedal whenever the car is slowed quickly from speeds of 50 m.p.h. or beyond. Replacing the two ventilated 9½" discs costs comfortably in excess of £100, so bear this in mind when haggling over a price with a vendor.

There were no inherent faults with the suspension system, but as components wear out, the handling becomes far less precise than it ought to be. Obvious wear within the dampers soon makes itself known by "floatiness" from whichever end of the car is affected, but less apparent is wear in the various bushes which feature within the suspension system; these get progressively softer, and the sharpness of response from the car gradually deteriorates.

Out on the road, the XR2 is great fun to drive, and surprisingly predictable in its road manners. Turn-in with the steering is direct and immediate, and providing everything on the suspension system is in good order, the driver is immediately aware of the attitude and intentions of the four road wheels. The car is also extremely responsive to tuning in both the chassis and the engine.

Being the good old Kent engine, there are abundant parts available to develop the power beyond the standard 84 b.h.p. A

When buying, it pays to start with the obvious weaknesses of the Mk I Fiesta range. Whilst no more susceptible to the dreaded rust than any other Fiesta, the XR2 which has not been subjected to lots of tender, loving care is likely to be showing signs of oxidisation on the lower edge of the tailgate, and on the leading edges of the front wings. Other weak spots are the joints between the front and rear valances and their respective side panels, and the arch edges beneath their special extension mouldings.

Being so mechanically simple, there is little to really go wrong with the XR2. A degree of noise from the top end of the engine is to be expected (this is curable by replacing the rocker shaft assembly with a kit which uses tubular spacers instead of the usual springs, but more of that later), but this is not usually harmful. A degree of wear is inevitable with the engine — the Kent is an old nail which will run forever — and this is best checked by running a compression test on the engine; look to a compression of about 170 to 180 lbs when the engine is hot, with no more than 10% variation between the four cylinders. Any dramatic loss in compression usually signifies excessive wear in the cylinder/piston ring assemblies, and is accompanied by much burning of oil and a drop-off in power. This means money, so be warned.

The transmission is quite durable, if a little prone to slipping out of adjustment; it can be obstructive and rubbery unless the gearchange mechanism is just right. However, if the shifter baulks and graunches going into second and third gear, beware — this could herald the imminent collapse of the transmission, which could result in a rather large bill.

THE XR OWNERS CLUB

There is a club which caters specifically for Ford XR models which can offer a selection of special benefits to owners of these cars, including events, special clothing, and information exchanges. A full information pack is available by writing to the club at 20a Swithland Lane, Rothley, Leicester LE7 7SE, telling them that **Performance Ford** sent you.

good starting point is to replace the standard exhaust system with a larger bore, 4/2/1 manifold and low-restriction silencing system, which ought to give an increase in the order of 10 to 12% without fuel economy being harmed unduly. From there, it is worth looking at a more substantial carburation system. Weber offer a choice, from the single twin-choke 34 DATR which offers a slight gain over the standard carburettor, through to the twin DCNF downdraught system which makes for a quite dramatic increase in power — although the gain is reflected in the substantial cost of the carburettors, manifold and air cleaner assembly. From there, it is a matter of removing the engine and carrying out major works such as installing a new camshaft with slightly greater lift and longer duration (both Kent and Piper offer a range of suitable camshafts, as do a number of smaller companies), or going the full distance and overboring the block, adding higher compression pistons as you go, and possibly even a bigger valve head — although take care with the latter, as it is very easy to lose bottom-end torque which would make the car a little unwieldy in traffic.

Another option to consider is to turbocharge the car. There are not, so far as we are aware, any kits available which bolt directly onto the Kent engine used in the Mk I XR2 (Turbo Technics' system for the XR2 is designed around the CVH engine used in the Mk II version of the car), but that does not mean that fitting a turbocharger will be impossible — it simply means that an exhaust manifold which holds the turbocharger will have to be fabricated, rather than cast.

▶

BUYER'S GUIDE

◀ Whichever route is taken with tuning, it is essential to uprate the rest of the car once the power goes beyond the 100 brake horsepower (at the flywheel) stage. There are a number of very good suspension kits available for the car, from a variety of manufacturers such as Bilstein, Spax and Koni, as well as Monroe. In some cases these are dampers only, whilst in other cases they are kits which also include new road springs which lower and stiffen the car. It is worth contacting a dealership which can offer a choice between several makes to discuss your specific needs before committing yourself to any one system — that way you will almost certainly get a balanced opinion on what is best-suited to your requirements and budget.

The one last area for improvement is the braking system. Due to the car being conceived as a left-hand drive machine, the master

cylinder assembly is situated on the opposite side of the car to the pedal block on right-hand drive cars, the components being connected by a pivoting rod mounted to the bulkhead. This is directly responsible for the poor pedal pressures and lack of feel which beset the XR2. It isn't that braking is particularly bad on the car — it just feels poor, as the system takes away any hope of a direct response between pedal application and the rate of retardation. The only sure way of improving feel is to add bracing around the mounts which retain the pivot rod at the bulkhead, but this is a major piece of work to carry out on a car which is intact; this is the sort of job to attempt whenever the engine is out of the car, and access to the bulkhead is thus far easier.

Braking effect itself is easiest improved by replacing the standard friction material with a set of Mintex's excellent M171 pads, ensuring that they are bedded in properly following the instructions which accompany each set. If your standard discs are showing signs of wear, then Mintex can help there too, as they are able to supply replacement discs as part of a wide range

which they are now carrying.

The only other changes which owners consider desirable on the car concern either body kits, of which a choice is available ranging from the mild Ford Rallye Sport bits which would replace the standard equipment right through to the radical "X" packs obtainable from Fibresports, or changes to the internal fittings of the car. Replacing the standard Ford steering wheel with a far more substantial RS item is another favourite move, as the rim of the original wheel soon becomes excessively slippery. Finally, some owners have added central locking and power windows to their cars, using aftermarket items as those two options were not listed by Ford themselves. Naturally, each of those items adds to the value of the car, and this ought to be taken into account when considering a purchase. ●

SOURCES

Mintex Don Limited ·
P.O. Box 18, Cleckheaton, West Yorkshire BD19 3UU
(Brake systems)

Janspeed Engineering Limited
Castle Road, Salisbury, Wiltshire SP1 3SQ
(Exhaust systems, tuning equipment)

Weber Concessionaires Limited
Dolphin Road, Sunbury-on-Thames, Middlesex TW16 7HE
(Carburation systems)

Turbo Technics Limited
17 Galowhill Road, Brackmills, Northampton NN4 0EE
(Turbocharger systems)

Magard Limited
372 East Park Road, Leicester LE5 5AY
(Bilstein dampers, special throttle linkages)

Monroe Auto Equipment Limited
Rosemary House, Lanawades Business Park, Kennett, Newmarket, Suffolk
(Monroe dampers and suspension systems)

Spax Limited
Telford Road, Bicester, Oxfordshire OX6 0UU
(Spax suspension)

Burton Engineering Limited
623 Eastern Avenue, Barkingside, Essex IG2 6PN
(Engine performance equipment)

Engines & Components Limited
10-14 King Street, Kettering, Northamptonshire
(Engine performance equipment)

Abbott Racing
Spinnals Farm, Wix, Manningtree, Essex
(XR2 performance tuning)

Please mention **Performance Ford** when contacting any of the above for details of their nearest dealer or distributor.

BETTER BY FOUR

FOLLOWING A SHORT INTERMISSION IN PRODUCTION, THE XR4x4 IS BACK — WITH THE 2.9 LITRE ENGINE AND A TOTALLY NEW TRANSMISSION. WITH THESE CHANGES FORD HAVE MADE A GOOD CAR GREAT, AS DENNIS FOY HAS BEEN FINDING OUT.

DENNIS FOY

It takes just one fast, hard run on demanding roads to appreciate the logic behind Ford's decision to adopt four-wheel drive for its premier models; in such a situation the XR4x4 is sharper, tidier and more neutral than any two-wheel drive model which the company has produced to date.

The format was first introduced to the Sierra range in the spring of 1985, as a replacement for the rear-wheel driven XR4i. Up until the middle of 1988 the XR4x4 was powered by the 2.8 litre fuel-injected V6, but that engine has now been superseded by the 2.9i version of the Cologne engine and it is the latter engine which is to be found beneath the Sierra's bonnet. The revised car has been a long time in coming (there was a break of something like eight months in the supply of XR4x4s), but I can hold my hand over my heart and say that the car was worth the wait.

According to inside sources, most of the delays in production were caused by difficulties with the new MT-75 gearbox which supplants the old five-speed of earlier models, but there were also apparently hiccoughs with the engine management system used on the car. This is the ubiquitous EEC-IV which controls the ignition and fuelling of the engine, a complicated piece of electronic hardware which is, in fact, two separate computers working in parallel. Fortunately, both problem areas have been thoroughly sorted out, and the XR4x4 is now back on general sale throughout the country.

The 2.9 Cologne engine is more than a slightly bigger version of the earlier unit – only the basic block remains the same. Six-port heads feature on the top of each of the two banks of three cylinders, which live at an angle of 60° from each other. The plenum chamber which feeds the heads with air and fuel is divided into two, feeding each head independently of the other; the EEC-IV was conceived in the days when it was considered ecologically sound to be able to shut down half of the engine. ▶

BETTER BY FOUR

and run on three cylinders only in the interests of saving fuel. Whilst that idea was shelved by Ford Europe some time ago, the 2.9i engine can be run thus, simply by reprogramming the engine management system.

Whilst the overall power output of the engine is exactly the same as that of the earlier engine, both producing 150 brake horsepower at 5700 r.p.m., the torque curve has been altered to provide more muscle at lower engine speeds; the current engine gives 172 lb/ft @ 3000 r.p.m., whereas the 2.8 gave 159 lb/ft @ 3800 r.p.m.

Backing up the engine is a 242mm single-plate clutch, which

feeds the power out to the all-new MT-75 transmission. From there drive passes to a central differential which apportions the power between the front and rear axles — 66% goes straight out to the rear axle, whilst the remainder is taken via a chain-driven propshaft to the front differential which is mounted within the engine's oil sump. The central differential has a viscous coupling integrated into its design to ensure that power splitting remains as intended, the differential limiting any slippage by locking gently and progressively. Another viscous coupling is to be found in the rear axle's differential to control wheelspin at that end of the car. The front differential is straightforward, Ford

feeling that the two viscous couplings already mentioned are adequate to control the excesses of all four wheels.

The XR4x4 shares the same basic suspension format of the lesser Sierras, with MacPherson struts at the front, and semi-trailing arms at the rear. There are, however, a number of special pieces integrated into the system, such as reworked front hubs, a re-shaped anti-roll bar, and stronger springs and gas-filled dampers. The rear trailing arms are unique to the 4x4 Sierras, in order to accommodate the rear disc brakes. Front ventilated discs of 260mm diameter are employed, with the rear 242mm solid items being linked via a diagonally-split hydraulic circuitry arrangement. Servo assistance is provided, and there is the option of electronic anti-lock braking control.

The mechanical picture is completed by the provision of a

> "Even when the tachometer needle is close to the redline the exhaust note is still a basso profondo, a low, menacing roar."

damped, power-assisted variable-rate rack and pinion, and a set of 5½" x 14" RS alloy wheels with 195/60 VR tyres — Uniroyals in the case of this particular test car.

At the time of its introduction in 1982, the Sierra hatchback bodyshell was considered a radical design. However, there are now so many on our roads that the appearance of one no longer raises eyebrows. The XR4x4 shows just what can be done with a chunk of strategic colour-coding and a dinky little rear spoiler — with the low stance of the car and those chunky alloy wheels the car looks exactly the sporting hatchback that it sets out to be.

Earlier examples of the XR4x4 were criticised for the relative lack of creature comforts when compared with its Ghia 4x4 Estate stablemate, and to counter these a good number of

SPECIFICATIONS
FORD SIERRA XR4x4

ENGINE TYPE	V6 overhead valve	BRAKING SYSTEM	Front ventilated discs, rear solid discs, dual circuit, servo assistance, ABS optional
BORE x STROKE	93mm x 72mm		
SIZE	2933cc		
BHP @ RPM	150 @ 5750	WEIGHT	2795 lbs
TORQUE LB/FT @ RPM	172 @ 3000	POWER/WEIGHT RATIO	118 b.h.p./ton
FUEL SYSTEM	Bosch L-Jetronic electronic ignition	WHEELBASE	102.7"
DRIVEN WHEELS	All	LENGTH	174"
TRANSMISSION	5-speed manual	WIDTH	75.6"
SUSPENSION: FRONT	MacPherson struts, anti-roll bar, gas-filled damping	HEIGHT	53"
		TEST MILEAGE	1,080 miles
REAR	Independent, semi-trailing arms, coil springs, gas-filled dampers	MANUFACTURER'S MPG	N/A
		TEST MPG	21.6
		PRICE AS TESTED	See text
		INSURANCE GROUP	6

MANUFACTURER: Ford Motor Company, Dagenham, Essex, England.

A little colour co-ordination and a rear spoiler combine with the alloy wheels and low stance to create the sporting hatchback image.

features have been carried over from the Ghia to the XR's cabin. The seats, which are trimmed in the same Astral and plain velour as the Ghia, now have adjustable lumbar support pads (operated by those funny, surgical applicance-style rubber bulbs), and the driver is able to adjust the height of his or her seat, as well as being able to alter it for reach and rake. This is just as well, as anybody over six feet tall will find their head brushing the cloth headlining if the seat is in anything but its lowest position. Standard features on the car now include power operation for all four windows, and there are switchable-delay courtesy lights on the rear doors as well as on the front. The front screen is now heated, as are the door mirrors, and the latter items are electrically adjustable. Naturally the tailgate has a wash and wipe attached to it, and the rear screen is heated. Central locking is standard, as are wipers and washers for the headlamps, and there is a tilt-or-slide sunroof with sliding visor. Tinted glass, a high-grade stereo system with six speakers and power amplifier, and a graphic display to warn of open doors, non-working lights, or ground frost complete the specification of the car's standard features.

The driver is presented with what is to all intents and purposes a standard Sierra Injection instrument binnacle, with the conventional gauges easily viewed through the two-spoke steering wheel. Primary controls are well-placed, with everything falling nicely to hand, but it is a bit of a stretch to reach the switches for the screen heaters and the auxiliary and high-intensity lamps. The gearlever of the new transmission is shorter than that of the old five-speed, and the overall throw is likewise shorter — this means that there is no undue stretching to engage any of the five forward or the reverse gears. The clutch action is pleasant, being light in operation but not at the cost of feel, and the throttle pedal has a nice progression to it, power output rising in direct proportion to the amount of pressure applied to the pedal. All three pedals are nicely set for height, and a smooth transfer from brake to throttle pedal and back is easy to execute. The only reservations that I have are that the pedals feel very slightly offset to the right-hand side of the car,

and there is not really anywhere comfortable to rest the left foot when on a long journey with no gearshifts being necessary. The provision of a "dead pedal", Porsche-style, would be a welcome addition to the car.

The 2.9 makes a gloriously deep sound when fired up, and the tone varies very little as engine speed increases — even when the tachometer needle is close to the redline the exhaust note is still a basso profondo, a low, menacing roar. Depressing the clutch pedal, the gearshift snicks positively into first gear and easing out the clutch with as few as 1200 r.p.m. has the car pulling away smoothly and evenly. When the car first arrived at P.F. Towers it felt tight, and the engine was a shade unhappy at having to pull quickly — this was hardly surprising, as there were only 1,200 miles registered on the odometer. By the time that the car went back to Uncle Henry a week later we had close to double the number of miles showing, and the engine had freed up appreciably, to the point where it would happily spin around to its redline in the lower gears, forward progress being restrained only by the rev-limiter which came in at 6200 r.p.m.

Although the principal advantages of four-wheel drive are discovered on open roads, when the additional traction offered by dividing the drive to all wheels raises the cornering abilities to a level unknown in most two-wheel drive cars, the system also proves itself useful when trying to emerge from a side road into a stream of fast-flowing traffic; as a gap appears in the road that you are attempting to join all that is required is to judge your speed and rate of acceleration, and to then punch the throttle. There will be no wheelspin (even on wet roads), merely instant traction which enables the car to be slotted neatly into the available space on the road.

Running in dense traffic in a town or city centre could never be described as a fun way of whiling away the time, but I can think of far worse cars in which to endure a traffic jam — the comfortable seats, light controls and good ventilation see to it that the occupants do not suffer unduly. Whenever a gap

BETTER BY FOUR

The 2.9 injection V6 sits neatly in the engine bay, and gives appreciably more torque than the 2.8 it replaces.

appears, the instant power and traction enable the situation to be capitalised upon — whether accelerating or braking there is no fuss or drama about this car; if you ask it to do something it will do it. Simple as that.

It was out on the motorway that the only negative aspects of the car manifested themselves. The first of these was a pronounced boom which came through the car's floorpan at 3000 r.p.m. — which is just about what the engine is rolling at when loping along at the legal limit in fifth gear. There is no booming either side of that engine speed, but the problem does occur in gears lower than fifth, which suggests that there is a minor fault with the engine mountings' damping action. To date this is the only example of XR4x4 2.9 that we have got our hands on, and so cannot really say whether or not the problem is peculiar to this particular example; there are no such booms from either the Ghia 4x4 Estate or the Granada 4x4 which we tried out at the time of the transmission launch, both of which have the same driveline as the XR, so only time will tell if it is a fault with the model as a whole, or just our test car.

The other downside to the car which showed itself on the motorway was when the engine was running at higher speeds (beyond 4500 r.p.m.) in the intermediate gears, as engine noise made its way into the cabin to a far greater degree than I would have expected in a car of this calibre. The noise emanates from the valvegear of the Cologne engine, and I daresay that it would be an easier move to add more soundproofing to the bulkhead than to try and eliminate the coarseness from the top end of the powerplant.

In all other respects the XR4x4 is a superb machine in which to take on the challenge of our over-populated motorway network. For all of its vestigal appearance that little tailgate spoiler is most effective at stabilising the car in crosswinds, aided by the four-wheel drive. Mid-range acceleration is good, thanks to the considerable amount of torque that the V6 pumps out — overtaking is a simple matter of rolling in a little more power, with a downshift being unnecessary for all but the most rapid of manoeuvres.

Out in the car's most natural habitat of rural roads, the driver is able to make the most of the four-wheel drive system. Being loaded in favour of the rear axle, the car behaves for the most part like a rear-wheel drive car with only tighter, faster bends making the driver aware that the car is being pulled as well as

pushed through the curve. The steering action of the car is little short of excellent, its weighting remaining constant at any speed above parking (at low speeds the wheel can be spun from lock to lock effortlessly, making the car an absolute doddle to slot in and out of parking spaces) and its turn-in being positive and direct. Ford's Special Vehicle Engineering have done their usual superb job on the XR's chassis, managing to combine nimble handling, positive feedback to the driver, and ride comfort in equal proportions. S.V.E. must surely be the most talented group of chassis engineers in the British motor industry.

Neither compact nor lightweight, the XR4x4 has the ability to behave on the road as though it was a much smaller machine, its sharpness and precision contradicting the fact that it weighs in at a ton-and-a-quarter before anybody gets aboard. The combination of the fast-acting steering and the precision of the gearshift (whilst the MT-75 isn't quite a match for the legendary 2000E 'box, it comes pretty close — close enough to put Ford back at the top of the gearshift league), make the car a joy to push hard through demanding bends, and if full use of the torque spread is made there can be few cars able to keep up with the XR4x4. It is very difficult to reach the wrong side of this car's handling envelope — only with an appreciably more powerful

PERFORMANCE
FORD SIERRA XR4x4

0-30	2.86 seconds
0-40	4.17 seconds
0-50	6.02 seconds
0-60	7.69 seconds
0-70	10.36 seconds
0-100	18.77 seconds
30-50 (2nd Gear)	3.14 seconds
30-50 (3rd Gear)	4.02 seconds
30-50 (4th Gear)	6.60 seconds
50-70 (3rd Gear)	4.21 seconds
50-70 (4th Gear)	5.81 seconds
70-90 (4th Gear)	5.40 seconds
Quarter Mile	15.79 seconds @ 89.3 m.p.h.
Maximum Speed	128 m.p.h.
50-0	2.96 seconds

engine will the car start to misbehave — but when the edge is overstepped, then the driver has a hell of a battle to regain control. This is for no other reason than the speeds involved being substantially higher than they would be in a two-wheel drive car. What tends to happen is that the XR remains neutral, neither under- nor oversteering, right up to very high velocities. As the edge is neared the tyres will start to sing, and the car will set onto a light, tip-toeing drift towards the outside of the curve — then suddenly bang! the car has gone, leaving the road in a sideswipe towards the nearest obstacle. But to get to such a situation the driver has to be devoid of mechanical sympathy and be extremely clumsy with the car's controls, and also travelling at a wholly unsuitable high speed.

As with the rest of the Ford range, anti-lock braking is available for the Sierra range at an extra cost of about £1,000. This is a fully-electronic system which ensures that none of the wheels actually locks up, and as a result full steering control is retained

> ## "The car's sharpness and precision contradict the fact that it weighs in at a ton-and-a-quarter."

even when panic-braking. It is easy to be a smartass and claim that a driver with skills to match the car will never get into such a dangerous situation, and there is much substance to such a statement. However, even the most adept of drivers cannot claim psychic powers, and so the facility of ABS ought to be

seriously considered if only as an insurance policy for that day when the unexpected happens.

The XR4x4 is much improved by the change in engine and gearbox, and the fuel economy figures add to the benefits of more power and greater driveability; during our week with the car we achieved an average of 21.6 m.p.g., an improvement of no less than 4.3 miles to every gallon when compared with our last standard XR4x4 test car, a 2.8-engined model which we tried a little over a year ago. Assuming an average mileage of fifteen thousand a year, a typical owner would save something like £100 per year in petrol costs by trading in an earlier XR4x4 for the newest model.

Reading between the lines, you may have gathered that I feel that the chassis could handle more power, and you would be right to make such an assumption — whilst the standard car is swift in its ability to accelerate — as our test-track figures prove — there will always be those who want more muscle under the bonnet and we are aware that several tuning companies are working on solutions even as you read this. Naturally, we will be bringing you our opinions on these cars as soon as they become available. For the meantime, anybody about to go out and order a new XR4x4 ought not be disappointed with what they find — whilst not exactly cheap (at the time of going to press the final price has to be announced, but is expected to be in the region of £16,000), the car represents excellent value because of its refined chassis and driveline. Leaving aside the RS Cosworth, this is probably the most satisfying mainstream driver's car that Ford are producing at the present time. ●

Ghia-specification interior is comfortable, although a little extra soundproofing wouldn't go amiss.

LIKE A CAT OUT OF HELL!
IS THIS THE ULTIMATE XR2?

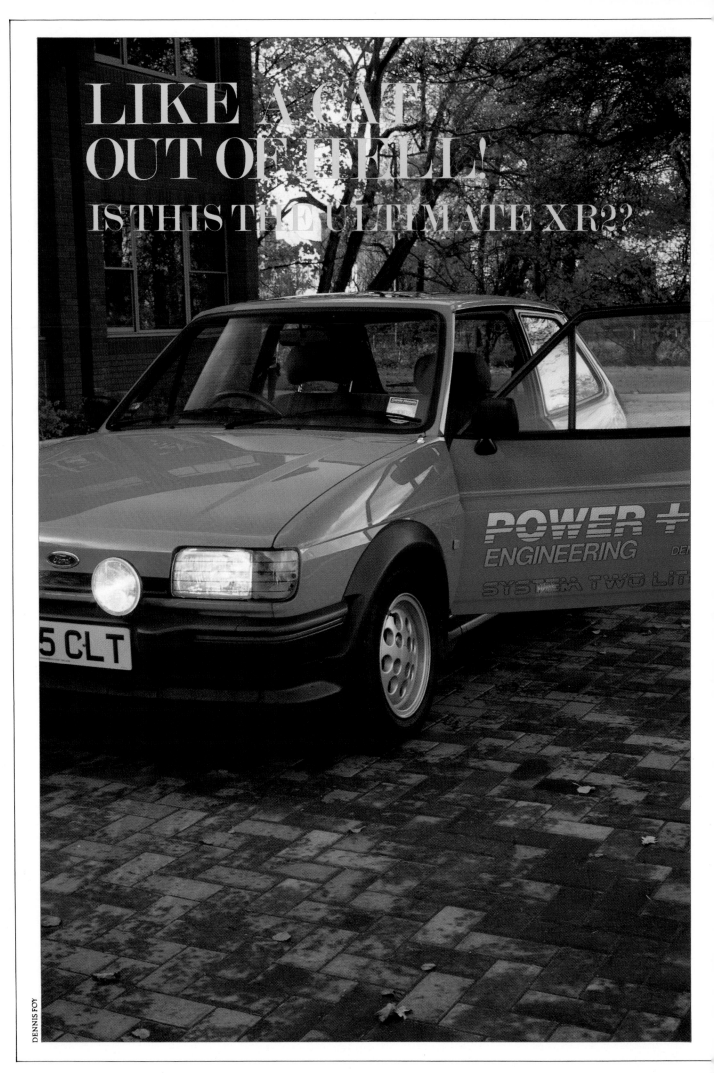

*POWER ENGINEERING
HAVE INSTALLED THEIR
SYSTEM TWO LITRE
ENGINE INTO A FIESTA
XR2, TOGETHER WITH A
TOTALLY NEW
HANDLING PACK AND
A BRAKE UPRATING KIT.
DENNIS FOY
HAS BEEN TESTING IT.*

That the Fiesta XR2 delivers a tremendous amount of fun per pound spent is beyond dispute. It is, however, quite a long way down the pile of hot hatchbacks in performance terms – its abilities have long since been eclipsed by a number of competitors from different stables.

With a totally new model of Fiesta just around the corner (the car will be on sale throughout Britain from April 1989), it is totally understandable that Ford's Research and Development staff have decided to leave the existing model to fend for itself, and concentrated all of their energies on the newcomer; it will be Fiesta III which will do battle with Peugeot, Volkswagen, and the myriad of Japanese contenders for the title of "King Of The Hill".

Which leaves the onus on the smaller, independent performance equipment companies to improve the chances of the existing model of XR2. Having already developed a two-litre conversion for the XR3i, which shares the same basic cylinder block as its smaller stablemate, it therefore seemed a logical development for Power Engineering of Uxbridge to insert one of their muscular motors into a previously unsuspecting late-model XR2.

A radically reworked Ford CVH engine, the overbored and longer-stroked 1951cc block puts out a shade over 130 brake horsepower from its flywheel – more than enough to develop a serious imbalance within the Fiesta's suspension system. Basically, the first time that the clutch was dropped with a serious number of engine revs being indicated on the car's tachometer, the car darted first left then right as the wheels scrambled for traction; in short it was a lethal combination. Being responsible types, there was no way that the team at Power could sanction the conversion's usage in that state, so they looked closely and seriously at the entire suspension system underpinning the little red car.

Working closely with the much-respected suspension design team at Spax, Power have developed a new set of coil springs and dampers which slot straight into the holes vacated by the original Ford items. The car sits a little closer to terra firma than a standard item, and when combined with a couple of front-end geometry changes which Power Engineering have devised, acts most effectively to control even the most wayward actions of the gallon which sits beneath the bonnet of this pint-sized powerhouse.

▶

CAT OUT OF HELL!

The car sits slightly lower than a standard XR2, thanks to the new handling pack with Power have developed in conjunction with Spax.

◄ I upset quite a few people during the ten day test period in which we had this car. They were all driving hot hatches, cars varying from a Golf GTi 16V through a collection of XR and RS Escorts, down to a small Japanese car of indeterminate parentage. On a twisting, winding piece of road, there wasn't a single one of them could effectively keep up, let alone seriously harrass me and my little red pocket rocker. One incident in particular still stands out in my mind, an incident which

involved a dark grey Fiat Uno Turbo. i.e. This car came up extremely close behind me at the start of a stretch of tight and twisting country lane not far from home. Whether he was merely curious or actually out to hassle me I'll probably never know. What I do know is that by the far end of the road, a distance of perhaps three quarters of a mile, I had pulled a lead of more than 150 yards on him ...

The amount of torque which this engine develops would do credit to many a tractor, and the manner in which it delivers it is nothing short of amazing; there is enough muscle to enable the car to pull away in high gear from as little as 1200 r.p.m., and by three thousand there is something like one and a half times the power of a standard XR2 coming down the line. That level of torque is held on a perfect plateau right through until a little over 6000 r.p.m., when the camshaft's hydraulic lifters declare that enough is enough. The impression gained is that the engine would be happy to keep delivering power by the bucketful forever, if the valve gear would only let it.

The standard clutch assembly of the Fiesta is retained, and pedal

> "In the wet, sense and sensibility limits road speed long before the edge of adhesion is reached."

pressure and bite is just fine, thank you. The gearshift is typical Fiesta, quite accurate and precise enough provided there is no attempt made to over-hurry its move from one gear to the next. It is an absolute waste of time attempting to be brutal with an XR2's gearchange, all shifts needing to be planned, deliberate and accurately paced. Break the rule, and the baulking from the gear level mechanism will attempt to break your wrist.

There is little to fault in the car's other main controls. Although there is a distinct extra surge at about 2800 r.p.m. as the carburettor's second venturi comes into effect, engine speed is always directly related to the amount of pressure being applied to the throttle pedal. The third pedal is usually the one which

SPECIFICATIONS
POWER ENGINEERING XR2

ENGINE TYPE	Inline 4 cylinder SOHC	**BRAKING SYSTEM**	Dual circuit, front discs, rear
BORE x STROKE	84mm x 88mm		drums, revised friction
SIZE	1951cc		materials, stainless steel
BHP @ RPM	132 @ 5000		flexible hoses, racing fluid
TORQUE LB/FT @ RPM	150 @ 3000	**WEIGHT**	1848 lbs
FUEL SYSTEM	Weber 2V carburettor	**POWER/WEIGHT RATIO**	157 b.h.p./ton
DRIVEN WHEELS	Front	**WHEELBASE**	90.1″
TRANSMISSION	5-speed manual	**LENGTH**	144″
SUSPENSION: FRONT	Uprated MacPherson struts, uprated	**WIDTH**	68″
	coil springs, amended geometry	**HEIGHT**	51.5″
REAR	Trailing arms, uprated coil springs,	**TEST MILEAGE**	1,421 miles
	uprated telescopic dampers, beam	**TEST MPG**	32
	axle, anti-roll bar	**PRICE AS TESTED**	See text
		INSURANCE GROUP	5/6 subject to engineers report

MANUFACTURER: Ford Motor Company, Dagenham, Essex, England.
EXTENSIVE MODIFICATIONS: Power Engineering, Uxbridge, Middlesex.

gives the owner of an XR2 cause for concern, but once again Power Engineering have addressed the problem and developed a package comprising uprated front pads and rear shoes, stainless steel flexible brake lines, and racing-specification fluid. When fitted to the car they result in a markedly improved stopping power coupled with a far more positive pedal action.

The final amendment which Power make to the car's original specification is to replace the original moulded "soft feel" steering wheel with a very neat leather-rimmed Nardi item. Whilst no new steering wheel can really counter the weird offset of the steering column head, the tactile pleasantness of the Nardi's rim goes a long way towards compensating for it.

Somehow or other, Power have managed to make the Fiesta feel as though it is blessed with a longer wheelbase than its actual ninety inches; this is the first Fiesta which I have driven that I could accurately drift, all four wheels acting in total unison. Once the apex of the bend is reached and the other end of the curve is visible, it is a simple matter of rolling on some power to have the car tighten on its line with absolute precision. Applying more pressure to the throttle pedal has the Fiesta clawing its way forward toward the beckoning open road ahead.

Even when the roads are damp or wet, it is still possible to make quite reasonable progress in the System Two Litre XR2 — progress which is proportionally higher than that of a standard example of the car. As with any Fiesta, it is the omnipresent fear of locking up the front wheels which limits road speed, rather than any other single factor; sense and sensibility take over long before the car's wet-weather limits of adhesion are reached. Over-enthusiastic use of the accelerator pedal will have the front wheels spinning and the car attempting to make a sideways detour if the roads aren't dry, but this car is still far better behaved than a standard version of the car, despite its far more substantial engine.

When roads are dry and conditions clear, this car is virtually unbeatable on the open highway, yet it is equally at home in heavy traffic; the light controls help matters considerably, aided by the tremendous reserves of power on instant call. The engine is at almost all times smooth and progressive, and enhances the Fiesta's inherent virtue of being able to slot neatly in and out of traffic. The only time that the red machine showed any reluctance to run smoothly was when it was cold; its auto-choked Weber carburettor has a distinct flat-spot halfway through its range which does not completely disappear until the

engine has reached its proper operating temperature. We have noticed this problem on a number of other Fiesta XR2s, and apparently it is a curable fault.

Out on the motorway the car is extremely usable, there being so much power available that downshifts to make overtaking manoeuvres are a redundant affair — simply leave the car in top gear, and let the torque do all of the work. The XR2's bodykit improves the car's stability at higher speeds when compared with a standard Fiesta, but even so the device is about as aerodynamic as a bespoilered housebrick. At speeds of more than a hundred miles per hour there is precious little downforce offered by the relatively vestigal spoilers of the little machine. ▶

PERFORMANCE

0-30	3.17 seconds
0-50	6.19 seconds
0-60	7.30 seconds
0-70	10.10 seconds
30-50 (2nd)	2.55 seconds
30-50 (3rd)	4.02 seconds
30-50 (4th)	6.23 seconds
50-70 (3rd)	4.06 seconds
50-70 (4th)	6.21 seconds
50-70 (5th)	6.78 seconds
70-90 (4th)	8.01 seconds
70-90 (5th)	10.32 seconds
Standing ¼ Mile	17.01 seconds @ 83 m.p.h.
Maximum Speed	129 m.p.h.

CAT OUT OF HELL!

and an astute driver will soon appreciate that the car is beginning to float a little too much for comfort. But then, apart from driving on certain autobahnen, such speeds are illegal on British and mainland European roads anyway, and you lot are law-abiding. Aren't you? Eh?

Readers in Germany would be best-advised to look at one of the more effective bodykits — Ford's own RS rear spoiler would be a good starting point, although the original tailgate trim of the

> "Having driven the Power Engineering XR2, I have come close to the same adrenalin burn as a skateboard superstar I once saw on Brixton Hill."

XR2 would have to be removed to allow its fitment. Beyond there, it is a matter of looking to the aftermarket for a suitable system which will give additional front-end downforce.

I remember a few years back seeing a cool kid on a skateboard, ghetto blaster in position within a couple of inches of his left ear, whopping down the middle of Brixton Hill in South London. In between six lanes of traffic, weaving and bobbing to avoid oncoming cars. I remember thinking to myself that even if undertaking a pretty novel form of suicide, the kid had a total mastery of his skateboard. I never mastered the device myself, managing only to fall off with any degree of professionalism on the few occasions where I tried that particular form of transport.

Having now driven the Power Engineering XR2, I reckon that I have come close to achieving the same adrenalin burn as that skateboard superstar presumably did. And no, I didn't try running the red car down the middle of Brixton Hill; I got enough kicks from pushing it hard through the lanes of Cheshire and Derbyshire.

The usual down-side to a converted car of this calibre is that fuel economy takes a nosedive. However, that is not the case with this particular car, as our average — which took in almost 1,400 miles of very mixed driving, from motorway trips through to fast runs in the country, and even included half a day at the test track — was an astounding 32 miles to the gallon.

There was one thing which we would like to have seen fitted to the car, and that was a soundproofing kit; even though the System Two Litre engine block is built to exacting standards, and closer tolerances than anything which comes out of Ford's plant at Bridgend, it takes the standard cylinder head assembly, and it is that part of the engine which sets up a raucous din at higher engine speeds. A long run can become a slightly tiring affair, thanks to the noise levels which emanate from beneath the bonnet.

SYSTEM TWO LITRE: THE CONCEPT

The basis of System Two Litre is a 1597cc Ford CVH cylinder block, which is totally stripped and cleaned before being inspected. Once passed as sound, it is bored out, fitted with cylinder liners, and rebored to a new size of 84mm. A totally new crankshaft is then installed, which takes the engine's stroke out to 88mm. Forged, specially-designed pistons are installed, along with specially-made connecting rods. New bearings, core plugs oil gallery plugs, and new bolts throughout. The engine can be either fitted by Power Engineering into your own car, or supplied direct to you on an exchange basis for your old cylinder block. When the latter route is chosen, the block comes to you in a specially-designed crate which will hold your returned block.

When the block is installed, a full set of new gaskets, a new oil pump and water pump, a new camshaft drive belt and all oil seals are fitted; when the block is to be customer-fitted, these parts all come within the crate along with the ready-to-fit cylinder block, on payment of a £175 supplement.

In addition to the block itself, Power Engineering are able to offer a selection of other parts for all of the XR2/XR3/XR3i/RS Turbo range, and the equivalent Orion models. These include two suspension systems (an adjustable one for the XR3i and RS Turbo, and a non-adjustable for all other models listed), a high-output camshaft, revised brake system kit, a high-torque fuel pressure regulator for the XR3i, a modified head for lean-burn engines, a stage three head for all vehicles, and an uprated clutch assembly. Then there are such addenda as a high-specification electronic alarm system, uprated headlamp conversion kit, and a choice of leather steering wheels.

A full information pack is available to potential purchasers which details all of the system, together with prices and specifications.

With a power-to-weight ratio approaching a hundred and sixty brake horsepower to the ton, and the ability to put the power down onto the tarmac so effectively, this particular Fiesta is brisk, to say the least. Indicative of the performance potential of the car is that we achieved a time for the standstill-to-sixty sprint of a mere 7.3 seconds — a solid two seconds quicker than Ford's own time for the standard car. A similar pattern repeated throughout the speed ranges, whether from a standing or a rolling start; the other benchmark time usually quoted is for the run from thirty to fifty in fourth gear. Ford reckon that the standard car takes 7.7 seconds, whereas our time for the same exercise in the System Two Litre car was a second and a half quicker. Up at the top end of the scale, whereas a stock XR2 can just about manage to reach 110 miles per hour, this particular example carried on going to almost 130 m.p.h.

The intended flagship for the new Fiesta range will be a 1.4 litre turbocharged model, but this won't be on sale for some time to come — certainly not before the end of 1989, as the machine is still under development with Cosworth Engineering and Ford Special Vehicle Operations. Until that car arrives, its space will be babysat by a car which is pretty much equivalent to the present XR2 in both specification and performance terms. Which means that Ford's return to the top of the hill could be some time off — which again leaves the responsibility for developing the performance potential of the 1600 carburated to the aftermarket, and the burden of expense to individual owners.

This being the case, there can be few ways which are more effective at increasing the performance of a standard XR2 Fiesta than Power Engineering's System Two Litre. Costs for the basic engine conversion vary from £1,200 to £1,600, depending upon who installs the new block. To this should then be added £340 for the suspension kit (an absolute necessity with the new engine), and a further £135 for the braking system uprating kit — another very desirable part of the package. Altogether, those three items would take the cost of a brand new Fiesta XR2 up to £10,500 — and the total performance of the car up to the level of something costing several times as much.

Some might say that ten and a half thousand pounds is an awful lot of money for a Fiesta, but they are, almost without exception, people who don't drive (or aspire to drive) an XR2 already; the car has developed quite a following in much the same way as the Capri did in the latter days of its lifespan. What the extra performance offered by System Two Litre offers is a means of owners of these little cars to endow their cars with a level of performance which put them back at the top of the hill.

If you are amongst that number of people who own an XR2, or intend to in the very near future — and want your car to have the split personality of being totally docile in traffic yet able to run like a cat which has had its tail singed by hell's inferno, get in touch with Power Engineering. You will not be disappointed.

Power Engineering are at Department P.F., Unit 9, 5a Wyvern Way Industrial Area, Uxbridge, Middlesex UB8 2XN. The company also has a Northern Agency, Lakeland Ford, who are at Department P.F., Mintsfeet Road South, Mintsfeet Industrial Estate, Kendal, Cumbria LA9 6NF.

●

OPEN PLEASURES

By adding a turbocharger to an Escort Cabriolet, together with a pack of improved suspension components, Turbo Technics have spiced up Ford's open car to RS Turbo performance levels.

DENNIS FOY

The story starts with the esteemed West German coach-building company of Karmann, who take a basic Escort estate bodyshell, add a mélange of their own specialities and Ford XR3i parts, and produce a desirable open tourer for four. The car is reasonably nippy, and by the time that the purchaser has delved into the Ford list of options, the Escort Cabriolet becomes a civilised mode of transport.

Turbo Technics have a few tricks up their sleeve for the car, too; by installing one of their turbocharger systems and a set of modified suspension components, they are able to multiply the fun factor quite appreciably.

The Cabriolet is the heaviest of the Escort range, thanks to the additional stiffening devices which Karmann add to the basic bodyshell to compensate for the loss in strength induced by the removal of the roof panel; a pair of steel beams are run lengthwise along the car inboard of each sill, a rollover bar is introduced between front and rear seats, and there are stiffening ribs on the front and rear bulkheads. By the time that the power hood motor, and similar devices to raise and lower the side windows, are added then the car is carrying a weight penalty of some 80 lbs.

As the car shares its driveline with the standard three-door XR3i, and thus has but a hundred and five horsepower upon which to call, performance is not quite as sharp as it might be — the weight penalty doesn't harm the "paper" performance figures, but does blunt the mid-range "zizz" of the car; it is only the low overall gearing which saves the day. Which is where Turbo Technics make their entrance onto this particular scenario.

One of the company's first-ever conversions was of an Escort, back in the days when we had XR3s, but no injection system.

In the intervening years the XR3 has become more sophisticated, and the same applies to the conversions engineered by Geoff Kershaw and his team in Northampton. In its latest form it is possible to extract upwards of 160 brake horsepower from the T.T.-developed CVH engine, but in an effort to retain practicality and tractability the installation in the Cabriolet has wisely been kept down to a sensible 130 b.h.p.

At the heart of the conversion is a tiny water-cooled Garrett T2 turbocharger which is modified by Turbo Technics. This has an integral wastegate, and offers very sharp throttle response; the concept of turbo lag is something of which this car has never heard. In the interests of simplicity — the less that you alter on a car, the less there is to go wrong — engine modifications are limited to a lowering of the compression ratio from 9.5:1 to 8.1:1 by re-machining the piston faces. The fuelling and ignition systems are revised to provide for the different requirements of a forced induction engine, and the front end of the standard exhaust system is modified to allow for the physical intrusion of the turbocharger, which is of course driven by the engine's exhaust gases. Turbo Technics' Geoff Kershaw has built up his company's reputation on the premise of not cutting corners, and this shows when the installation is inspected closely; the manifold which carries the turbocharger is cast from a high-nickel iron, and all of the necessary induction system plumbing into and out of the intercooler is purpose-designed. If you are looking for bodges, then you are wasting your time.

A major weakness of the Escort range in general is the suspension system, in particular that at the front end of the car. Despite the stiffening added to the bodyshell by Karmann the Cabriolet is particular prone to twisting, and in consequence torque steer becomes problematic. To minimise ➤

OPEN PLEASURES

this, Turbo Technics have developed a suspension system which comprises uprated dampers for both ends of the car, a pair of softer rear springs with complementary rear anti-roll bar, and stiffer bushings throughout. Whilst these do not totally eradicate the problem, the package does help make the car more controllable and positive.

Out on the road, the first thing that impresses is the willingness of the engine; the tiny turbo is set to deliver a total of seven pounds of boost, and according to T.T.'s own figures it is delivering the majority of this at a mere 1800 r.p.m. — enough to endow the engine with a better torque curve than Ford's own RS Turbo. The overall power output is rated at a hundred a thirty brake, which is within a whisker of that achieved by the RS Escort, and in consequence the performance figures are very similar indeed; the Cabrio hits sixty from standstill in 8.3 seconds when the second-to-third upshift is achieved cleanly (an identical figure to that of the RS), and the 30-50 time of the Turbo Technics car is actually better than that of Ford's own turbocharged Escort, with 5.5 seconds versus 6.3 seconds for the fourth gear burst. Maximum speeds are virtually identical, the Cabriolet

from that of a standard Cabriolet, or any other standard XR3i for that matter; if the power is applied at the apex of the bend then the front wheels become unsettled as they strive to put down the extra power, and this leaves the driver battling with a steering wheel which is not impressed by the desires of the pilot to follow an intended line. Instead, it is better to adopt the classic Porsche Turbo policy of slow in, fast out from a curve or bend — deal with the braking in a straight line, handle the deviation on a trailing or very light throttle, and then pile on the power when the car is pointing straight ahead again. That doesn't cost any time in cornering manoeuvres — and makes progress a far more safe and smooth process.

The revised suspension bushes improve steering feedback, and the driver is constantly aware of what the front end of the car is doing. There is no vicious snatching action to be felt through the steering wheel, even on the most irregular of surfaces. The car also handles with a surprising neutrality; even at high cornering speeds the anticipated ploughing understeer (the car is an Escort ...) didn't materialise. On sweeping curves and less-than-tight bends it is possible to have the car adopt a gentle four-wheel drift on a trailing

managing to get to 124 m.p.h. — one less than the RS Turbo.

But it ain't what it does so much as the way that it does it that becomes that elusive quality, the Fun Factor. Rushing along sweeping country roads with nothing above your head but the clouds, the birds and the occasional aeroplane is the perfect antidote to the tedium of day-to-day life — seven pounds of boost and as much headroom as you can handle is guaranteed to sweep away the blues and to put a smile on the driver's face. The power delivers crisply and neatly, and punching the throttle has the car urging forward appreciably more swiftly than any standard XR3i Cabriolet could manage — the 25% power boost equals 10% more fun.

The driving style called for by this car is appreciably different

SPECIFICATIONS

ENGINE TYPE
Transverse four cylinder SOHC
BORE x STROKE
80mm x 79mm
SIZE
1597cc
BHP @ RPM
130 @ 6000
TORQUE LB/FT @ RPM
136 @ 3200
FUEL SYSTEM
Turbo Technics/Garrett T2 water-cooled turbocharger, Bosch K-Jetronic electronic fuel injection
DRIVEN WHEELS
Front
TRANSMISSION
5-speed manual transaxle
SUSPENSION, FRONT
Uprated MacPherson struts, anti-roll bar
SUSPENSION, REAR
Independent transverse arms, uprated dampers, revised coil springs, anti-roll bar
BRAKING SYSTEM
Front discs, rear drums, servo assisted, mechanical anti-lock system
WEIGHT
2135 lbs
POWER/WEIGHT RATIO
134 b.h.p./ton
WHEELBASE
94.5″
LENGTH
158″
WIDTH
72″
HEIGHT
55″
TEST MILEAGE
671 miles
MANUFACTURER'S MPG
N/A
TEST MPG
23.7
PRICE AS TESTED
£16,102
INSURANCE GROUP
7
MANUFACTURER
Ford Motor Company/Karmann Coachbuilders
Modifications carried out by Turbo Technics, Northampton

throttle, which changes to a wave of solid forward motion when the throttle pedal is depressed.

To Turbo Technics' great credit, the car is quite content to potter along when circumstances dictate, showing no tendency whatsoever to anything untoward; there is no build-up of excess heat from beneath the bonnet, nor is there any fluffing or misfiring. The engine simply does what it is supposed to when it is supposed to do it, regardless of road speed.

In common with just about every other turbocharged car which we have driven, there is an air of disproportionate pressure-to-performance about the throttle action at higher engine speeds; beyond perhaps three thousand revs per minute, the action of piling more pressure on the go pedal has the car pulling ahead at a rate which is greater than the amount of throttle which has been given to the engine. Sometimes this is unnerving, but most of the time it enhances the adrenalin burn as the boost really takes hold. Much the same sort of thing happens in reverse, too; running on full throttle and then lifting off from the pedal has the engine braking the car more rapidly than would happen with a naturally-aspirated engine.

The ride quality of the car is high, with the revised damping

> ''Seven pounds of boost and as much headroom as you can handle is guaranteed to sweep away the blues and to put a smile on the driver's face.''

and rear springing being, if anything, an improvement over those of the standard car — there seem to be less crashes and bangs making their way into the car from the road surface than there were in the last standard example of Cabriolet which we tried a year or so ago.

The car which we have been trying came from new with a variety of Ford options, the single most useful of which was the power hood; this enables the car to be closed quickly and effortlessly in the event of a sudden shower or downpour; the car must be stationary with the engine switched off, and the quick-fitting tonneau cover must not be in place. All that is then needed is to press a button and wait for ten or twelve seconds whilst the hood raises itself, and drops down into place. Two neatly-designed handles then lock the leading edge onto the screen rail, and that is that — the car can be driven away, keeping the worst of the rain out.

Unfortunately, despite at least three attempts at re-designing the leading edge seal, the hood will still let in a drip of water on either side of the car, onto the left leg of the passenger and right leg of the driver respectively. We have driven but one example of Cabriolet which hasn't leaked in this manner — and are beginning to suspect that it was a fluke model ...

Other options which have been added to the car are the attractive five double-spoke alloy rims, heated windscreen,

power windows, and central locking. Since this car was built, the latter three items have been added to the list of standard equipment at no extra cost. Can anybody tell me why the central locking on the Cabriolet doesn't extend to the bootlid? That the system operates only the two doors seems a little ridiculous to my way of thinking ... The one other addendum to the car is, to us at P.F., the single most effective £400 which it is possible to spend, and that is the provision of anti-lock brakes. If during the lifetime of the car they prevent but one accident, then their provision will have more than been paid for — and we feel that it is sheer folly not to take up the option on any car, performance machine or not, when they cost less than the price of a good quality stereo system.

Most open cars are not really practical propositions for everyday transport — the great majority will carry two people and maybe an overnight bag, but little else. Being based upon a mainstream Escort model, the Cabriolet offers excellent practicality — it seats four with as much interior space as that found within an XR3i, and it is able to carry a surprising amount of luggage within its boot. There is a reasonable amount of stowage space available within the car for odds and ends, and there is the provision of a locking glovebox lid so that the car can be left unattended with the roof down without fear of losing small items from within, to passers-by with a penchant for magpie-like behaviour.

A pair of Recaro-style sports seats do a good job at locating the front occupants of the car, being supportive and comfortable — their initial firmness is forgotten after a few miles, and the occupants can reach their destination several hours after leaving base feeling quite untired. What is more, unlike the Recaros to be found in an RS Turbo, there is no intrusion from the side bolsters when the driver is attempting to make a gearchange or to use the handbrake; RST owners soon learn to keep the left elbow a couple of inches further outboard of the body than normal!

Ahead of the driver is the same fascia that is found on virtually all Escorts, with a binnacle containing the speedo, tachometer, fuel and temperature gauges — only the steering wheel, which is a thick-soft-rimmed item, differs from that of lesser ➤

PERFORMANCE

0-60	8.3 seconds
0-100	21.8 seconds
50-70 (4th)	5.5 seconds
50-70 (5th)	7.0 seconds
70-90 (5th)	5.8 seconds
Maximum Speed	125 m.p.h.

OPEN PLEASURES

Escorts. The ergonomics of the car are good, with all of the controls falling neatly to hand, and only the pilot lights for the screen heaters being obscured from view by the rim of the steering wheel.

Because the additional power loading is not putting a great deal of extra strain on the driveline of the car, the transmission and brakes remain just as Ford produced them. There are no great problems from brake fade during normal use; it is only when a driver uses predominantly tight and twisting roads which call for frequent applications of the middle pedal that the effectiveness of the brakes becomes reduced, and a set of good quality anti-fade pads will soon sort out that problem. Much the same applies to the transmission. This is not prone to breaking up, and there seems to be no need to go as far as installing a viscous coupling as neither front wheel is given to undue amounts of spinning. Or at least not in the dry.

As with most performance cars, the Cabriolet's wet weather behaviour can become a little less predictable — it pays to keep the speed down and the level of caution even higher than normal. But such an attitude is no more than commonsense

anyway ... Attempting to press on quickly will induce wheelspin, just as it would in a standard XR3i, and this will cause the front of the car to dart sidewards — which endangers other road users. Combining this characteristic with the fact that rearwards visibility when the hood is raised is much-reduced should be reason enough to be prudent with the right foot whilst the rain is falling.

Motorway stability of the car is good, better than most Escorts, and the car seems to be virtually impervious to crosswinds. The turbocharger endows the car with sufficient power to make short work of most overtaking manoeuvres, minimising the need to make downshifts — even in fifth, it takes but seven seconds to whip up from fifty to seventy, and

the test-track figure from seventy to ninety in fifth was a mere 5.8 seconds — impressive for a 1.6 litre engine. Rapid lane changes, whenever circumstances dicate, can be executed quickly and safely — whilst the chassis can feel a little twitchy, the car still obeys the instructions given via the steering wheel without actually upsetting the car.

The Turbo Technics Cabriolet is an impressive package, combining a lively engine and a good suspension system with what is undoubtedly one of Ford's more desirable models from the Escort line-up. As with all of T.T.'s current range of conversions the car runs on lead-free fuel of regular (95 octane) grade, and will give a quite creditable level of fuel economy if driven reasonably lightly; we were seeing about 27 miles to each gallon for much of our test period. It was only when we took to driving the car hard, in the interests of being able to bring you performance figures and an impression of how the car behaves under pressure, that the figure dipped to a tad below twenty to the gallon. A survey conducted several years ago by, I seem to recall, Saab, indicated that once the initial buzz of owning a turbocharged car wore off — once the honeymoon was over, so to speak — then the amount of time that the blower was actually working hard boosting the incoming charge was down to something in the region of five or six percent of the total running time of the engine. If this is the case with this car, then the fuel economy figure achieved by an owner of a Turbo Technics TT130 Cabriolet such as this ought to be much the same as that for a standard car.

There ought also to be no problems with routine maintenance of the car, as so little is changed; provided the servicing is carried out to Turbo Technics' specifications and recommendations, and a good synthetic lubricant is used, then there will again be little that is different from a standard example of the car. The car comes with the company's own assurance policy to underwrite the engine conversion, and the company also co-ordinates the British operation of Turbocare, an international network which encompasses aftermarket sales and servicing of turbochargers. When the unit reaches the end of its working life a service exchange unit can be obtained at an appreciably lower cost than that of a brand new unit.

The bottom line of any conversion is the amount on the invoice, and in the case of the Escort Cabriolet the price of the engine conversion is £1,795, with a further £440 for the handling pack — both of which exclude V.A.T. By the time that these are added to a new Cabriolet's £12,337 price tag (plus a further £440 for the anti-lock brake system, £530 for the power hood, and £265 for the alloy wheels) we have a total of £16,102. Of this amount £13,532 is going direct to Ford — and the balance is not a bad price to pay for the extra performance and crisper handling. After all, we now live in an age where performance doesn't come cheap. What will doubtless encourage one or two people is that most insurance companies worth dealing with tend to appreciate that converted cars such as this are no longer to be greeted like some kind of evil on four wheels, but instead group them alongside cars of similar value and performance — they may require an engineer's report before they will issue a policy, but they will class this car alongside an RS Turbo. Mention a turbocharger to an insurance company five or six years ago, and they would be reaching for crosses and cloves of garlic ...

What Turbo Technics are able to offer is a car which offers the best of both Escort worlds; RS Turbo performance with Cabriolet charisma. For full information on this, or any of the other Turbo Technics conversions for the Ford range, contact Turbo Technics (P.F.), 17 Galowhill Road, Brackmills, Northampton NN4 0EE.

BIPLANES OVER THE ATLANTIC

The Sierra XR4i and its American-market counterpart the XR4Ti have developed something of a cult following — and for more than just the biplane rear spoiler. We look back on the XR4i, compare it with the Merkur model which is still on sale in the U.S.A. — and attempt to find some answers to the mysteries surrounding the car.

By Dennis Foy.

T here are two questions concerning the XR4i Sierra which have often been asked, and it is highly likely that neither will ever be satisfactorily answered. The first is why we got the car in the first place, and the second is why it was killed off after such a short life.

As with the standard Sierra range which had gone on sale in 1982, public reaction to the twin-winged fire-breather which appeared in showrooms from the beginning of May 1983 was mixed. People were still getting used to the idea of a car with a hatchback and an abundance of compound curves which had replaced the much-loved, squarecut three-box Cortina — and the boundaries of acceptability were pushed back still further by a three-door version of the car which had not just the twin-level rear deck and screen spoiler, but also the entire lower section clad with plastic panels, along with a rather strange looking side window treatment which combined etched stripes and an additional quarterlight — in standard three-door Sierras, the rear panels were given a single window apiece.

When asked the loaded question of why we had such an overtly sporting version of the car, one senior Ford executive suggested that the concept of XR4i was to replace the ageing Capri model, and that the 2.8 injected car was a tester to gauge market reaction; if the public liked that car, then smaller engined (and thus cheaper) versions of the car would follow in due course. As is so often the case with such semi-official comments, some of the executive's reply was based on truth — yet some was also inconsistent with other developments within the company's product range. It was an ill-kept secret that Ford wanted to kill off the Capri, as the car was not selling in anything like the numbers that the board of directors considered worthwhile. In an effort to jolly along sales, they had gone to the trouble of having S.V.E. re-engineer the flagship of that range, and the result was the 2.8i Capri as a replacement for the old three-litre version of the car. This was

an effective move, and fresh interest arose in the Capri model range, with the result of an increase in sales levels.

It was also true that a variety of different powerplants had been tried in the Sierra. The original XR4i project was based around the 2.3 litre version of the Cologne V6; in his highly informative book, *XR: The Performance Fords,* my colleague Jeremy Walton regales us with a conversation between the man in charge of the programme, Hans Gaffke, in which J.W. was told of the long and abortive attempts to satisfy Ford of Europe's Chairman Bob Lutz, who was insistent on using that particular engine. The decision to drop the 2.3 in favour of the 2.8 engine was taken in the light of a total inability to get the smaller engine to produce adequate torque — tipping the scales at about 2700 lbs, the Sierra three-door needed at least 150 lb/ft of torque, some twenty more than the 2.3 engine could muster. Another engine which was tried was the 2.3 litre turbocharged overhead cam engine from the 1980/81 ➤

BIPLANES OVER THE ATLANTIC

◀ Mustang, but that also was discounted for the European market. That powertrain was eventually used in the XR4Ti Merkur — but more of that later. For now, back to the main plot.

It had never been Ford's intention to introduce the XR4i at the same time as the rest of the Sierra range; this is a standard policy Ford adopt, as the launch of the latest Fiesta shows — whilst the rest of the range has been on sale since April of this year, it is likely to be late autumn before the XR2i is available through dealerships.

When it finally arrived in 1983, the Sierra XR4i showed great promise. The 2792cc V6 was rated at 150 brake horsepower and 159 lb/ft of torque — less than the official figures for the same engine in the Capri, which was credited with a superior exhaust manifolding and silencing system. Backing up the engine was a standard five-speed transmission and 9½″ single plate clutch, and at the rear of the car a tallish 3.62:1 final drive gearset was installed in the differential. The Capri, incidentally, had a 3.09:1 final drive ratio, which accounted for the different performance statistics of the two cars — differences which have been a source of arguments between respective owners of the two models ever since the 4i appeared on the streets!

The suspension system of the car is fundamentally the same as that of the rest of the Sierra range, in that it has MacPherson struts at the front of the car, with a rearward-mounted anti-roll

also tidied up, and the result was not just a claimed improvement in stability, but also a gain of 0.02 in the drag coefficient.

Ford's aim was to produce a car which was in the classic GT mould — a true Grand Tourer which would waft four or even five people along at high speeds across countries and even continents. There was certainly enough space within the cabin of the XR Sierra, and the large, heavy doors opened wide enough to make access to and egress from the rear seats reasonably easy — and certainly no more difficult than any other large two-door car. In the intended style of the car, the front seats were supportive sports seats with more lateral support than those of lesser Sierras, the driver's seat was height adjustable, and both had adjustable lumbar support. The chosen trim fabric was a soft velour with a relief square pattern woven into the main facings, and the same theme was repeated on the door liner panels.

As befitted a car of the XR4i's intended status, there was a lengthy list of standard equipment, and another list of almost equal length which detailed optional extras. Alloy wheels, a remote tailgate release, variable speed intermittent wipers, twin door mirrors, a high-grade stereo system, extra driving lamps integrated into the spoiler and a locking fuel cap were all standard issue. Amongst the available options were a fuel computer, power steering, tinted glass, a sunroof of the tilt-and-slide variety, power windows, and central locking. As so often happens with Ford of Europe, the price and

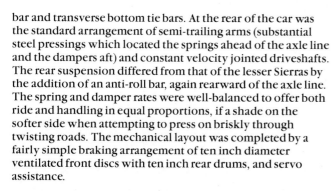

"Ford's aim was to produce a car in the GT mould — a true Grand Tourer which would waft four or five people along at high speed across countries or even continents."

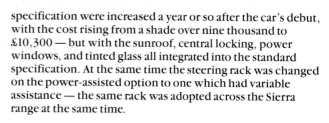

bar and transverse bottom tie bars. At the rear of the car was the standard arrangement of semi-trailing arms (substantial steel pressings which located the springs ahead of the axle line and the dampers aft) and constant velocity jointed driveshafts. The rear suspension differed from that of the lesser Sierras by the addition of an anti-roll bar, again rearward of the axle line. The spring and damper rates were well-balanced to offer both ride and handling in equal proportions, if a shade on the softer side when attempting to press on briskly through twisting roads. The mechanical layout was completed by a fairly simple braking arrangement of ten inch diameter ventilated front discs with ten inch rear drums, and servo assistance.

Whilst the Sierra bodyshell offered a creditably low drag coefficient of only 0.34, that slipperiness was achieved at the expense of high-speed stability in a straight line, especially when there were crosswinds to be contended with. To overcome this and give the car a stable cruising performance, Ford's team went back into the wind tunnel and developed that biplane rear spoiler which effectively split the air coming down over the gently-raked rear hatchback, cleaning up what is in aerodynamic terms a "dirty" area. The frontal area was

specification were increased a year or so after the car's debut, with the cost rising from a shade over nine thousand to £10,300 — but with the sunroof, central locking, power windows, and tinted glass all integrated into the standard specification. At the same time the steering rack was changed on the power-assisted option to one which had variable assistance — the same rack was adopted across the Sierra range at the same time.

For the other side of the Atlantic the turbocharged 2294cc Mustang engine did eventually get installed into a Sierra three-door bodyshell, and was exported to the U.S.A. The engine utilised a single turbocharger with intercooler (the earliest examples of Mustang to be equipped with this engine had no intercooler, and thus ran into dreadful reliability problems) and produced, in 1985 form, about 160 brake horsepower. Today that figure has been improved further, thanks to better engine management systems, to a claimed 175 brake horsepower — but worth considering is that the American way of measuring horsepower differs from the European method, as across the Atlantic measurements are taken from a bare engine with no ancilliaries, whilst here the readings are taken from an engine driving its generator, power steering pump, and so forth. It therefore follows that the nett power developed by the 2.3 engine was close to that of our 2.8i V6.

The mechanical layout of the Merkur XR4Ti (as the car is sold) was broadly similar to that of our own car. In view of the different weights of the turbo-four and the V6 engines the front spring rates were different, and the transmissions also differed between the two cars; whilst the European-market car was cursed with the dreadful Ford five-speed gearbox which was used on all inline applications until it was usurped by the new MT-75, that found in the Merkur was the vastly superior Borg Warner T10 five-speed — the same gearbox which is still used today in the Cosworth Sapphire as well as the Mustang model range. Unlike the British car, it was also possible to order a Merkur with an automatic four-speed transmission. When the manual gearbox was specified the car came with the same 3.62:1 final drive ratio.

The interior of the car was again broadly similar to that of the European models of XR4i, although the fascia switches differed in detail — and the tachometer incorporated a little boost gauge into its top corner, just like our original whale-

The Sierra was designed to take a V6 engine from the outset — hence the neat manner in which the Cologne 2.8i sits within the bay. This car has a K&N filter and a Janspeed exhaust system in place of the standard item — giving a power gain of almost thirty horses.

tailed Cossie Sierra. Trim details varied, but anybody stepping into a Merkur XR4Ti after driving a left-handed version of the European car will be on comfortable, familiar territory.

By a bizarre providential twist of fate, we are able to bring you pics of the two cars alongside each other. This came about following a letter from one of our readers, Simon Coughlan, telling us about his 1985 XR4i — and his mentioning, as a postscript, that there was a neighbour of theirs with a Merkur of similar vintage just around the corner!

Simon has owned his car since July 1986, having bought it from a Ford main dealership in the Salisbury area. Whilst the car was withdrawn from the British market in February 1985, the model remained in production for the West German market for some months afterwards, until the XR4x4 successor achieved mainstream production status, and it was possible, albeit with a degree of pressure and a lot of patience, to obtain an example of the car — which is exactly what the principal of that particular dealership did for himself. When the time came to change his car, Simon stepped in and bought the XR.

His neighbour James Benson is an American working here in Oxfordshire with his company, and he bought his car back at home in Carolina. He is so attached to the car that he had it shipped to England when he was transferred to his employers' British branch office. James has owned the car from new, and it is unchanged from its original 1985 specification.

Simon Coughlan's car illustrates some of the changes which were executed by Ford during the car's lifetime. The first examples had the white lines across the rearmost pair of side windows, but by the time that Simon's car was built in the summer of 1985 the lines had been removed in the interests of improving visibility whilst reversing. Similarly, the interior of the earlier XR4is abounded with red stripes and keylines around the instrument panel, but by the 1985 models these too had been toned down from a vivid red to a more subtle cherry colour. Finally, the lower mouldings themselves were changed from mid-grey to a much darker shade which is charcoal in colour.

As might be expected of a car ordered as personal transport for the head of a main dealership, the XR4i has all of the options — which means that it has the fuel computer and air conditioning featuring in its specification, along with the variable-rate power steering rack. The American car features air conditioning too — but then cars from the U.S.A. rarely ▶

The interior of the Merkur is familiar territory to anybody who has driven a LHD Sierra — only the 85 m.p.h. speedo and the tach with a boost gauge gives away the fact that this is no ordinary Sierra.

BIPLANES
OVER THE ATLANTIC

◀ seem to appear without that feature, especially those intended for a life in the climatic extremes of the southern states.

Whilst James Benson has left the mechanical specification of his car unchanged, Simon has made one or two subtle alterations to his. The first of these was to replace the standard air filter element with a freeflow K&N item, and the second was to ditch the entire exhaust system (the very components which were responsible for the down-rating of the Cologne engine to 150 b.h.p.) in favour of a Janspeed system. He then went on to have the car re-tuned on a rolling road, and the nett result of the changes was a boost in power of almost thirty brake horsepower. At under £300 for the exhaust manifolds and system and another £30 or so for the filter element, this represents excellent value for money at only £11 per horsepower gained. What is more, the Janspeed exhaust system worked out cheaper than the Ford price for a standard exhaust system!

Early examples of XR4i were criticised for their twitchiness, particularly from the rear axle of the car, and so there were a few detail changes made as it progressed through its short lifetime. These were principally in the valving of the gas-filled Bilstein dampers; interestingly, these are still available from Ford dealerships, but appear to be unavailable direct from Bilstein agents. It is also understood that there were very slight alterations made to the rear camber settings. These changes from the original XR4i specification were incorporated into the Merkur XR4Ti right from the first examples of that car rolling off the production lines.

In both cases, the cars are both quick and fast; the European version of the car was able to get to sixty in a shade over eight seconds — one magazine which tested an example in 1983 actually registered 7.7 seconds for the sprint — whilst the American version is rated at hitting the same sprint in 7.8 seconds. The maximum speed for the XR4i is a touch under 130 m.p.h., and according to American colleagues the Merkur version is capable of a not-dissimilar figure — even though the speedo on Jim Benson's car, in keeping with most other newer American cars, only reads up to eighty five miles an hour!

The cars both have very similar handling characteristics, with a neutral stance giving way to gentle understeer as cornering speeds increase; this is much as expected given that the car has a weight split of 55% front/45% rear — the difference of 100 lbs in weight between the Cologne and Merkur engines is compensated for by having the V6 sit slightly further back in the chassis of the European car than the four cylinder motor of the XR4Ti does.

As with any powerful front engined, rear wheel drive car, caution must be exercised in wet weather, as the dry-road understeer gives way to chronic oversteer when over-enthusiastic use is made of the right foot. The powered steering rack is fairly low geared, and much wheel-twirling is called for if the errant tail of the car is to be caught before it creates serious havoc on the roadside. Being gentle with the car in the wet is the rule here, with either of these XR Sierras — save the rapid action stuff for the dry when good traction is guaranteed.

American cars are generally appreciably cheaper than they are here in Britain, and much the same goes for the cost of spares. Except when you happen to own and drive a Merkur, which is sold as a special import through the Lincoln-Mercury division of Ford Motor Corporation. For a start, the car (along with the other main German-built Mercury, the Scorpio) is available at only seven hundred selected Lincoln-Mercury dealers throughout the North American continent — a mainstream model such as the Cougar is available from any of several thousand outlets.

James was unfortunate enough to have a minor parking altercation with his car whilst still living in the U.S.A., and needed a new front moulding for the lower part of the car, along with a couple of lamp lenses. Would you believe more than $500 for the moulding, which here in Britain would cost a little under £100? Or $18 for a trafficator lens that costs £8 here? Much the same applies to routine servicing items (except engine items, which are native American), and so James will doubtless stock up on items such as brake pads and other consumable items before his contract in Britain expires and he returns to his homeland.

The one other aspect of the car that annoys James is the size of

The latest version of the Merkur XR4Ti is more subtle, and uses the XR4x4 rear spoiler in place of the previous biplane item. Cosworth RS 500 wheels are another new addition for the current model year.

FORD PHOTOGRAPHIC UNIT

the fuel tank. This is the same sixty-litre item that is fitted to all bigger-engined Sierras, and for European applications, where sustained runs of longer than 250 to 300 miles are uncommon, this is quite adequate. However, mainland North America is a vast place, and when you work in Tennessee and want to visit the folks back home in Carolina then having to make frequent fuel stops becomes tiresome; there was more than one occasion when he wished that his car had an appreciably bigger tank such as those fitted to typical American saloons. That point aside, he is very happy with his XR4Ti, enjoying its blend of individuality, performance and handling — James Benson can think of few cars from the present line-up on offer from the major American manufacturers with which he would happily replace his Merkur.

Simon Coughlan is also very fond of his car. He went through a phase a little while ago where he felt it was something of a waste of time having such a powerful Grand Tourer which wasn't being used for anything like the amount of time that the car deserved, and so he traded it in against a new, smaller, far more sensible and practical car. And promptly regretted it. His work situation changed, giving both he and his wife Lucy more time, and the new car (a non-Ford of British origins, the details of which are best kept undisclosed in the interests of good taste and decency) proved to be an unmitigated disaster zone on wheels. After a bit of detective work he managed to track down the XR4i again, and persuaded the new owner — who had only done a few hundred miles in the car in the seven months of ownership — to part with the car again. The car had been looked after meticulously, and the Coughlans have jointly decided against the idea of parting with the car again.

Simon likes the package, praising the torquey engine, which offers simplicity and efficiency in one package — there is no need to go over to high-tech, multi-valve, multi-cam engines in Simon's book. The chassis works well, although there is scope for improvement in the braking department; a set of anti-fade pads and linings, Goodridge braided brake lines and racing-specification fluid are already on the shopping list. Whilst undoubtedly rapid, the car's performance can start to feel a little less than the owner really wants with any car, and Simon is no exception to that syndrome and so he is looking into ways of getting more power from the 2.8 engine. He doesn't want to radically alter the car in any way, merely extract a little more power.

He too, like James Benson, likes the package that the XR4i offers — and is able to report that his car's fuel computer is one of those extremely rare beasts that is accurate! Being something like six feet two inches tall he appreciates the space provided within the cabin, and also likes the good all-round visibility — apparently he soon learned to modify his junction positioning to compensate for the restrictions of the rear quarterlights.

So we have two happy owners — and if our postbag is anything to go by, they are typical XR4 owners. Which brings us neatly back to the question of why the car was axed, quietly and with a minimum of fuss, just two years after it first appeared. After all, by the point of its demise in 1985 people were accustomed to the appearance of the Sierra, and the emergence of one onto the roads no longer raised eyebrows. The XR4i had been slowly refined, and in fact the XR4Ti is still very much alive and well in the U.S.A. and Canada, so the Ford Motor Company cannot even claim that it was uneconomical to produce — had that been the case, then the North American continent would no longer be able to get their version of the ➤

A late-model example of the car, Simon Coughlan's XR4i is more subtle than that of the earlier models. Those big doors weight heavily, and to protect the hinges from premature wear and tear it pays to keep them closed for as long as possible.

BIPLANES OVER THE ATLANTIC

◄ car.

Part of the answer would have to lie with the success of the Capri 2.8i. Originally, that car would have been a limited edition model, possibly the swansong for the entire model range. As it happened, thousands and thousands more Capris were to be sold right through until the car was finally axed in 1987. The anticipated trend to the XR4i from the two-eight

Capri never materialised, and the total sales of XR4i Sierras in Britain barely scraped past the twelve thousand mark — whilst apparently there were close on twenty thousand 2.8i Capris sold in the period from spring 1983 to autumn 1985.

Another part of the answer had to come from the car's successor, the XR4x4. This was a package aimed at the same market sector which was first conceived during the early days of the XR4i programme — and which was originally intended as a showcar "simply to prove that Ford could do it", according to one well-informed inside source. As the prototype took shape it began to dawn on the higher echelons within Ford of Britain that they could have a winning package — not just in the showrooms, but also in motorsport. And successful motorsport cars generate more interest in showroom cars ... I'll save that story for another time in the near future — for now suffice to say that there was little enthusiasm within Ford of Britain for the rear-wheel drive XR Sierra, but a great deal of faith in the four-by-four version of the car. Cutting a long story very short the 4i was allowed to dwindle away with no particular marketing push to bolster sales — and the 4x4 Sierra was waiting in the wings during 1985.

The XR4i was undoubtedly a good car, and had it been given the benefit of some time and energy by Rod Mansfield and the team at Special Vehicle Engineering, then it could have been great; as it was, the German-engineered chassis was good, but lacking that special something which can give a car that special edge in the marketplace. As it was, the car found itself fighting the Capri 2.8i and the XR4x4 — and it couldn't beat either of them out of the showroom. ●

THE LONG GOODBYE

Production of the XR2 has now ceased, and the XR2i waits in the wings, ready to take its first bow. We take a last look at the Mk II — and decide that the new car has a tough act to follow.

By Dennis Foy.

I have come to appreciate the XR2 in much the same way as I felt about the Capri 2.8 injection – it is a car which I like in spite of, rather than because of, itself. Noisy at speed, cramped and jiggly, the XR2 can infuriate with its apparent disregard for driver and passenger comfort. Yet the same car can also lead to the appearance of a split-ear grin across the face of just about any red-blooded driver who has the chance to take a fast run in one in the right circumstances — for which read a twisting, winding country road. Character? It has it by the bucketful.

Firing up the ignition and blipping the throttle, the XR2's exhaust note sets the tone, and hints at the car's nature by sounding like a yapping little terrier eager to be let off its leash. The steering wheel, although alluding to a sportscar feel, is in fact a slightly flimsy piece of apparatus not aided in the slightest by the jaunty angle at which it sits atop the steering column; the driver's right hand needs to be about an inch, perhaps slightly more, forward of the position of his or her left hand, when the

wheel is held in the anatomically-correct "quarter to three" position. What is more, the wheel feels a little higher than instinct says it ought to be. However, the driver soon gets the feel for the car, and the odd angle of the column gets forgotten in the quest for pleasure.

Equipped with a five speed transmission identical to that of the Escort XR3i, the Fiesta is able to make more of the available ratios than its bigger brother thanks to the reduced weight it has to carry about. A surprisingly precise gearshift marked our test car, along with a pleasantly-weighted clutch pedal mechanism. Light and airy, with good all-round vision, the car is fine in traffic, and downright simple to park and unpark. If only the Escort had as immediate, light and effective a steering system.

In heavy traffic, the Fiesta is agile and nimble. In XR2 form, it is the same but more so: there is a greater precision to the steering, more rapid acceleration, and sharper reaction from the brake pedal. Running quickly in dense, but fast-flowing traffic, there can be few cars capable of maintaining the XR2's rate of progress. The car could never be accused of having a good ride quality or level of comfort, and it proves to be an extremely difficult car to drive smoothly if speedy progress is required — yet learn to live with the car's little foibles (and if you are carrying passengers warn them to grip hold of the nearest grab-handle, to avoid being unnecessarily tossed about), and your reward will be

making the journey from one side of town to the other as quickly as it is possible to make it.

The XR2 is a car with a cherry disposition, and some of its sunny side is bound to rub off onto the driver the first time that the machine is given its head on twisting country roads. It is as predictable as the next Stock, Aitken and Waterman production: the details may change, but there is a consistency that never goes away. The driver knows, for instance, that putting the right foot down with the gearlever in the appropriate slot will elicit a burst of acceleration that gets the job done — the performance isn't exactly earth-shattering from the XR2's noisy 1.6 litre engine, but it is generally sufficient to satisfy most drivers' needs and immediate wants.

The handling is another safe, predictable area: it takes a ham-fisted fool to get into serious trouble with one of these cars, as it has surprisingly high reserves of grip. Certainly an unsympathetic driver will have the car twitching nervously, but if the person behind the wheel heeds the many signals that come through from the wheels, engine and transmission, then the car will never be put into a position whereby it becomes a dangerous weapon. Only if the car is deliberately unbalanced by, for example, braking too late and too deep into a bend, does the machine become a liability.

Having such a short wheelbase (a mere 90"), it pays to heed the ▶

THE LONG GOODBYE

basic principles of performancing driving – brake in a straight line, in slow, hold a light throttle until the exit to the curve is in sight, and then out quickly, but not over-hastily. It definitely pays dividends to have the car in a gear whereby the tachometer is showing between 2500 and 3000 immediately before applying the power to make the exit from a bend, as the car is starting on its serious torque curve in that band: the peak figure of 100 lb/ft is reached at 4000 r.p.m. Attempting to throttle out of a curve with under 2500 indicated has the engine pausing momentarily, and that can be enough to make a pig's ear of the bend. Too much throttle on the apex of the bend will have the car understeering a little too much for comfort – with the resulting battle for traction and line again upsetting the car's balance.

off having fun – oops-sorry-serious-testing – there were no problems with the manner in which the car stopped.

Where the XR2 is least happy is on motorways. Once again it is the car's size – or rather lack of it – which catches it out, particularly in stiff crosswinds. Despite the various bits of aerodynamic addenda such as front and rear spoilers and side skirting, the car is still close to a shoebox in its ability to cut a swathe through the air, and is happy to be shoved sidewards by a gust of wind, or the draught from a truck being overtaken. The driver soon learns to keep both speed down and a reserve to redirect the car onto its intended line when pushing along a motorway at any speed much beyond 55 miles per hour.

The braking action of the car is generally very good, although a series of fast, tight bends in rapid succession will have the slowing distances steadily increasing as the friction materials begin to fade. In all other situations that we encountered during our week with this particular XR2 – and believe us, we try hard to put the car into as many situations as possible in the interests

Admirable though the car's suspension system is at dealing with twists and turns along the highway, it is not terribly good at coping with rough road surfaces – every imperfection of the road is passed straight through into the cabin, and distributed on a fairly even basis between all occupants. Even on smooth roads the car could never honestly be described as comfortable – it

HIGH-TAILING

Richard Grant Accessories have introduced a new rear spoiler for the Fiesta Mk II. Manufactured in semi-rigid polyurethane, the new spoiler comes complete with all fitting equipment and instructions, and retails at £62.70 plus V.A.T. For full details of the range of R.G.A. spoilers and bodykits, and how to fit them, contact R.G.A. at Department P.F., Moor End, Eaton Bray, Dunstable, Bedfordshire LU6 2JQ.

merely becomes less uncomfortable to travel in.

The front suspension system is also to blame for another of the XR2's faults, that of torque steer in wet weather. In the dry, the car can achieve traction with its front wheels surprisingly easily, right up to high engine speeds and quite rapid clutch-dropping. However, trying anything other than a feathered start in wet weather — or even on damp roads, come to that — and the car will dart to either side, and make progress in any which way but ▶

FORD FIESTA —
A POTTED HISTORY

It would perhaps be a little unkind to accuse Ford of sitting on the fence waiting for the rest of Europe's major manufacturers to make whatever mistakes there were to be made, before making their own début into the marketplace for front wheel drive minicars, but at the time of the Fiesta's launch in 1976 there was more than one pundit who noticed the apparent time lag. Those same members of the press corps also noticed that the Fiesta was hardly innovatory by industry standards. Yet for all of its design conservatism, its engine which was merely another variant on the good old crossflow Kent unit, and its styling which was angular and simple, the Fiesta went on to become the envy of the rest of Europe's major car makers. The reason was simple; it sold.

Tooling up for a completely new product line was, and still is, a staggeringly expensive business, and so to ensure that they were working along the right lines Ford commissioned a massive, pan-European market research study to not only assess the market as it stood at the beginning of the 1970s, but also the way in which it was expected to develop. Their conclusions were that the marketplace sought a car which was roomy, versatile in its load-carrying ability, and cheap and easy to run. It got the Fiesta, which was launched just as the western world was reeling from another kick in the economic crotch administered by the oil-rich Arab states.

As might be expected from a company which has an international reputation for triumphing marketing over engineering, peeling back the razamatazz of the car's launch revealed a range which consisted of two cars — the 950 and the 1100. The rest of the "range" shown to the press and public was created, in time-honoured fashion, by varying the trim and equipment levels, offering certain colours only on certain models, and so on and so forth.

It was autumn 1977, some six months after the first cars had gone on sale, before the 1300 was offered to British buyers, and not until 1981 could a customer order a serious sporting Fiesta, the XR2. In between, Ford did offer the Supersport, but even that didn't appear until the beginning of 1981, and so enjoyed a far shorter lifespan than it deserved.

The first major change to the range came in autumn 1981, when the 1982 model year cars were announced. Although these differed only slightly from the model which had been introduced some five years previously, they did have a much-improved ride quality and handling, when compared with the earlier models.

In 1983 the entire range was revamped, being given a more rounded appearance thanks to a new nose section and fresh tailgate and light cluster arrangements.

The interior of the entire range was also changed, and there became two distinct groups of Fiesta, even though Ford may not have intended that to happen; the economy models came with a very basic fascia, whilst the upper range, which have subsequently become the ones bought as fun cars, or as second cars, have a more up-market dashboard with such equipment as a radio, tachometer and so forth as standard issue. At the same time as the restyling, there were mechanical changes including the general availability of a five-speed transmission on all but the most basic models, and the use of the CVH engine from the Escort in place of the Kent 1600. ▶

THE LONG GOODBYE

forwards. On bendy bits of road a similar trait is apparent, as the car will understeer quite chronically unless the driver is particularly light-footed. Our test of the Power Engineering System Two Litre XR2 in the last issue proved that this need not be so; altering the spring and damper rates, along with a

FORD FIESTA — A POTTED HISTORY

When the Mk III Escort received its first facelift in 1986, some of the new equipment for that car made its way down to the Fiesta, most notably the 1.4 version of the CVH engine, which was used to replace the 1.3 crossflow in the interests of better fuel economy. Shortly afterwards the 1.4S Fiesta appeared, as an alternative to the overtly sporting XR2 model. Cheap, cheery and nippy, the car proved so popular with buyers that Ford were unable to offer examples out for press evaluation.

The last major change to appear on the Fiesta came in May of 1987, when the CTX (Continuously variable TransaXle) automatic transmission became available.

Much of the continuing development of the Fiesta range has been in the interests of ensuring that the public didn't have too many revelations to deal with once the new Fiesta finally made its bow in December 1988, but the changes have also ensured that the car has stayed right up there at the top end of the national sales chart — Fiesta has figured in the top three almost without fail since its introduction, selling several to every one Nova or Metro.

The third generation of Fiesta, which goes on sale in April, continues the tradition by breaking little new ground, but does incorporate quite a number of desirable features which have been seen on larger Fords. These include the award-winning Stop Control System of anti-lock braking, power windows, heated front screen, central locking, and so forth. The new car is appreciably bigger than the ones which have become so familiar on our roads, and has a wheelbase a full six inches longer than the "old" Fiesta.

Interior space is much improved, as is luggage area — although the anticipated version of the car with a boot in place of the hatchback was dropped, at the eleventh hour, by Ford because they did not feel the format to be economically viable. For the first time there will be a four passenger door version of the car available, and the XR2 model, temporary flagship until the Cosworth-developed 1.4 Turbo model goes on sale in a year or so, has gained not just electronic fuel injection, but a five brake horsepower advantage over its XR3i stablemate. According to reports from several enthusiasts who have actually managed to drive the car, the XR2i is a fine-handling, crisp little performer well worth waiting for. We hope to bring a full test of the newcomer in our April 1989 issue. •

re-setting of the front geometry, makes for a Fiesta which will deal almost as well with wet roads as it does with dry. But as we presumed in that feature, the chances are that the XR2 hasn't been looked at by Ford's chassis development people in quite some time, given that its replacement was already on the way. So once again, it is down to the aftermarket and the private owner to correct the wayward tendencies of the car.

Whilst the initial brief which Ford followed for the car included the requirement of a roomy interior, it is an honest assessment of the Fiesta range (as it now stands) that the description would not really describe the car which we have known for the past twelve years or so. Unless, of course, you happen to be a pigmy, and only ever carry fellow members of the tribe around in your XR2.

The level of equipment in the XR2 is as good as you'll get in a Fiesta, but even so, it doesn't stand too close an inspection, or comparison with other equivalent models by different manufacturers. Which is why there will be features such as central locking and power windows available for the car's successor — Ford have at last realised that even though people are buying the baby of the Ford family, they have a right to demand features such as these in their car. Interestingly, there are switch blanks for power windows moulded into the centre console of the XR2, but that feature has never been offered on the car.

The car has, for all of its faults, foibles and general shortcomings, served its makers well, and the XR2 in particular

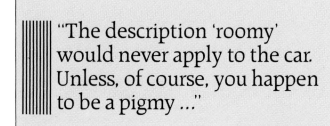

"The description 'roomy' would never apply to the car. Unless, of course, you happen to be a pigmy ..."

has developed almost a cult following in much the same way as the Capri did. This is purely and simply down to the fact that the car has a charismatic character, something which very, very few cars today have. We live in an age where a homogenised, sanitised, predictable and usually boring car is being offered by a manufacturer, and in a world filled with such machinery the Fiesta XR2 stands out from the crowd because it has an identity. Get into most small cars, and without reading the badges it is hard to tell quite what you are driving. Yet you know immediately that you are behind the wheel of an XR2, from the moment that you first blip the throttle and let out the clutch. This car will be sorely missed. For all of its faults, it is still a fine little car that will be difficult to match for sheer fun. It is to be hoped that the new generation, when it appears on the roads in April, will have at least some of the character of this model. •

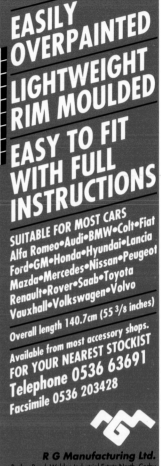

ARRIVISTE!

Ford's newest hatchback has finally arrived — the XR2i is now on general sale. Do we rate it?

By Dennis Foy.

It was just after passing through the sleepy, closed-season, seaside town of Cushendon on the Antrim coast that I started to fully appreciate how good the chassis of the new XR2i is, to realise just how much better the newcomer is when compared with its predecessor.

That stretch of the Ulster coastline is sparsely populated, and the smooth surface of the deserted road shone slightly from the fine, steady, drenching drizzle which had been falling for some hours. Here and there a patch of matt tarmac indicated where one or other of the utilities had been digging up the road, whilst subtle changes in the sheen hinted at deviations in camber on the abundant sweeping curves. The road lured me, and I rolled on a little more power to see if I could get the car to misbehave.

I couldn't. Instead the small black device simply did what it was bidden to do with a pleasing consistency.

Given the province's reputation for autumnal rain, the choice ➤

ARRIVISTE!

of Ulster as a launch venue for a new car could be construed as a brave one. Whilst many cars can feel quite allright when being driven on dry roads, attempts to push those same cars hard when the highways are covered in water can highlight all manner of handling deficiencies. Ford were obviously confident in the abilities of their latest hot hatchback. Their confidence is well founded.

The XR2i follows the same basic format as the rest of the Fiesta range, which first appeared in the Spring. The standard three door bodyshell is distinguishable from its lesser brethren by a stylish set of additional body trim panels, whilst on the interior of the XR2i there is abundant use of the same Zolda fabric which is to be found within the XR3i Escort. There is also a price tag which is some £986 heavier than that of its next most expensive member of the Fiesta family, the 1400 Ghia.

This is the first Fiesta to gain the benefit of electronic fuel injection, and this is controlled by a variation on the ubiquitous EEC-1V engine management system which also looks after the ignition system. The use of this black box packed with electronic gizmos, microchips and suchlike is allied to a redesigned intake system and exhaust manifold which allows the 1596cc powerplant to make an appreciable gain in specific power output; in this form, the aluminium-headed, iron-blocked CVH (Compound Valve, Hemispherical) engine develops 110 b.h.p. at 6000 r.p.m., and 102 lb/ft of torque at a credible 2800 r.p.m. It also achieves these figures on a permanent diet of low-octane unleaded fuel — although it will happily run on normal leaded fuel when lead-free is unavailable.

The XR2i shares the same transmission as the rest of the range of CVH-powered Fiestas, and has the same 4.06:1 final drive

FORD PHOTOGRAPHIC UNIT

gearing as the 1.4 models — only the 1.6S and the 1.8 Diesel have taller overall gearing, at 3.82:1 and 3.59:1 respectively. Drive is handled at one end of the transmission by a 220mm single plate clutch, and at the other end by a pair of driveshafts to the front hubs.

The hubs are connected to the rest of the car via a pair of MacPherson struts, which make use of single-mount upper bushes to avoid spring winding when the steering is on full lock. At the bottom of the struts are the acclaimed L-shaped locating arms which do a far more positive job of controlling wheel angle than the ''traditional'' single tie bars ever could. These arms make use of sealed Rose joints which allow movement in all of the desired planes, but without the usual trade-off of deviations in wheel angle. The nett result is a system which is far less prone to torque steer than most front wheel drive cars. A 15mm diameter anti-roll bar aids the springing at the front of the car, which is appreciably uprated from that of standard Fiestas.

At the rear of the car is a rather complex arrangement of a torsion beam axle, a pair of trailing arms, and a pair of outboard-mounted struts which locate into turrets either side of the load area. When compared with the previous Fiesta XR2, the revised suspension is not only more efficient, but also more widely spaced — track is wider by 1.4″ at the front and 2.6″ at the rear, and the wheelbase is a substantial 6″ longer, at 96.3″. To allow the car to retain a tight turning circle of 32 feet, the steering rack has a slow 4.2 turns from one lock to the other. Whilst we have discovered this rack to be

> ''The additional body detailing gives the new car an overtly sporting appearance, and the image is completed the moment that the key is turned.''

ponderous on lesser Fiestas in the range, the uprated springs, lower ride height and lower profile tyres of the XR2i disguise matters quite effectively, and in practice the car feels nimble and responsive.

Braking from the 240mm ventilated front discs and 203mm rear drums is servo assisted, and both weighting and bite is excellent; pedal response is sharp without being prone to grabbing, even when the system is cold. There is also the option of Ford's excellent mechanical Stop Control System, a mechanical anti-lock braking facility which adds a reasonable £400 to the £9,995 purchase price of the car. This operates on all four wheels of the car (when it was first introduced on the Escort and Orion only the front wheels were thus protected against skidding), and works very well. The standard wheels which come with the car are steel, but for the payment of another £200 the buyer can take delivery of the new car with the neat, sculpted aluminium alloy rims which are unique to the model. Tyres are the same regardless of wheel type (both steel and aluminium rims are 5.5″ x 13″), being 185/60 HR 13s. All examples of XR2i that we have so far seen from the production run have been shod with Pirelli P600 rubber.

Ford have long since proven their mastery of the concept of taking an ordinary car and making it look appreciably different by appending a few strategic bits of additional bodywork. In the case of the XR2i, a new front bumper with integral additional driving lamps (one pair of spotlights, the other pair being foglamps) is paired with a deep rear bumper moulding, the two ends of the car being linked by a pair of side mouldings which follow the shape of the front and rear arches, and which flare out along the rocker panels to form sideskirts. These are all colour-keyed to the bodywork (which in XR tradition is available in only four shades, red, white, black or metallic grey), and have insert strips of bright blue. The same blue is used inside the car, as an insert strip dividing the upper and lower halves of the door liner panels. Regardless of body colour, the same shadow grey shade of Zolda fabric is used, with co-ordinating grey carpets and plastic mouldings.

The additional body detailing gives the new XR2i an overtly sporting appearance, and the image is completed the moment that the ignition switch is turned and the engine bursts into life.

The injected CVH engine has always been a free-revving unit, and this aspect of its behaviour combines with a rorty note from the car's squared-off tailpipe to immediately convince occupants and bystanders alike that this is a car which has a sporting disposition. A quick dab on the lightly-sprung throttle pedal is enough to have the tachometer needle whipping around towards the redline if the transmission is in neutral.

Ergonomically, the XR2i has made a quantum leap forward from the earlier model of Fiesta. The seats are comfortable and supportive, and the pedals and thick-rimmed steering wheel fall nicely. The gear lever (with its "map" in the same shade of blue as the insert strips along the door liners) is also nicely positioned, as are most of the ancilliary controls — only the window lifter buttons mounted on the centre console are a stretch away from the driver's seat. The additional interior space provided within the new bodyshell has been used to allow a greater degree of fore/aft adjustment

PERFORMANCE

0-60	9.0 seconds
30-50 (4th)	7.1 seconds
Maximum Speed	119 m.p.h.

For: Good looks, good package, fun factor
Against: Noise levels

for the seats, and the car is thus able to accommodate both shorter and taller drivers than those who would have been able to drive the earlier model of XR2. Headroom is adequate for drivers of up to about 6'2" in height, which is much the same as that found in Escorts and Sierras. The main controls are also nicely weighted, with the pressures of the three pedals bearing a good relationship to each other.

Pulling off from standstill, the gearknob has already slotted itself nicely into its intended position, and the clutch has proven itself progressive enough to allow a smooth take-off. Clean and judder-free gearshifts, whether up or down the box, are easy to accomplish in this car. If circumstances dictate that pottering about is the order of the day, then the XR2i will happily oblige with all of the docility of a 1.1LX Fiesta. Yet when the open road beckons — as it did for me that few miles north of Belfast — the car will adopt an air of urgency which is totally in keeping with its appearance.

In the stop-light grand prix, the car can make the sprint to sixty in nine seconds exactly, which is much the same as its predecessor would manage; the extra horsepower doesn't make its presence felt in such situations but the revised front suspension does, by neatly ironing out any tendencies for the wheels to weave and dart about. Even with the diminishing traction afforded to the P600s on Antrim's wet roads the car was still aiming accurately forward under hard acceleration. In the dry it takes an awful lot for the nose of the car to do anything untoward.

Where the additional power afforded by the engine modifications really makes itself known is in the mid-range; whereas the previous XR2 was lively and nippy through the gears, it was prone to running out of breath at higher engine

speeds. No such problems afflict the injected engine, which simply keeps delivering power in a most pleasing manner. A cursory check of mid-range acceleration times showed that the extra fourteen horsepower is enough to clip a second or two off the performance of the old XR2. However, what is more important is that the torque-spread is now much improved, and thus the rate at which a sequence of bends can be negotiated is now appreciably better.

The car really comes into its own when there are bends to attack. The combination of a wide track, long wheelbase and lightweight bodyshell powered by a responsive engine allows the driver to set the car up beautifully for a curve or a corner with equal ease, and the chassis simply does what the driver tells it to with total complicity. Even when the limits of adhesion approach, the car is still behaving itself, and the driver is still in control; it would take an awesome degree of insensitivity on the part of the driver to actually unstick the car at that point, such is the strength of signal that is being transmitted back to the steering wheel rim.

At the moment of diminished adhesion the car will be ➤

ARRIVISTE!

understeering, but only just; if the power is held at the same level until the end of the bend then the car will present no problem to the occupants of the car, any other people in the vicinity, or indeed the surrounding countryside. Only when yet more power is rolled on whilst the car is still in mid-bend will it start to run seriously wide of the intended line — and as I have already stated, the chassis is already screaming that enough is enough, thank you very much.

As has been Ford's philosophy over the past half-dozen years, the chassis is extremely user-friendly — if the driver decides to back off in mid-bend the XR2i will tuck its nose back into the curve, and carry on as though nothing has happened. It won't tell on you if you won't, and it is all rather impressive.

One of the usual problems with small, powerful front wheel drive cars emerges when a little too much power is applied on tight bends; the usual upshot is that the inside front wheel will begin to patter and bounce as it battles to gain some kind of traction. Whilst the new bottom links on the front struts have not totally eliminated this syndrome, they have dramatically reduced it when compared with not just the earlier XR2, but also with most of the other small hot hatches on the market.

Equally impressive is the car's braking ability. Although the car is now in something of a minority in its class by still having drum brakes on the back axle, the system still works very well, and it takes a real panic stop to break traction with the front pair of tyres — even when the road surface is wet. Most of the time the application of some pressure to the middle pedal will simply scrub off some speed in direct proportion to the amount of weight being applied by the right foot. In emergency situations there is the failsafe back-up of anti-lock braking available to those prepared to forego a new stereo and spend £400 on that option instead. Whilst not as sensitive as an electronic system — which is appreciably more expensive, which is why Ford offer it only on Sierra and Granada models — S.C.S. is certainly a sensible addition to the car's standard specification, which is better than no system at all.

So what didn't impress us about the newcomer?

Principal moans concern the noise levels within the car, which can soon become intrusive when the going is fast. Most of the aural overload comes from beneath the bonnet, but there is also a considerable amount of tyre roar to be contended with. A few strategic sound-deadening pads would doubtless help here, and I can foresee the manufacturers of soundproofing kits gaining a substantial amount of business from owners of the new XR2i. Then there is the niggling matter of the door mirror adjusters. These are fiddly little toggles which emerge through the cornerplates of the door windows, and they prove extremely difficult to fine tune; any attempt to reposition the mirror lenses has the driver going through a process of trying to stop them going too far up, down, or sideways. The provision of electrical adjusters such as those found on other Fords would be an immediate solution to the problem, and would complete what is an otherwise satisfactory level of trim and equipment. The only other complaint that we can make is that, from the inside, it is difficult to tell that the driver is not in one of the lesser Fiestas, such as the 1.6S. I feel that there will be quite a few XR2i owners who crave a slightly more distinctive cabin for their cars.

In all other respects, the new car is a worthy contender. Its standard specification includes such items as a sunroof, electric windows, central locking, remote tailgate release, and a System 2005 stereo cassette with four speakers and keycode protection. Stowage for odds and sods is ample — although we would have liked to see somewhere to store cassette tapes — and accommodation for four adults is good, considering the overall compact dimensions of the car.

SPECIFICATIONS

ENGINE TYPE
Transverse four cylinder SOHC
BORE x STROKE
80mm x 79.5mm
SIZE
1596cc
BHP @ RPM
110 @ 6000
TORQUE LB/FT @ RPM
102 @ 2800
FUEL SYSTEM
Ford electronic EEC-1V injection
DRIVEN WHEELS
Front
TRANSMISSION
5-speed manual transaxle
SUSPENSION, FRONT
MacPherson struts, L-shaped lower brackets, 15mm anti-roll bar
SUSPENSION, REAR
Torsion beam, MacPherson struts, trailing arms
BRAKING SYSTEM
Front discs, rear drums, servo assistance, option SCS anti-lock
WEIGHT
1958 lbs
POWER/WEIGHT RATIO
124 b.h.p./ton
WHEELBASE
96.3″
LENGTH
148″
WIDTH
73″
HEIGHT
52″
TEST MILEAGE
180 miles
MANUFACTURER'S MPG
28.5
TEST MPG
N/A
PRICE AS TESTED
£10,725
INSURANCE GROUP
5
MANUFACTURER
Ford Motor Company, Dagenham, England

The car looks the part, and combines respectable — if not quite earth-shattering — performance with all of the virtues of the new Fiesta range. The new range has been engineered to minimise servicing costs by sealing for life many of the main components, and the insurance companies have rated the car as Group Five, which is quite reasonable considering the overall performance of the model. When fully loaded with all of the options (alloy wheels, heated windscreen, anti-lock brakes and either black or metallic paint), the car still comes out on the right side of £11,000, which again compares favourably with the competition.

Most of all, though, the car is endowed with that most elusive of qualities, a fun-filled character. The XR2i has a cheeky disposition which immediately comes across the moment that the driver starts to pile some power on along an open stretch of road. Its responsive steering, good suspension (it jiggles a bit on bumpy roads but tends not to deviate from the intended line) and willing engine feed the driver a set of sensations which are bound to appeal to anybody with red blood coursing through his or her veins.

Ford aim to sell some thirty one thousand XR2i models in the coming year — the model is expected to account for 20% of all Fiesta registrations — and they report advance firm orders for more than ten thousand cars before the model even went on sale. On the strength of our experiences so far with the new XR2i, there will be few dissatisfied customers.

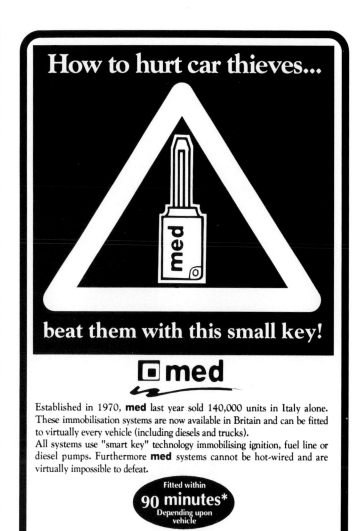

4x4 + 2 = HEIGHTENED PLEASURES

Turbo Technics have taken the latest generation of XR4x4 and added a matched pair of T.02 turbochargers — an equation which results in a 50% power increase. A full test follows ...

There is a certain pleasure gained when driving Ford's XR4x4, from setting it up for a bend, getting the braking over by just the right point on the approach, and then drifting the car lightly, almost on tiptoes, until the moment when it is just right to roll on the power. There is the certain knowledge that traction from all four wheels will propel the machine forward, tight on its intended line — and appreciably more quickly than most two wheel drive cars would achieve with the same minimum of fuss. When the XR4x4 happens to have a pair of tiny turbochargers forcing

DENNIS FOY

the air and fuel into the engine, then that certain pleasure is heightened considerably — as are the speeds which can be achieved on the exit of a curve.

The latest generation of XR4x4, with the 2.9 litre Cologne engine and the slick new MT-75 transmission, is a natural for the Turbo Technics treatment — after all, the company has already gained a great deal of experience building turbocharged versions of the earlier, 2800cc models of the car. A variety of performance levels were offered on that particular car, from two to three hundred + horsepower. With that car the induction side was handled by a large Garrett AiResearch T.03 turbocharger, and the various levels of performance were achieved by subtle alterations to the size of intercooler, compression ratio settings, and ultimately the levels of boost which the turbine was allowed to create before being told to desist by the electronics of the management systems.

For the new car, Turbo Technics have decided against simply carrying over the old system, and instead started with a clean sheet of paper; there are a number of reasons for this, but the principal one lies in the quest of the serious turbocharging tuner to totally eradicate the old bugbear of turbo ''lag''

The accepted reason for the phenomenon of ''lag'' is the amount of time that it takes the turbocharger to spin up to a sufficient speed for its induction side to make the transition from vacuum to positive boost — and as a general rule, the bigger the turbocharger, the greater the problem. By installing a pair of the diminuitive Garrett T.02 turbos — units which are intended for use on engines of up to 1800cc — Turbo Technics are able to endow the engine not only with adequate airflow, but also with turbos which will spin up to positive boost speed far more quickly than a single larger unit would be able to achieve.

In keeping with T.T.'s tradition, the turbochargers are mounted on a specially-cast pair of manifolds which are tuned for optimised pulse separation, and which couple to the car's original exhaust downpipes. The induction system starts with a modified air cleaner assembly, and then passes through dual outlets into the turbochargers. From there the air passes into a large, purpose-built air-to-air intercooler which reduces the temperature of the incoming charge to a manageable level. From the intercooler the air joins up with the standard 2.9i twin-plenum intake manifold, where the fuel is added; this needs to be appreciably greater in quantity once boost levels are achieved, and the standard EEC-1V engine management system has thus been overridden by electronics of T.T.'s own specification.

This aspect of tuning the 2.9i has perplexed just about everybody who has attempted to make the unit behave differently, and I recall a conversation with Geoff Kershaw, head of Turbo Technics, at last year's Motor Show in Birmingham during which he outlined to me some of the difficulties that they were having in persuading the EEC-1V to obey revised signals. From our test of the car, I am able to report that their patient approach appears to have paid off as the car seemed to behave perfectly with no flat spots or hesitations at any point throughout the rev range.

Supplementary fuel injectors feature as part of the T.T. solution, along with a remapped fuel injection programme and boost-retard ignition settings.

Actual engine modifications are limited to a reduction in the compression ratio from 9.5:1 to 8.6:1 in order to handle the increased thermal load of the forced induction. The nett result is an increase in power of exactly 50%, from 150 to 225 brake horsepower. Torque is likewise increased substantially, from 172 lb/ft to no less than 273 lb/ft. To handle this the clutch is uprated, but the rest of the driveline is able to cope admirably with the surge in power — the MT-75 transmission is rated at 300 lb/ft capacity, and so is still safely within its design parameters.

Firing up the engine is no different from that of an ordinary example of 4x4; a twist of the key and the motor bursts into life. As with any engine it pays in the long term to allow the engine to reach its proper operating temperature before making it really work for a living, and out of deference to the car we deferred using the engine hard until it had been awake for a few minutes.

►

''Pottering around town it was difficult to tell the car apart from any other example of XR4x4. Hit the open road and it was a completely different story ...''

PERFORMANCE

0-60	6.8 seconds
0-100	15.1 seconds
50-70 (4th)	4.3 seconds
50-70 (5th)	5.3 seconds
70-90 (5th)	4.6 seconds
Maximum Speed	145 m.p.h.

4x4 + 2 = HEIGHTENED PLEASURES

Pottering around town, with low revs and frequent gearchanges, it was difficult to tell the car apart from any other XR4x4 — only the heavier clutch pedal pressure gave any kind of hint that this was a different sort of car. Hit the open road and it was a completely different story. Turbo Technics tend not to install boost gauges in their demonstration models, and so it was difficult to say for certain at what point in the rev range the induction system makes the change from vacuum to positive boost, but the seat of my pants tells me that things start to happen at as little as two thousand revs per minute — an *exceptionally* low point in the engine's speed scale for a turbocharged car.

Fans of older-style turbocharged cars, who get an adrenalin burn from the sudden surge in power as the turbine kicks in, may feel slightly disappointed in this car — not because the performance is any less than it would be, but because that sudden rush is absent. Instead of a slight flatness and then a sudden rush this car has an ever-increasing solid wave of power that is most impressive. This allows a conventional driving technique to be maintained when pushing the car through a series of bends — it is no longer necessary to anticipate that split second when the engine will make the transition from normal aspiration to turbocharged, a moment which must be judged finely if tidy handling is to be maintained.

If the braking is dealt with in a straight line this car can, just like a standard XR4x4, be lightly drifted through to the apex of a bend, and then the power can be rolled on progressively — the depth of travel of the throttle pedal being governed only by the state of the road ahead or the driver's state of mind. There are no special tricks necessary with this car, save for those which will be familiar to anybody used to driving four wheel drive cars; for the uninitiated, a 4x4 will behave quite differently from a rear wheel drive Sierra. Whereas a rear driven Sierra will eventually oversteer if adequate power is available following a period of understeer, a four wheel drive car will pull its nose forward and adopt a neutral posture at much higher speeds. When the limits of adhesion are reached the car with two wheels being driven will usually go tail first if there is adequate power on tap, or nose first if there isn't enough muscle to throw the rear of the car out of line. A four wheel drive car will let go sideways, and there is rarely a thing that can be done about it, apart from putting your head between your legs and … well, we'll leave the graphic details for another occasion.

This car has no trick components within its suspension system — everything on each corner of the car is just the way that it was when the car rolled off Ford's production line.

The pair of tiny Garrett water-cooled turbos nestle in the engine bay, one feeding each bank of cylinders. Note the additional injector plumbing at the head of the plenum chamber.

Therefore it figures that the cornering speeds are just the same as they would be on any example of the machine which was fitted with the excellent BFGoodrich Comp T/A radials. What is different is the car's acceleration out of the bend — roll the power on and the car hurtles forward with an eagerness which is totally in keeping with the massive amount of torque on instant call. And the straights between the bends suddenly become much shorter, so reaction times must be honed to a corresponding level.

For such a powerful car the suspension on this particular XR4x4 was a little softer than we would have liked — the amount of roll as the car enters a curve is somewhat at odds with the accelerative powers of the car. Turbo Technics offer a revised suspension system for the car, one which keeps to the same basic format but which offers firmer springing and stiffer damping — but for some reason the test car had been left in its standard form. I cannot help but feel that a more rapid progress through the bendy bits would be possible with an uprated suspension system — and our experiences in a number of thus-modified Sierras shows that there need not be any great "trade off" against ride quality and comfort when the handling is improved.

The "Sierra According To Turbo Technics" is equally at home on the motorway as it is on the backroads of Britain, eating up the miles without any difficulty — some two-thirds of our 1,050 test miles were undertaken on motorways, and we would have soon discovered any weaknesses in that area had they existed. When circumstances allow, the car is capable of running at as much as one hundred and forty five — which means that at a legal seventy the car is running at under half of its potential. This in turn can be translated into the fact that when a sudden burst of power is needed, in order to drive away from a tricky situation, there is plenty to call upon. The tall overall gearing of the XR4x4 (the final drive ratio is 3.62:1, and fifth gear is overdriven) allows the car to lope along at

seventy with the tachometer hovering at three thousand on the scale; keeping within the letter — as distinct from the spirit — of the law does wonders for the fuel economy. However, keeping within even the *spirit* of the law is not easy in this car, such is the willingness of the engine — it finds its own level at about five thousand cruising revs per minute. With about twenty four miles per hour as the car's fifth gear cruising figure per thousand revs, the nett result is a highly illegal "natural" cruising gait …

The car's braking system is again standard, just the way that Ford made it — but there is obviously so much over-engineering in the all-disc Ford system that it is patently able to deal with just about anything that is thrown at it. Even the occasional high-speed run along a demanding series of twists and turns won't catch the system out; it simply scrubs off as much speed as it is told to do, immediately. There is also the highly-desirable optional extra of anti-lock braking available for the Sierra — and anybody who considers that they have the skill and acumen to never need such a facility is fooling nobody but themselves; the system has only to preclude an accident once to pay for itself — and bear in mind that in today's world a thousand pounds (which is the cost of having ABS factory-fitted to a new XR4x4) doesn't buy an awful lot of body repair work.

The XR4x4's cabin is a nice place to be. Whilst some of the control gear is beginning to show its age (the Sierra and ►

The car's driveline is engineered to take more than the standard hundred and fifty horsepower, and so T.T. have been able to leave everything but the clutch standard. Stiffer springing would improve rate at which car could negotiate bends.

4x4 + 2 = HEIGHTENED PLEASURES

Sapphire are the only Fords to still have the old three-stalk controls for lights and wipers), and whilst some of the secondary controls are something of a stretch to reach, the ergonomics of the car are still pretty good. The steering wheel is fixed, with no tilt or reach adjustment, but the driver's seat can be adjusted for reach, rake, height and lumbar support — which means that just about everybody can achieve their ideal sitting position. The semi-bucket seats offer good, firm support for both front seat occupants, and their side bolsters are high enough to provide good lateral location without intruding any further than they need to. The three pedals are neatly placed in terms of matched height and spacing, and the short-throw gear lever of the MT-75 falls nicely to hand. The thick-rimmed steering wheel feeds orders out to the ground via what has to be one of the best power-assisted steering racks in the business, a system which allows the driver to know precisely what is going on at ground level without ever

''When circumstances allow, the car is capable of running at as much as a hundred and forty five — which means that at the legal motorway limit it is running at under half of its potential.''

becoming involved in a struggle against the wheels; it gives both light action at parking speeds *and* sharp reactions when the car is travelling briskly.

In terms of equipment the XR4x4 scores quite highly, offering power assistance for the mirrors and all four side windows, heated front and rear screens, a tilt-and-slide sunroof, masses of warning lights, and a high-grade stereo system with four speakers amongst other items. Externally, the XR is immediately identifiable by its colour-keyed front and rear spoilers, the pair of extra washers and wipers on the headlamps, and that smart set of RS alloy seven-spoke rims.

In its basic form, the Turbo Technics car adds some £2,950 to the £15,750 price tag of the XR4x4 — which would bring the total value of this car, as tested, to a little over £20,300 by the time that the V.A.T. on the conversion and the supplements of £995 for ABS and £175 for metallic paint have been added. That is a lot of money — but then it is a lot of car. It has a level of performance which is definitely in the supercar league — its acceleration is as sparkling as it ought to be, and is a perfect match for the maximum speed.

What is more, the car will run happily on a permanent diet of unleaded fuel, which is not only ecologically far preferable to regular four-star, but is also some ten pence to the gallon cheaper. In terms of the amount of fuel which it uses, the car proved itself to be less eco-conscious, returning an average of 17.08 miles to each gallon — a figure which compares less than favourably with the 21.6 miles of unleaded fuel distance which we achieved in our last full test of the standard XR4x4 2.9i.

So to the bottom line. The Turbo Technics treatment will add twenty per cent to the basic cost of the car, and fuel bills will rise by a similar percentage. However, the power increase is no less than fifty per cent — and the amount of extra enjoyment

that having all of that extra power on tap is impossible to quantify in bald mathematical terms. In its basic form the XR4x4 is virtually viceless; only its thirst and its cost can really be held against it. It is an exciting and stimulating car to drive — and the pair of twin turbochargers which form the heart of the Turbo Technics conversion enhance the car's appeal much further. The car is not like earlier examples of T.T. conversion that we have tried in that it is often difficult to sense exactly when the boost comes in; that sudden rush is not there. Instead, it feels as though the car's engine has been made appreciably bigger — a feature which particularly suits the XR's chassis. It is a car which is as easy to drive as any normal XR4x4, but which offers substantially sharper performance levels. To discover the pleasures of running a Turbo Technics XR4x4 for yourself, contact the company at 17 Galowhill Road, Northampton NN4 0EE, telling them that *Performance Ford* sent you. ●

SPECIFICATIONS

ENGINE TYPE
Inline six cylinder Vee pushrod
BORE x STROKE
93mm x 72mm
SIZE
2933cc
BHP @ RPM
225 @ 5500
TORQUE LB/FT @ RPM
273 @ 2750
FUEL SYSTEM
Turbo Technics/Garrett twin T.02 water-cooled turbochargers, modified Ford EEC-1V management system, additional injectors
DRIVEN WHEELS
All four
TRANSMISSION
5-speed MT-75 manual
SUSPENSION, FRONT
MacPherson struts, anti-roll bar, gas-filled dampers
SUSPENSION, REAR
Independent semi-trailing arms, coil springs, gas-filled dampers
BRAKING SYSTEM
Front ventilated discs, rear solid discs, servo assisted dual circuit hydraulics, optional electronic anti-lock braking system
WEIGHT
2820 lbs
POWER/WEIGHT RATIO
180 b.h.p./ton
WHEELBASE
102.7"
LENGTH
174"
WIDTH
75.6"
HEIGHT
53"
TEST MILEAGE
1,046 miles
MANUFACTURER'S MPG
N/A
TEST MPG
17.08
PRICE AS TESTED
£20,312
INSURANCE GROUP
Special quotation
MANUFACTURER
Ford Motor Company
Modifications carried out by Turbo Technics, Northampton

X CERTIFICATE

The System X Sierra XR4x4 provides serious, grown-up acceleration, speed and handling.
What do we make of the latest offering from Power Engineering?

By Dennis Foy.

ratio of the engine in order to deal with the dramatically-increased chamber temperatures. This hurts the bottom-end power output of the engine, a characteristic which can be accentuated by the need for the turbine to spin up to speed before it starts to supply boosted air to the engine — depending upon the installation, the engine power below two to three thousand revs can be appreciably lower than that of a similar engine running its standard compression ratio.

The temperature of the incoming charge from a belt-driven supercharger is lower than that of a turbo at any given boost pressure, which as a general rule means that there is no need to alter the compression ratio of the engine. By careful selection of the pair of pulleys which are joined by the driven belt, it is also possible to have the supercharger unit start developing positive boost at very low engine speeds — and these two factors combine to create a powerplant which starts to develop usable power right at the bottom end of its speed range.

What is more important when driving along twisting, winding roads than brake horsepower is torque, and the supercharger, for the reasons already given, produces a highly impressive amount of torque; at 4300 r.p.m. the engine is developing a massive 305 lb/ft of torque, and even at as low as 1500 r.p.m. there is more than double the torque of a naturally ➤

O ccasionally, in an idle moment, I have paired up pieces of music to particular cars. For instance, Springsteen's anthem Born To Run can only ever really be applied to a street-racing Plymouth Belvedere with a 426 Hemi under a lightweight, grey-primered hood. The TVR ''S''? That would go well with Steve Earle's Copperhead Road, or perhaps something from the repertoire of ZZ Top. The subtlety of the Sapphire Cosworth would tie in nicely to the classic elegance of Beethoven's Ninth, the Choral Symphony, which soars and sweeps along with understated urgency. And this red supercharged XR4x4? Well, there is only one piece of music which would really suit it; The Ride Of The Valkyries, by Wagner. It was no accident that the lunatic commanding officer in the film Apocalypse Now had his helicopter gunships blasting out that particular theme when they went on raiding missions over Vietcong positions — Wagner's pièce de résistance has a menacing, awesome might to it. And so does the supercharged four-by-four.

Our photographic session was undertaken up in the hills between Macclesfield and Buxton at an altitude of about 1,800 feet, just a little higher than the famous Cat & Fiddle pub which is one of the highest inns in England. To get to our location involves a ten mile run uphill from the edge of the Cheshire Plain along a road which is none too wide, and packed with tight, twisting bends — there is even the odd hairpin to contend with. To get the best out of the road a car needs to have excellent handling, surefooted grip, and a punchy, powerful engine endowed with masses of bottom-end punch. The System X supercharged XR4x4 has all three qualities in abundance — factors which enabled us to make our trip to and from our photosession site (a run we make regularly) more quickly, more accurately, and altogether more effectively than I have ever been able to before.

The Sprintex supercharger is, for those not already familiar with the device, a means of forcing pressurised air into the engine, boosting the power output of the Ford V6 from its normal 150 b.h.p. to something in excess of 250 brake horsepower. Turbocharging achieves the same end, but by a different means; whilst a turbo is driven by exhaust gases, a supercharger is belt-driven from the engine's crankshaft pulley. A turbocharger generates a tremendous amount of heat (although the more sophisticated installations use an intercooler to partially reduce the temperature of the incoming charge, back down to manageable levels) which brings about the need to reduce the baseline compression

X CERTIFICATE

Wider than standard, the Italian-made alloy wheels are shod with 205/50ZR15 Yokohama AVS tyres rated to 170 m.p.h. Wheels are also an inch greater diameter than standard Ford seven-spoke RS alloy rims.

Twist the key, fire up the engine, and there is just the slightest hint that the car is something out of the ordinary; as the machine bursts into life there is a sharp rasp from the blower belt-drive before everything settles down to a steady idle. The already deep exhaust note of the V6 deepens still further, suggesting that there is Muscle with a capital "M" lurking beneath the expanse of Radiant Red bonnet. Yet the noises are never so loud as to create any suspicion amongst passengers who do not share the driver's penchant for fast cars — and the illusion can be held even after moving off, should the circumstances dictate that it is advisable to have things that way.

Depress the standard-weighted clutch pedal, snick the short-throw lever of the MT-75 into first, and the car can be pottered out into a line of traffic, actions arousing no interest from anybody. If, however, you drop the clutch more sharply with a rapidly-increasing number of revs indicating on the large clear tachometer then the story which unfolds is one of scintillating

> "A standard XR4x4 is quick through the bends, but this specimen is appreciably more rapid."

◄ aspirated 2.9i V6 coming through the Sierra's driveline. In practice, these figures mean that if you stomp on the loud pedal there is an instant sharp reaction at road level, with the beefy Yokohama tyres digging into the road surface and lunging the red car forward.

As a tribute to Ford's policy of over-engineering the XR4x4, Power Engineering have needed to make few changes to the driveline of the car. The clutch, transmission, transfer box and front and rear differentials are all just as they come from the factory, and cope easily with the seventy seven per cent increase in torque. However, the standard handling of the XR is, whilst perfectly adequate for the standard engine, clearly overstretched when treated to such a dramatic increase in power. The brakes too could handle a little outside help when the car is being expected to pull down from appreciably higher velocities.

To bring the handling up to the required level, Power have developed a new suspension package which puts together uprated springs with Koni adjustable dampers, a combination which appreciably stiffens the car whilst cornering, yet which has no particular adverse effect on ride comfort. To make the most of the improved handling, the roadholding is upgraded by replacing the standard wheels and tyres with a set of stunning-looking Italian aluminium alloy wheels shod with the excellent new Yokohama AVS 205/50ZR15 rubber.

Braking is upgraded by replacing the standard pads with racing-grade friction material, and replacing the standard flexible lines with stainless steel braided items. Finally, racing fluid is used in the system (which incidentally does not affect the ABS if the car is thus-equipped), as this has a higher resistance to boiling than regular-grade hydraulic fluid. Although they graunch from time to time, the brakes never fail to arrest the car's speed consistently, and appear to be totally fade-free.

acceleration as the ton-and-a-bit of Sierra hurtles toward the horizon with an urgency normally reserved for the dragstrip. A sharp getaway with a floored throttle will see each ten mile an hour increment of the speedometer pass a second after the last one right through to the sixty miles per hour, and if you do happen to be on a dragstrip then the car will trip the shutdown lights at the other end of the quarter mile 14.7 seconds after starting on its sprint, at a terminal speed of more than ninety eight miles per hour. Impressive stuff by anybody's standards.

Unfortunately, the combination of that glowing red paintwork, the wide offset alloy wheels and the various decals proclaiming "Power + ", "System X", "Supercharged" plus of course our own P.F. stickers, combine to be an effective red rag to anybody of a bullish nature who happens to pull alongside it at a set of lights — we even had a Lada 1200 have a go at us during our tenure of the car!

PERFORMANCE

0-30	2.36 seconds
0-40	3.89 seconds
0-50	5.01 seconds
0-60	6.20 seconds
0-100	14.97 seconds
30-50 (2nd)	2.65 seconds
30-50 (3rd)	4.76 seconds
50-70 (3rd)	3.65 seconds
50-70 (4th)	4.22 seconds
60-80 (4th)	4.30 seconds
Standing ¼ Mile	14.73 @ 98.1 m.p.h.
Maximum Speed	145 m.p.h.

Of course, there is something of which regular drivers of extremely rapid motorcars will already be aware, and that is not to rise to every challenge; blowing away a Lada at the lights is a hollow victory at the best of times. Instead, there is the safe knowledge that there is but a small number of other cars on the road that could actually give this car a hard time. And a few of those would be very hard put to match the in-gear, up-and-running times that this particular machine is capable of achieving.

The most useful of the overtaking bursts of speed tend to be from thirty to fifty, from fifty to seventy, and from sixty to eighty. This car manages to accomplish each of those in well under five seconds in the appropriate gear — and even if you are feeling lazy and decide to leave the car in fifth, the times will still be on the right side of eight seconds!

This ability to convert a prod of the throttle into immediate forward motion makes the car a jolly useful tool for motorway work, and for covering mile after mile of highway driving. However, the other side of the car's nature — which was hinted at in the early part of this tale — has the enthusiastic driver looking for excuses to leave the major roads, and search out winding stretches of back road. Then the real pleasures of motoring can be rediscovered. Floor the throttle and the car will rocket towards the first bend, the approach to which is dealt with effortlessly by a quick push on the middle pedal, and a downshift to another gear — and it seems not to matter that much which gear, such is the amount of instant torque available.

The car will turn into the curve nicely — the sticky Yokohamas not being particularly affected by whether the road surface is wet, damp or dry — without so much as a hint of drifting even at indecently high speeds. Once at the apex the power can be ➤

MANAGEMENT SKILLS

The XR4x4, in common with the rest of the current line-up of Ford fuel injected engines, uses the EEC-1V computer unit to control its fuel and ignition systems. As a direct result, any attempts to seriously tune the engine result immediately in the EEC-1V failing to understand the revised signals which its various sensors send to it, as they are outside the parameters which it is programmed to receive. It consequently either shuts the engine down completely, or puts it into ''limp home'' status.

Tuners on both sides of the Atlantic have fallen foul of the EEC-1V, and in a number of cases have discarded the complete system in favour of another, more easily programmable ''brain'' such as the British-built Zytec engine management system. Power Engineering contemplated such a move at one point during the protracted development programme of their supercharged 2.9i V6, but eventually opted to persevere with attempting to interface with the EEC-1V in an effort to keep the servicing of the completed cars as simple as possible, and to ensure that Ford continued their approval for the conversion.

The eventual cure came from ERP of Brighton, with whom Power Engineering have worked closely for some years. They have produced a complex, and fully adjustable, second management computer which interfaces with the Ford unit. This second management unit does not come into play until the supercharger unit starts to develop positive boost pressure; until that point it is not needed, as the engine is to all intents and purposes standard, and is thus able to run happily on the EEC-1V alone.

However, once boost is developed, the signals which are going back to the EEC-1V vary tremendously — especially once the engine reaches the point of needing additional fuel, and of needing a different ignition map to ensure that there is no detonation. By intercepting the signals and providing the changes to the fuel and ignition systems so that the Sprintex supercharger will continue to do what it is supposed to do, and multiply the power output without the EEC-1V interfering. In short, the Ford management computer is fooled into thinking that everything is running just normally, when in fact the power output of the engine is appreciably greater than the EEC-1V would like it to be.

Each ERP unit is provided completely unset, and Power are able to programme it for each specific application via a purpose-built test rig. Such is the nature of the beast that additional fuelling and specific ignition timing points can be programmed in at each increment of the engine's speed scale. This allows Power to run the engine at optimised boost levels close to the edge of the detonation pocket without actually endangering the engine — which means that power output levels and overall engine efficiency are optimised without any waste of fuel. ●

X CERTIFICATE

Neat detailing of supercharger installation includes all alloy castings being plastic coated, and specially-developed air trunking, as well as braided hoses and K&N filters.

◄ rolled on, and what was left of the curve is straightened out instantly, as the Sierra surges towards the next deviation. Body roll exists, but in moderation; it never becomes excessive — which is reassuring in a way, as it gives the driver an impression of the sort of cornering forces that he or she is expecting the car to deal with. If the car maintained a totally flat attitude through the bend, it would lead to an all-or-nothing situation where there would either be traction and grip, or a car which has been remodelled around the nearest tree. In short, this is the best-handling XR4x4 we have ever tried.

Steering response of the standard XR4x4 is pleasing, and the revisions made to the suspension system of this particular car have left that response sharper still; the driver is constantly aware of what the footprints of the front tyres are doing — sensations are also heightened by the excellent Personal Imola steering wheel which Power have fitted in place of the standard-issue Ford plastic item. Whilst offering full power assistance at parking speeds, the rack and pinion arrangement used on the XR4x4 progressively gets left to its natural resistance as road speeds increase, which means that there is none of the high-speed "woolliness" normally associated with power-assisted systems.

There is no tendency for the car to tramline, either, despite the wider offset and broader footprint provided by the new wheels and tyres fitted to the car; even rutted stretches of A-road can be handled confidently by the chassis of the XR4x4. Much the same applies to the braking, which can be dealt with by a simple shove on the middle pedal with no fear of weaving or darting — any over-zealous use of the pedal is dealt with by the excellent anti-lock system which is a £1,000 option on the Sierra range, but which comes standard on both of the four-wheel drive versions of the car.

Start to make a seriously quick run on a demanding road, and

you will immediately feel the benefit of four-wheel drive, as the front wheels pull to correspond to the pushes made by the back pair. A standard example of the car is quick through the bends, but this specimen is appreciably more rapid; the combination of instant power and high cornering abilities make this the quickest four door saloon that we have ever tried on cross country routes. The power split adopted by Ford gives the front of the car 34% of the available muscle, with the balance favouring the rear axle. This can allow the tail of the car to flick out slightly when provoked, but it is easily rectified by the simple process of easing off the pressure on the throttle pedal by just a slight amount. Whereas with a

"Stomp on the loud pedal and there is an instant, sharp response at road level."

standard XR4x4 a driver can push the right pedal to the floor on the exit of a curve with relative impunity, there is so much torque on call from the supercharged powerplant that it is rarely necessary to use it all from the apex of the bend.

Press on the pedal just as much as is necessary and the car will swoop elegantly along even the most demanding stretches of road, eating up the miles and slower traffic with an ease approaching disdain. The Valkyries of Nordic legend were the handmaidens of Odin who would seek out victims to be slain by his soldiers, and they did their hunting in chariots. The driver of the System X Sierra 4x4 can do his or her hunting in air conditioned comfort, cossetted in a supportive seat which

happened during fast runs along tightly-turning roads, where the driver is constantly going on and off the power. This was directly attributable to the second engine management system (see sidebar for more details) and has since been cured by further revisions to the mapping. In all other respects the car proved to have excellent manners and responses.

One usual adverse side-effect of tuning an engine by such a dramatic degree (brake horsepower has risen by 66%, and torque is up by more than 75%) is that the fuel economy suffers. The standard example of XR4x4 which we tried back in April 1989 returned an overall average during our test period of 21.6 miles to each gallon of fuel and we expected the supercharged car to fall in somewhere slightly below that level. We were therefore pleasantly surprised to discover that our average consumption during the two-week, 1,500 mile test period was a little under 24 miles per gallon — an improvement of just over ten per cent.

The quality of engineering applied by Power is exceptionally ➤

is padded in all the right places and surrounded by hand-crafted walnut trim fillets.

The XR is a full five seater, and comes complete with such nice little touches as additional map reading lights, a full centre console with cassette stowage, a high-grade stereo system with power amplifier, power windows all round, and a tilt and slide sunroof. Trimmed in a pleasing grey fabric, the cabin is a comfortable environment in which to spend time whilst travelling. The only thing which detracts from the pleasure of being there is the noise level coming through from the engine and from the transmission.

Quite how Ford have managed to get away with producing a pushrod, cast iron engine at the start of the 1990s eludes us; the Cologne engine has long since been eclipsed by far more sophisticated units from the likes of Honda and even — shock horror! — Volvo. The pushrod Ford power unit becomes very noisy at anything over 4500 r.p.m., and the clatter spills through the soundproofing of the Sierra's bulkhead into the cabin — especially when the supercharger encourages the driver to exploit the available power to the full. Add to this noises from the transfer box mounted adjacent to the MT-75 transmission, and the noise levels which result are at odds with the rest of the car's nature.

There is a distant rasping whine from the supercharger's belt drive at speed, but this is often drowned out by the din from the valvegear of the V6. The supercharger itself is virtually silent in operation, because of the way in which its drive gears run in oil, and because the rotors are very closely set, but never actually touch.

There was only one aspect of the car with which we were less than happy, and that was the way in which the engine would occasionally surge slightly on the over-run; this only ever

SPECIFICATIONS

ENGINE TYPE
Inline six cylinder Vee pushrod
BORE x STROKE
93mm x 72mm
SIZE
2933cc
BHP @ RPM
250 @ 4300
TORQUE LB/FT @ RPM
305 @ 4300
FUEL SYSTEM
Ford electronic fuel injection, ERP secondary management system, Sprintex supercharger
DRIVEN WHEELS
All four — 34% front, 66% rear
TRANSMISSION
Ford MT-75 manual five-speed
SUSPENSION, FRONT
Uprated springs, anti-roll bar, adjustable gas-filled dampers, independent by MacPherson struts
SUSPENSION, REAR
Uprated springs, adjustable gas-filled dampers, independent by trailing arms
BRAKING SYSTEM
Ventilated front discs, solid rear discs, uprated friction materials, racing grade fluid, stainless steel braided hoses, electronic anti-lock system
WEIGHT
2825 lbs
POWER/WEIGHT RATIO
195 b.h.p./ton
WHEELBASE
102.7"
LENGTH
174"
WIDTH
75.6"
HEIGHT
52"
TEST MILEAGE
1,532 miles
MANUFACTURER'S MPG
N/A
TEST MPG
23.7
PRICE AS TESTED
£22,270
INSURANCE GROUP
Special quotation
MANUFACTURER
Ford Motor Company
Modifications carried out by Power Engineering, Uxbridge

X CERTIFICATE

The interior is substantially enhanced by the walnut trim panels which cap the doors, rear ashtrays and window winder switch panel. Fascia insert over engine management system is not popular with all who have seen the car.

◄ high; in addition to the Scottish-designed Sprintex supercharger unit, which sits on a specially-made set of brackets to the nearside of the engine bay, the installation also includes specially-made air trunking and cast aluminium alloy connections to the original Ford plenum chamber. All of the castings and the plenum chamber are finished in black nylon coating which effectively seals the surface, and also looks very nice. The installation is finished off by the adoption of braided stainless steel hoses and K&N filters and the overall effect is of a factory product, rather than an aftermarket conversion.

Naturally, the amount of work which has gone into the conversion is reflected in the price; the engine conversion (which also includes the braking system uprate) comes with a price tag of £3,550 fitted. The uprated suspension system, which includes four new springs, four adjustable dampers, fitting and realignment, adds a further £550 to the cost of the car, and those wider wheels and tyres cost £985 — which brings the overall cost of the mechanical changes to the XR4x4 up to £5,085.

Our test example also benefited from the installation of a set of very high-grade walnut trim panels and fillets to the door cappings, window switch panel and rear ashtray cappings, as well as the management system cover on the fascia ahead of the front passenger. That last item was the subject of some discussion during our tenure of the car, some feeling that it was a little too much, and that whilst the door cappings and small fillets definitely added to the appearance of the car, the fascia panel was a little over the top, and would look better left in the original grey plastic. The cost of the wood trim kit is £395. The Personal Imola steering wheel — which is one of the most pleasant aftermarket wheels we have ever used — is a reasonable £95.

If you add all of those costs to the price of a new XR4x4, you end up with a bill of £22,270. Whilst that might sound a lot, it compares favourably with not only the price of similar conversions, but also very favourably indeed with the expected price of the forthcoming Sapphire RS Cosworth 4x4 — that car is expected to come out of your nearest RS dealership upon payment of between twenty five and twenty six thousand pounds. It is also appreciably less than the current list price of the two-door Audi Quattro, with which the System X begs comparison. That particular comparison is another story, one which we will be undertaking in the fairly near future.

Meanwhile, if you would like to learn more about the supercharged XR4x4 — which incidentally is Ford approved — contact Power Engineering at Department P.F., Unit 9, 5a Wyvern Way, Uxbridge, Middlesex UB8 2XN. They or their network of dealers will be happy to provide more information and possibly even a test drive. ●

IAN KUAH

RADICAL CHIC

Outrageous and stylish in one, the Rieger Escort F40 could be the shape of bodystyling to come. Will it be as big in Britain as it is in Germany?

By Ian Kuah.

It is a widely-held theory amongst car enthusiasts that the machinery produced by a country tends to exhibit the national characteristics of that land and people. From this theory it is easy to understand why the Latins, with their nationalistic brio and fiery temperament, make cars which are such fun to drive. The British reserve is exemplified by connolly hide and burr walnut, as found in Jaguars and Aston Martins. And the Germans? Precise people that they are, they seem to revel in producing beautifully designed and built cars which give the impression that they will last forever.

Yet theories are not always reliable, for despite their legendary serious approach to life it is the Germans who have to take the credit for producing what has to be the most dramatic piece of aftermarket bodystyling to hit the western world in years.

The instigator of this current German trend to producing

For quite a while, the wide-bodystyling school was the exclusive territory of the top end of the market, with expensive and exclusive cars getting the treatment; an additional £15,000 onto the already high price tag of, say, a Mercedes SL didn't appear excessive. However, as time has gone on then so the concept has been applied to less expensive cars, with such vehicles as the Gutmann Peugeot 205 GTi, Mohag Sierra and Rieger Tuning Volkswagen GTi Golf and Scirocco appearing.

Those latter two cars made their British débuts at GTi International, an event organised by VW Audi Magazine and the GTi car clubs. The interest shown in those cars was enough to prompt a London Volkswagen tuning business, Steiner Engineering, to take up the offer of the U.K. distributorship of Rieger Tuning's products. When Steiner's

radical wide-bodied versions must surely be one Vittorio Strosek, a graduate of the Wuppertal Industrial Design School who went on to work with the great Italian designer Luigi Colani. Striking out on his own in the early '80s, Strosek found work with Willy Koenig — who was just about to embark on his first radical Ferrari project, making changes to the driveline, suspension and bodystyling of a Maranello machine at the behest of a number of Ferrari-owning friends who had come off worst against a Koenig special at club race meetings. It was Vittorio's wide-bodystyling approach which appealed not just to Koenig but also to his clients, and by the time that the two gentlemen parted company in 1986 the look had been applied not just to Ferraris, but also to the products of BMW, Mercedes-Benz, and even Lamborghini. Strosek, meanwhile, turned his attentions to the Porsche range, and his wide-bodied 928, 944 and 911 models have become almost legendary in Germany.

Barry Mickoo offered me the opportunity to join him on a trip out to Rieger's headquarters about a hundred kilometres north of Münich, suggesting that I might like to see some exciting Ford products which they had available, I could not resist.

We arrived at Rieger's headquarters in Hebertsfelden in sub-zero temperatures, the ploughed fields which surround the building being covered with a heavy dusting of frost and the air laden with the threat of impending snow. Toni Rieger, a tall and friendly dyed-in-the-wool car nut, greeted us and immediately started to show us around his facilities. The whole business operates from the family farm, and huge outbuildings which once would have held agricultural implements have been turned over to car production facilities, with trimming, fitting, prototype development and warehousing all being carried out on-site. Only painting is undertaken away from the farm.

Toni rolled back the doors of a four-car garage to reveal an ➤

trafficators have been replaced by new amber lights set into the spoiler/bumper arrangement. There is also a less-radical alternative which retains the standard light clusters.

At the front, the wheel arches are extended outwards by some three inches — but by the time that one's eyes reach the back of the car it becomes obvious that the bodywork is six inches wider than standard on each rear quarter. A long horizontal stroke emanates from the front of the doors, culminating ahead of the rear wheel arches just above a substantial (but dummy) air intake. The side sill mouldings are deeply sculpted, following the revised lines of the bodyshell. A one-piece rear valance and bumper mouldings finishes off the styling, this having four black wire mesh filled apertures below bumper level, which helps to not only add feature to the panel, but also looks pretty good with the exhaust's twin tailpipes appearing through them. For a more balanced effect, it might be worth considering adding a second, dummy, set of tailpipes on the opposite side of the car to the real system's outlets.

The revised bodywork means that there are cavernous arches to fill, and so Rieger fit 15″ x 9″ front wheels and 15″ x 11″ rear wheels, both from the esteemed marque of B.B.S. These support 225/50 x 15″ and 285/40 x 15″ tyres respectively. Much care has gone into the selection of the B.B.S. wheels to ensure that the correct proportions of inset and offet are retained, without the need to employ spacers which would apply undue strain on the wheel bearings. These wheels were specially commissioned by Rieger, and B.B.S. have granted exclusive rights to Rieger.

Known as the Rieger Escort F40, the bodystyling system is only available in Britain from Steiner Engineering, who in addition to their Ford and VW activities are also an official TVR service centre. The team have consequently accumulated a great deal of tuning experience, and are thus able to offer a range of specialised services ranging from cylinder head gas-flowing right through to a 1.9 litre CVH conversion which promises more than 140 brake horsepower. As an aside, amongst their recent projects was the addition of a Motech fuel injection system to a TVR 420SEAC, a package which gave staggering results.

But back to the Rieger Escort. Naturally, given the high cost of laminating the body panels (glassfibre is very labour-intensive), and then the tremendous amount of work involved in fitting such a radical kit to an unsuspecting Escort, it is unsurprising to learn that the basic set of panels costs £1,550 or thereabouts (prices vary depending upon the strength of the Deutsch Mark) and that the bill for the three weeks it will take to fit to a guaranteed high quality and then paint the car will add another £1,800 to the price. To this should then be

RADICAL CHIC

◀ absolutely stunning Escort Cabriolet finished in metallic blue. The car started immediately that the key was turned, and he drove it out into the yard so that we could examine its sleek lines properly.

The front of the car has a dramatically deep spoiler which has been moulded integrally with the bumper, and which also contains a set of brake venting ducts. Naturally, the finished style of the spoiler will vary, depending upon whether the car in question is a Mk III or a Mk IV Escort; the earlier cars have the spoiler finishing at upper bumper height, where it is then topped off by a replacement grille containing four rectangular headlamps, but retaining the standard wrap-around trafficators. Later cars with their drop-down bonnet leading edge use a similar design of spoiler, but with an integral grille, which is finished off by a set of special new headlamp binnacles. These wrap around onto the wings, and the

added the considerable cost of the required wheels and tyres, and finally the dreaded V.A.T.

You will therefore be looking at a total cost of anything up to £6,000 before you start to upgrade the engine or the suspension. A lot of money — but it will virtually guarantee turned heads where ever you drive the car.

I was very impressed with Toni Rieger's operation in Germany. He has developed a totally professional organisation which is geared to servicing his agents quickly and efficiently — the number of Rieger panel kits which we have seen at European Volkswagen shows bear this out. Only time will tell if Britain's imagination will be fired by the wide-bodystyling phenomenon. To find out more about availability, contact Steiner Engineering on 01-741 5242, and tell them that *Performance Ford* sent you.

QUICKSILVER!

A Mercurial XR2

By Dennis Foy

We have tried and tested a number of entertaining Fiestas since *Performance Ford* first appeared on the news stands three years ago, one of which was the Turbo Technics XR2 which we featured in our September 1987 edition. Our overall impression of that car was that it was tremendous fun — but it needed to be in the right hands if the best was to be gained from the car.

The standard XR2 had very good roadholding and handling, and this could be exploited further when the car had been treated by Turbo Technics to a thirty five per cent boost in power. However, as tested the car had little roadholding left in reserve — all that it had was being used when the car was being pressed into hard service. We felt that the power-to-weight ratio, at almost 155 b.h.p./ton, was about as much as the car could cope with — and anyway, most owners would be content with a Fiesta able to run at 122 m.p.h., and capable of the yardstick zero-to-sixty time of 7.8 seconds.

There are always exceptions to the rule, and Paul Smith is one such exception.

Paul, a twenty two year old cycle retailer, bought his car a couple of years ago as one of the showroom-standard Turbo XR2 Fiestas which Turbo Technics had prepared for the Ford main dealer network. As with most owners he was totally

content with the car in standard form — but as tends to happen, he became accustomed to the performance of the Mercury Grey machine and began to wish for just a little more ''oomph'' for overtaking, just a couple more miles per hour on the top speed, just a little bit sharper handling ... He wanted more.

A natural starting point in the quest was Turbo Technics, who steered him towards their nearest dealership, Geoff Bloor Garages in Nottingham — and so far as Paul is concerned this was the best move he ever made with regard to his car as that business have proven to him that they not only have a thorough grasp of the complex business of tuning turbocharged cars, but that they also speak in an understandable language; not for them the habit of using ''tech-speak'' as a means of confusing the customer into parting with more money than intended.

The Fiesta XR2 was carburated, and this same means of measuring fuel is used when the car is turbocharged; the carburettor is the same Weber 32/34 DFT/4B twin-choke that has also been used on the carburated XR3 Escort — and it was the XR3 turbo system which Turbo Technics adapted for use on the Fiesta. The turbocharger itself is a Garrett AiResearch T.25 unit, which fits onto the forward edge of the engine between the block and the radiator. As with all Turbo Technics conversions a specially-developed exhaust manifold is used, cast from high-nickel-content iron and designed to optimise pulse separation, and the system also has an intercooler to keep the charge down to an acceptable temperature.

In its ''standard'' form the car developed a hundred and thirty

> ''165 brake horsepower takes a lot of harnessing when it is pushing its way out through an XR2 chassis.''

brake horsepower, and at the time of the launch Turbo Technics felt that this could be stretched further, to as much as a hundred and forty five horses, by increasing the boost pressure from the normal 0.45 bar (just six pounds per square inch) to perhaps 0.55 bar.

But Paul Smith wanted a little more.

To extract more power from a turbocharged engine the boost must be increased, but there is also the scope to release more power by improving the breathing. Hence Geoff Bloor's first move, which was to remove the cylinder head, strip it down, and then carefully rebuild it after opening out the ports to optimise gasflow. The valve sizes remain the same as previously, in the interests of longevity; installing bigger valves reduces the bridge between them to a dangerously small distance, and with the increased temperatures induced by turbocharging there is a very real danger of cracks developing.

Another effect of increased chamber pressures is the need to lower the compression ratio to cope, and so this too was attended to by machining away surplus material; from the normally-aspirated engine's compression ratio of 9.5:1, the engine has been modified to give a maximum of 8.2:1. This ensures that the revised package will be able to deal comfortably with the uprated boost of 0.675 bar, of 9½ lbs in English. The intercooler has been increased in size to help control the temperatures within the intake tracts.

The camshaft within the engine has been left as it was, for two very good reasons. One is that it was in very good order, with ▶

QUICKSILVER!

◄ no wear or tear being detected after a close inspection. The second is that the timing of the standard camshaft is ideally suited to turbocharging applications, having the right blend of duration and overlap to suit the forced induction system.

The carburettor jetting has been revised to increase the amount of fuel which is making its way through to the engine, and to ensure that the resultant mixture is ignited precisely when it ought to be the distributor has been overhauled, and given a new advance mechanism. A rolling road dyno tune has proven that the engine is developing no less than 165 brake horsepower at the flywheel — and that amount of power takes a lot of harnessing when it is pushing its way out, through an XR2 chassis.

Turbo Technics has already made a number of changes to the basic car's suspension system, primarily in the area of the bushes — all being replaced by stiffer items — and by increasing the size of the Panhard rod at the rear of the car. The rear also benefitted from the addition of a tubular tie-rod, whilst the front gained uprated track control arms. To improve matters further, Geoff Bloor Garages replaced the original set of dampers with four Koni items which are adjustable, and the springs were replaced with a set of similar poundage, but which site the car an inch closer to the ground.

The brakes of the standard XR2 could not honestly be described as confidence-inspiring, and so this area too was overhauled; a set of Tar-Ox discs have been fitted, along with matching pads, braided steel hosing, and uprated rear shoes. The final amendment to the running gear was to fit a set of RS seven-spoke aluminium alloy wheels with 195/55-13 Pirelli P600 tyres.

Special badging, blue trim in place of the usual red, colour-coded panelwork, RS alloys with P600 rubber and a stainless exhaust all conspire to make the car stand out from the crowd.

To bring the exterior of the car up to the standard of the mechanical areas, the body trim pieces, the bumper mouldings, mirrors, additional RGA rear spoiler and everything else that is normally black (including the post at the rear of the door on each side) has been colour-keyed in the same Mercury Grey as the rest of the bodywork. The red keylines which normally feature in the car's bumpers have been replaced by electric blue ones, and special decals have been procured in the same shade of blue. The overall effect is very pleasing.

Also pleasing is the way in which the little machine now goes.

> "The car's behaviour is as predictable as the next Jason Donovan record."

As with most of the bigger horsepower conversions, the car features a "granny switch" which allows Paul the choice of either "pottering" along with about 130 b.h.p., or doing some serious running with all 165 brake horsepower on call. For normal, everyday use Paul keeps the power maximum on its lower setting — this is perfectly adequate for running in traffic on his way to and from work, and other similar activities.

However, when the opportunity arises he simply flicks the switch and brings in the next thirty five horses — which incidentally gives the XR2 a better power-to-weight ratio than a Sierra Cosworth — then goes in search of supercars to humiliate. Impressive though the straight-line acceleration is — the sprint to sixty takes probably seven seconds — the car is really happiest when out on the run, on winding roads or on the highways.

Because of the basic design of the front suspension, with its MacPherson struts located at the bottom by track control arms and the pair of tie-bars, a degree of torque-steer is inevitable and no matter how well-sorted the suspension system this will never be totally eradicated; that old adage about making a silk purse out of a sow's ear keeps coming to mind. With the "granny switch" on its lower setting the syndrome is controllable, but when the switch is flicked to high a hard launch results immediately in a wild ride — the grippy Pirellis rapidly lose the battle for traction, and the car weaves erratically from side to side as serious amounts of power start to course through the driveshafts and out onto the road.

Paul has come up with a rather neat way of compensating for this, though; he launches the car with 130 b.h.p. on tap, and then once moving at a reasonable pace throws the switch to bring in the balance of the available power. The effect is like that displayed at least once in every episode of Knight Rider, the television programme which was rather popular a couple

of years ago — there is a sudden (but totally controllable) surge of extra performance lunging the machine forward as the switch to "superboost" is thrown.

On the open road, there are very few cars which would be able to keep up with this pocket rocket if Paul Smith was in the mood for a burst of serious running. The handling is about as good as it is possible to achieve with a Fiesta; there are few dampers which suit the XR2 chassis quite as well as Koni's products, and the springing has a pleasing amount of progression with the degree of roll being in total sympathy (or synergy, to use this year's trendy word) with the rest of the package. The stiffer bushes effectively eradicate any slack within the system, and this contributes greatly to steering precision and feedback which the driver is able to enjoy.

On tight and twisting roads the car displays a pleasingly neutral stance provided the engine is kept on its wide powerband; only if the revs are allowed to drop below 2000 r.p.m. will the nose of the car become a little wayward. If the power is being progressively wound on as the car exits a bend it will hold its intended line with as little bias as that exhibited by a member of the United Nations Peacekeeping Force in a buffer zone.

On sweeping curves the car's behaviour is equally sure-footed, and as predictable as the next Jason Donovan record. Putting on a little too much power a shade too early — that is before the apex is reached — there will result a gentle understeer which increases in direct proportion to the road speed of the car. This is rarely uncontrollable, the simple process of winding on a little more steering being all that is required to trim the car's line.

Overtaking manoeuvres in this car are simple and effective;

MODIFICATIONS

- Two-stage boost turbocharger system developed on Turbo Technics blow-through installation. Low setting gives 130 b.h.p., high setting 165 b.h.p.

- Lowered springs, Koni dampers, revised Panhard rod, tubular rear tie-bar, uprated bushes throughout.

- Tar-Ox discs, road/competition grade disc pads, uprated rear linings, stainless steel brake hoses.

- Performance clutch assembly.

- Colour-keyed exterior, RS alloy wheels, Pirelli P600 195/55-13 tyres.

find the slot in the traffic, engage the appropriate gear, and then simply zip past the slower vehicles. It really is that easy.

If the car has an Achilles' heel it is the difficulty it exhibits when dealing with sudden changes in road surface; hitting a typical badly-repaired patch of tarmac on an otherwise smooth stretch and the car will wiggle and jiggle and generally feel quite nervous. This is a trait which we have experienced in other examples of the XR2, especially specimens which have been fitted with wider and lower-profile tyres, and seems in the main to be attributable to the lamentably short wheelbase of the model. Paul's car is only worse than other examples because it is usually travelling at a higher speed than a standard XR2 would be in a similar situation.

One of the usual stumbling blocks for smaller cars is the sudden lane change, the sort of situation which arises when a vehicle suddenly pulls out immediately ahead and evasive action must be taken. This particular car acquitted itself surprisingly well when we simulated such a manoeuvre, making the deviation without the expected nervousness or sudden unloading of the chassis.

And the brakes of this particular machine are nothing short of excellent. In place of the usual spongy pedal is a firm one with a sharp and direct action, and the whole system is endowed with a directness so sadly lacking in examples of the standard car of similar age; when the middle pedal is prodded the car will scrub off speed immediately, and the harder it is pressed the quicker the retardation process. As for fade, the system just does not know the meaning of the word.

The other pedals too are pleasantly progressive. The standard clutch of the XR2 is quite enough to deal with perhaps 125 brake horsepower, but woefully inadequate when it comes to dealing with a further forty. Therefore Geoff Bloor installed a competition-specification clutch assembly at the time of the car's reworking. This is not a great deal heavier than the standard item in operation, but is more than able to cope with ➤

The larger intercooler sits neatly to the side of the original Fiesta radiator.

◄ the flywheel output of the uprated engine. The throttle cable of the car is standard, and so that pedal is also light and progressive in its action.

In fact, being in the driver's seat of this diminuitive demon is a rather pleasant place to spend time. The standard seats are comfortable, and the tactile pleasures are enhanced by the three-spoke RS steering wheel which now sits at the head of the column. The car has all of the go, handling and stopping power that anybody could ever want, and is reasonably well equipped. And if the rorty note from the big stainless steel tailpipe starts to become a little boring, there is always the sound system to listen to, for in the place normally occupied by the ESRT-32-PS Ford radio-cassette unit there now lives a Pioneer unit which has radio, cassette and compact disc. The latter item is a front-end only, with the actual player mechanism being situated in the boot of the car; the dash-mounted unit selects which track from whichever of the half dozen discs is required. Backing up the fascia unit is a high-power amplifier and a custom-installed set of radically uprated speakers.

Paul professes to be happy with his car, and is fulsome in his praise for Geoff Bloor Garages. Paul has been taken seriously on his every visit and during his every telephone conversation, and has basically been made to feel that he is important, and a valued client. If he has asked for anything that is practicable it has been sorted, and if it has been impossible he has been told precisely why it is impossible. And you cannot ask for more than that ... ●

Geoff Bloor Garages are at Pavilion Road, West Bridgeford, Nottingham NG2 5FG. Telephone: 0602 821803. Please mention Performance Ford when making enquiries.

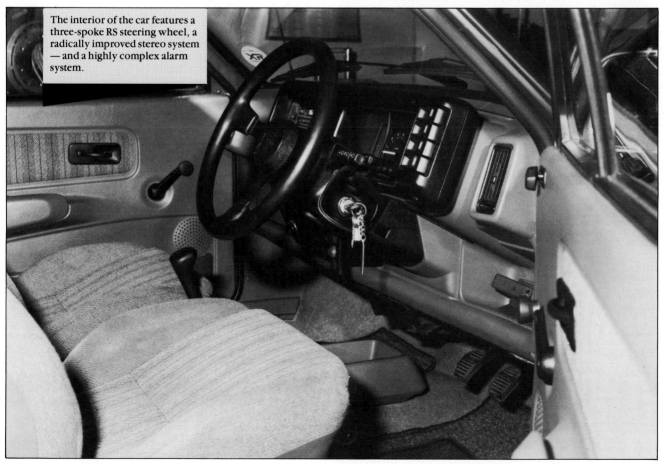

The interior of the car features a three-spoke RS steering wheel, a radically improved stereo system — and a highly complex alarm system.

A TWO HORSE RACE

Is there a distinct advantage between the XR3i and its nearest in-house rival the Orion 1.6i? We attempt to find an answer.

Although they both offer similar levels of performance, share a similar mechanical specification, offer similar levels of accommodation and cost within £500 of each other, the XR3i Escort and the 1.6i Ghia Orion are two very different cars, with very different characters. And even after covering comfortably in excess of a thousand miles in each we are still unable to say that one is definitely better than the other.

Both cars make use of the latest version of Ford's proven 1596cc CVH engine, a lean-burn four cylinder powerplant which is controlled by the EEC-1V electronic management system, and both share the same transaxle system which houses five well-spread gear ratios, a set of clusters which make the most of the available hundred and eight brake horsepower. However, at the end of that powertrain lives the component which contributes most to the difference in the two cars' behaviour and character — the final drive assembly.

Conceived as a contender in the Hot Hatchback stakes back at the beginning of the last decade, the XR3i has been given a "short" final drive ratio of 4.27:1, whilst the Orion 1.6i was evolved as more of a cross-country machine and has been given the benefit of the taller 3.82:1 final drive gears. In practical terms, this means that the Escort has the sharper edge to its acceleration at the expense of high-speed cruising comfort, whereas the Orion is able to cruise along at high speed using less engine revolutions than would the XR3i at a similar speed. The downside is that the in-gear acceleration of the Orion is slightly dulled by comparison with its hatchback stablemate.

Because both cars come with the same wheel and tyre sizes as part of their standard equipment, the variation in final drive gearing means that the two cars' in-gear maximum speeds vary quite substantially — the XR3i runs out of steam in first at 32 miles per hour, whereas the Orion can manage 35 m.p.h. before requiring second gear to continue its progress. In second the XR can make 52 m.p.h., whilst the Orion is able to reach 57 miles per hour, and in third the respective figures are 78 m.p.h. and 83 miles per hour. By fourth the gap has opened up by no less than ten miles per hour, the Escort managing 105 to the Orion's 115. Only in fifth, presumably because of the combination of aerodynamics and the heavily-overdriven gear (0.756:1) is the balance redressed, both cars being rated by Ford at 117 miles per hour maxima. We say rated by Ford at that speed because our figures proved different — but more of that later.

The two cars share the same arrangement of a MacPherson strut front suspension (with the bottom links being the familiar combination of track control arms and the anti-roll bar) and a trailing arm rear suspension which uses inboard coil springs and separate vertically-mounted dampers. Both cars — which are built alongside each other on the production lines at Halewood and Saarlouis — also share the same braking arrangement, ventilated 240mm x 24mm front discs with single-piston sliding calipers being augmented by 203mm rear drums, with full servo assistance and dual-circuit hydraulics. The Escort and Orion also have the desirable option of a Lucas Girling-Ford anti-lock braking system, a mechanical system which costs a reasonable £435.

Externally, it does not take an ''A'' level in art and design to detect the differences between the two cars; the XR3i is a compact three-door, which comes complete with substantial rear spoiler and sporty aluminium alloy wheels modelled after the set which are to be found on the RS Cosworth

stalks which control the lighs and the washer/wiper set (including the tailgate wiper on the XR3i) and in the centre of the fascia are the heater controls below which lives the stereo system. On our two test cars this was the 2007 auto-reverse radio-cassette unit, with the matching five-band graphic equaliser. Below the stereo comes the ashtray and lighter, and then comes the four-slot cassette rack. The centre console of the range has recently been extended rearwards, and now concludes level with the rearmost edge of the seat mountings;

''The XR3i excels on sharp bends, whereas the Orion is happiest on sweeping curves.''

Sapphire saloon, whilst the Orion is a nicely-proportioned conventional four door saloon with boot, and no extraneous bits which hint at power. A really subtle car if ever there was, the Orion continues the illusion right through to its tidily styled pepperpot alloy wheels.

The insides of the cars, whilst again sharing a number of common features, are quite distinct from each other; the sporty nature of the XR3i is highlighted by its pseudo-Recaro bucket seats, whilst the Orion has the wide and soft seating which is also to be found within the Escort Ghia. Regardless of the model, the driver is presented with the same basic fascia which has a quadrant tachometer to the left of its instrument binnacle, a central speedometer, and then a pair of small round gauges which monitor the fuel tank's remaining amount of low octane unleaded petrol and the temperature of the coolant.

On the left hand face of the instrument pod are the switches for the heated front and rear screens and for the rear high-intensity lights, whilst on the right hand side is to be found the door mirror adjuster switch and the fuel computer. This latter item is a multi-functional piece of equipment which gives range, fuel used, instant and average fuel economy data in either metric or imperial measures, and unlike early examples of the device, which were infamous for their bleeping that there was a mere fifty miles left when there was patently sufficient fuel to cover more than twice that amount, the Ford electronics people seem to have sorted the thing out nicely and in both cars it proved surprisingly accurate.

To other side of the plasticky steering wheel are the stubby

this has tidied up what was hitherto a rather sparse area around the handbrake mechanism.

By the time that this specification has been topped up with such details as the tilt-and-slide sunroof, the power windows, the abundant storage space and the pleasant quality of trim, the cars look like quite good value; after all the Orion ALB is listed at £12,125 and the Escort ALB is £11,689 — but wait. These cars are straight off the press fleet, and are thus fully loaded. The metallic paint finishes, the alloy rims, the enhanced stereo systems, the XR3i's fuel computer, these all add up to a different picture. With the aid of the Ford Cars ➤

A TWO HORSE RACE

catalogue and a calculator, we are able to deduce that the actual prices of the cars as tested are, in fact, £12,639 for the XR3i and £12,410 for the Orion. And that is before the delivery charges, number plates and so forth have been paid for — those charges will put another £350 or so onto the costs by the time that a one-year road fund licence has been stuck in the corner of the screen.

So round one, the price factor, falls just slightly in favour of the Orion 1.6i Ghia.

Out on the road, although they are mechanically similar the two cars behave quite differently. The XR3i acts like a little street racer, lighting up its front set of Dunlop D8 tyres easily and without too much provocation in the dry. In the wet the driver has only to think about moving off from a standstill to set the wheels spinning and scrambling for traction. The Orion proved a little better, its taller gearing ensuring that the car did not let loose quite so readily. The better traction of the Pirelli P600 tyres in wet weather also seemed to help matters.

In terms of standing start acceleration, the advantage of the XR3i's low final drive is countered to a degree by the difficulty in gaining traction; our back-to-back runs showed that although the XR3i was a second quicker to forty and to fifty than the Orion, the car had great difficulty gaining traction and so was often outrun by the Orion. By the time that the two cars were running at sixty miles per hour, they were virtually neck and neck, the Escort rushing forward like a

terrier with the Orion lunging forwards in the more graceful manner of a greyhound. In the dry it is the XR3i which has the slight advantage, but when the roads are wet the Orion is actually the quicker car.

In the mid-range, it is all swings and roundabouts; the advantage goes to the car which is happily sitting with the tachometer needle at around 4500 r.p.m., by which point it is close to its torque peak — and it is torque, not outright horsepower, that makes for accelerative qualities. As an illustration of this, Ford claim — and we concur — figures of 7.7 seconds for the 30-50 burst in the XR3i, and a slower 9.3 seconds for the same run in the Orion. Yet when the increment is moved up one, to 50-70 miles per hour, the balance shifts in favour of the Orion which achieves the burst in eight seconds exactly, whereas the XR3i takes all but a second longer.

It is when the speedometer is pointing towards its first three-figure marking that the most vital differences between the two cars manifest themselves, for whilst both are rated by Ford as being capable of running to a maximum of 117 miles per hour the XR3i takes an awfully long time to touch that figure

The more luxurious interior of the Orion is shared with the Escort Ghia, and is generally better-equipped than that of the XR3i — what the Orion buyer gets is often an extra in the Escort. ▼▼

The interior of the XR3i has Recaro-style seats in the front, with a distinctive trim fabric. Ahead of the driver is the same basic fascia arrangement found in all Escorts and Orions.▼

SPECIFICATIONS
FORD ESCORT XR3i, FORD ORION 1.6i GHIA
(Where applicable, data peculiar to Orion is given in brackets. Otherwise, information applies to both cars.)

ENGINE TYPE
Transverse four cylinder SOHC
BORE x STROKE
80mm x 79mm
SIZE
1596cc
BHP @ RPM
108 @ 6000
TORQUE LB/FT @ RPM
105 @ 4800
FUEL SYSTEM
Ford EEC-IV electronic management system
DRIVEN WHEELS
Front
TRANSMISSION
5-speed manual transaxle
SUSPENSION, FRONT
MacPherson struts, anti-roll bar
SUSPENSION, REAR
Independent transverse arms, tie bars, coil springs, separate dampers
BRAKING SYSTEM
Front discs, rear drums, dual circuits, servo assistance, optional Stop Control System mechanical anti-locking
WEIGHT
2090 lbs (2110 lbs)
POWER/WEIGHT RATIO
114 b.h.p./ton (113 b.h.p./ton)
WHEELBASE
94.5″
LENGTH
159.4″ (165.9″)
WIDTH
72.2″
HEIGHT
54.1″ (54.8″)
TEST MILEAGE
1,121 miles (1,342 miles)
MANUFACTURER'S MPG
26.6 (28.0)
TEST MPG
25.8 (26.2)
PRICE AS TESTED
£12,639 (£12,410)
INSURANCE GROUP
5
MANUFACTURER
Ford Motor Company, Dagenham, Essex

whereas the Orion is still pulling past that point — and in fact we were able to claim an honest 122 m.p.h. on several occasions during our performance testing session. In short, by a hundred miles an hour the Escort felt as though it was running out of steam whilst the Orion still had plenty left to deliver. It couldn't possibly be that Ford's Marketing Department have interceded to ensure that the XR3i is not seen in too adverse a light when the two cars are compared by prospective customers, could it?

Which gives us something of a tie for round two, the cars' performance figures.

When the roads change from being straight — which is every few yards on Britain's back roads — there can be two types of deviation, either sharp bends or gentle curves. The XR3i excels on the former, whilst the Orion is happier on the latter. Both cars feature sports suspension packages, but the system on the 1.6i Ghia feels softer than that of the XR3i — a state of affairs which is exaggerated by the tall overall gearing of the transmission. The upshot of this is that it is easy to be caught off the power band when running on tightly twisting roads which leaves the car floundering a little — and the chassis of the Orion is definitely one which needs a quantity of useable power running through it to perform at its best.

Because the Escort's springing feels more firm, and because its gearing makes it a lot easier for the driver to keep the revs above three thousand, it thus keeps everything nice and taut. On sweeping curves, the Orion is far more balanced, and will swoop happily along in a deceptively quick manner without the engine sounding particularly strained. The XR3i in a

> "The XR3i acts like a little street racer, lighting up its tyres easily. The 1.6i Ghia did not let loose quite so readily."

similar situation will behave extremely well, but the driver is constantly aware of the road speed because the engine noise is so much higher — yet another legacy of the accent on sprinting rather than on cruising which has been engineered into the car.

On both cars the steering is good, but we would like to try two examples on the same make and model of tyre before saying for certain whether the parking-speed heaviness of the Orion was attributable to the car or to the tyres, for there was no such problem with the Escort. In either car, the turn-in of the steering gear was reasonably sharp, but on the XR3i tended to feel a little "over-centred" at times, and would weave and bounce if a pothole was encountered in mid-bend. Could this again be attributable to the tyres? In terms of tyre behaviour the Pirellis of the Orion seemed to have the advantage in both the wet and the dry over the Escort's Dunlops — the latter car tended to skitter when attempting wet-weather rapid progress on a series of bends.

In view of the controversy over the tyres — we would like to try the Orion on D8s and the XR3i on P600s before making a positive decision — the third round must again be considered as a draw.

The braking performance of both cars was good, very good — what the tyres lost in braking traction was more than made up for by the Stop Control System. Under all but the most severe braking manoeuvres the standard disc and drum arrangement was left to its own devices, able to decimate the speed of the car quickly and efficiently; only when a panic stop was being simulated were we able to feel the front wheels start to lock up, and the SCS mechanism come into play to prevent a skid.

The aluminium alloy wheels of the Escort, a £250 extra, have to be the most difficult things to clean ... Even a power-wash machine needs a considerable degree of help if all brake dust is to be efficiently removed.

Pedal feel was always good, with lots of feedback without any excessive weighting.

Another draw.

So far we have majored on the dynamics of the car. But what about the practicalities of the two body styles? The neat two door hatchback of the Escort has its distinct advantages, especially when you have odd-shaped and bulky loads to move about — the tailgate can be left open for short journeys. However, the first time that you try to load a couple of passengers into the rear of the car when the weather is wet you will appreciate the disadvantages of a two door car; a front seat partner has to wait until the rear bench is occupied and the front seatback has been dropped into its normal position before he or she can become installed. The accommodation in the rear of the XR3i is slightly more cramped than that of other Escorts, in view of the thicker-backed front seats — which means that there is less space for a pair of adults. Older passengers who are not too adept at impersonating Harry Houdini also tend to find that emerging from the rear of an XR3i is an uncomfortable experience because of the limited access afforded by the two door format.

The Orion, on the other hand, has the advantage of a door for each passenger, which means that the pair destined to travel in the back can be left to their own devices in wet weather. Although a shade on the narrow side, the rear doors are adequate for most needs — although a slightly wider angle of opening would be appreciated. Orion rear seat passengers also have the advantage of their own opening windows, too — a pleasing contrast to the XR3i's fixed rear quarter glass. Although it lacks the height advantage of a tailgated car, the Orion's bootlid opens quite wide, and the backs of the rear ➤

PERFORMANCE

	Escort XR3i	Orion 1.6i Ghia
0-30	3.4 seconds	3.2 seconds
0-40	5.0 seconds	5.9 seconds
0-50	6.7 seconds	7.7 seconds
0-60	9.6 seconds	9.5 seconds
0-70	12.3 seconds	11.6 seconds
30-50	7.7 seconds	9.3 seconds
50-70	8.9 seconds	8.0 seconds
Maximum Speed	117 m.p.h.	122 m.p.h.

A TWO HORSE RACE

Underbonnet view of either car is similar, as both use the same package of 108 b.h.p. engine with EEC-IV management system, coupled to a five-speed transmission.▲

◀ seats allow long loads to be carried — provided the load is not higher than about eighteen inches, the Orion can handle the task every bit as easily as the Escort. Luggage space for normal loads such as suitcases and bags is weighted in favour of the Orion, which has a slightly longer boot floor.

It is the factor of the different body formats which tends to influence the buyers of these cars, and as a general rule the XR3i appeals to the single person, or the couple who rarely need to carry about elderly passengers. Conversely, the Orion's buyer tends to be the family who need a four door car for its practicality, yet who do not wish to sacrifice performance; they are attracted to the 1.6i Ghia because it gives the best of both worlds.

So that matter too has to be considered as a tie, the two bodyshells being very definitely suited to their specific markets.

And really, the whole exercise can be summed up in the phrase ''horses for courses''. Neither car has a definite performance advantage over the other, both cost much the same (although the balance can shift dependent upon the specification of the car), and both offer similar running costs; even the overall test mileage was very close, the Orion turning in just over twenty six miles to the gallon and the Escort just under that figure during our test period.

There is one last aspect of the two cars which is worthy of consideration, though, should you be planning to buy one or the other; to the boys in blue the XR3i screams boy racer, whilst the Orion will slip quietly by, attracting no undue or unwarranted attention ... ●

Superchips

The SUPERCHIP range for the Ford EECIV computer controlled cars consists of a unique solution to the problem of reprogramming these management systems. No one else can offer any sort of reprogrammed module for these cars testifying to the superiority of the SUPERCHIP product.

The module simply plugs onto the back of the computer and can be fitted and removed in seconds. When it is in place it switches off the internal program and switches on the SUPERCHIP revised version which alters the fuelling and the timing for the very maximum performance and to enhance smoothness when driving. The overrun cutoff is removed for maximum driving pleasure and the rev limit is raised to help extract every ounce of power available.

SUPERCHIPS ARE AVAILABLE FOR THE FOLLOWING MODELS:
Fiesta Turbo
All 1.6 Escort/Orion injected engines with Electronic injection with or without catalytic converters
2 Litre single cam engine gains 13 BHP
2 Litre twin cam engines
2.9 V6 engine gains 15 lb ft midrange torque

The SUPERCHIP is a highly developed modification to your car's engine management system giving increased power and performance. Some cars respond well to electronic tuning and give significant power gains. Some drive considerably better with all of the gains in mid range torque and no absolute power increase. Whenever we reprogram a computer we always remove the overrun cutoff and tune it for extra driveability to remove flat spots, hesitations and jerkiness at low speed and we always increase the rev limit wherever possible for maximum driving pleasure all at no extra cost.

**WE HAVE DEALERS NATIONWIDE
SO CALL FOR DETAILS
OF THE ONE NEAREST TO YOU**

SUPERCHIPS LTD, Buckingham Industrial Park, Buckingham, MK18 1XJ Tel: (0280) 816781, Fax: (0280) 816764.

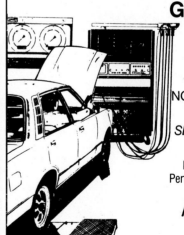

FIRST CLASS HONOURS
//////

Oxford. City of dreaming spires, of Inspector Morse, of punting on the Isis — and of Oselli Engineering. Appropriately titled The Graduate, Oselli's version of the 2.0 XR4x4 takes the car to the degree of performance which will more than satisfy the most demanding of buyers.

DENNIS FOY

When we tested the two litre version of Ford's XR4x4 back in November of last year, it is fair to say that our overall impression was that we were underwhelmed by its performance; although a competent enough performer around town, the car's cross country abilities were disappointing. And we were not, it would appear, the only ones to feel that way about the car, for David Oldham and the team at Oselli Engineering also felt that the car could do better.

One of our oldest established tuning companies, Oselli work closely with Turbo Technics, and were aware that T.T. were busy engineering a system for the 2.0 DOHC engine almost as soon as the powerplant became available. This, felt Oselli, could form a most useful plank towards developing an effective uprate for the car. In its standard form the Turbo Technics-developed version of the engine produces 165 brake horsepower, which is enough to give a substantial improvement in both acceleration and driveability in two-wheel drive Sierras and Granadas. However, Oselli felt that the effectiveness would be reduced in a four-by-four application, in view of the way in which Ford's all wheel drive system saps some thirty four per cent of the available power.

So they decided to take the Turbo Technics engine, and see just how much further they could go in search of meaningful amounts of power.

Whilst the basic installation is very much a bolt-on process, to extract more power still from the engine would be a far more complex affair; the standard compression ratio of 10.3 is acceptable with low levels of turbocharger boost (the 165 b.h.p. engine has a peak boost level of 0.45 bar), but if any more induction pressure is to be generated, then detonation would be a very real problem. So the engine has to come out of the car so that a set of remachined pistons can be installed, and some work done on the cylinder head to ensure a revised compression ratio of 8.7:1. New exhaust valves are installed, and the engine is then reassembled prior to receiving its new induction system.

The turbocharger is a Garrett T.25, a watercooled device which offers good low speed development of positive boost, and this is mounted on a Turbo Technics high-nickel alloy cast manifold which ensures optimised pulse separation, and thus smooth and even power deliveries. A two-stage electronically controlled wastegate is integral with the turbocharger, with a preset maximum boost level

of 0.75 bar on the higher stage.

Pumping additional air into an engine brings with it a need to add extra fuel, and in the case of the Oselli engine this task is handled by an extra set of four injectors mounted to the intake manifold, and injecting a mist of fuel direct into each port. A cast throttle body adaptor and idle speed air valve are fitted, and the entire assembly is then reinstalled back in the waiting engine bay. Once in the exhaust manifold is hooked up to a new big-bore stainless steel silencing system, and the revised electronic control unit is hooked up; the map of that item has been substantially rewritten to ensure that fuelling and ignition timing is kept just on the right side of detonation, and to ensure that the engine will still meet the relevant emission control regulations. The fifth injector of the standard Turbo Technics conversion is retained at the head of the plenum chamber.

To lubricate and cool the turbocharger, the main engine oil feed system is tapped into using braided hosing, and the water system is likewise plumbed into. The last change to the engine concerns its spark plugs, with the standard items being supplanted by wide heat range items.

The nett result of these efforts is a power output of 205 brake horsepower, and 215 lb/ft of torque — not bad, considering that the standard engine's relevant figures were 125 b.h.p. and 128 lb/ft of torque. Which means that Oselli have been able to entice an extra sixty five per cent horsepower, and more torque still.

➤

FIRST CLASS HONOURS

/ / / / / / / /

◄ Equally impressive is the fact that they have been able to extract that power without the usual penalty in terms of fuel consumption; our test mileage on the standard 2.0 XR4x4 was 28.3, and our mileage for the Oselli Graduate was 26.9 miles per gallon.

As good as the standard XR4x4 chassis is, it was designed to cope with no more than a hundred and fifty horsepower, and the speeds which such an engine can propel the car to. When the stakes have been raised by increasing the power to almost half as much again as the design maximum, then clearly there is a need to do some work on the chassis — and Oselli have been in the game for far too long not to realise that. The front springs have been stiffened, Koni top-adjustable dampers have been fitted in lieu of the standard equipment on each corner of the car,

and a set of heavy duty bushes have been fitted to the front track control arms. At the rear of the car the location bushings have been replaced by heavy duty items.

The nett result is a chassis which positively tingles with feedback to the driver; the perfect foil to an engine which responds positively and immediately to any prod of the "go" pedal.

Despite the fact that our test period coincided with absolutely foul weather, we were able to fully exploit the potential available. Our favourite cross-Pennine run was unavailable to us — it had been closed by snowdrifts a week before the car arrived, and was still closed a fortnight after the car was safely returned to Oxford — but even so, we were able to find other, almost equally demanding, roads.

Although clear of snow, these lowland roads in Cheshire were rain-sodden for much of the time, but this did not present any kind of traction problem to us, because of the wheel and tyre combination which had been selected for The Graduate; those attention-grabbing wheels have been wrapped in the excellent Yokohama AVS tyres. The idea of the package was to ensure that every last ounce of available horsepower made it through whatever was lying on the road surface and onto the tarmac below, and this was totally successful because at no point during our test period did the asymmetrical tread of the Japanese-made tyres break from their tenacious grip of terra firma. No matter how we tried — and believe us, we did try — we were unable to induce anything other than absolute fidelity of line from the four corners of the car; no matter where we pointed the car, it went.

Power delivery from the two litre turbo is on a par with that of a Cosworth, but with less lag; whereas we have observed that precious little happens below three thousand revs in the standard Ford product, with the Oselli Graduate positive boost starts to come in at about 2,000 r.p.m. The lowered compression ratio of the engine means that very low speed torque development is impaired when compared with that of a standard example of the 2.0i twin-cam Ford engine. However, because of the haste with which the T.25 turbocharger spins up to positive boost, the driver soon learns to "drive around" that potential problem area.

THE POWER BROKERS

IN THE FIRST OF A NEW SERIES WE GO BEHIND THE FRONT DOOR OF OSELLI ENGINEERING, AND SEE WHAT THEY HAVE TO OFFER.

F ounded almost thirty years ago by David Oldham, Oselli have been synonymous with their home city of Oxford right from the beginning; the name of the company is in fact a very loose anagram of Oxford Engine Services' acronym, and was coined because in

1962, when the company was first formed, anybody who was anybody in the tuning business had an Italian connection. The initials were tossed around, and came out as Oselli — a name sufficiently close to such genuine Italian names as Abarth, Ansa, and Osca to convince the wealthier undergraduates that the company had the right credentials.

Of course, had the business not been able to deliver the goods, then it would have foundered as quickly as it had been founded. But Oselli could deliver; a string of successes in events such as the R.A.C. Rally, and even the Monte Carlo, underscored their abilities as engineers. Throughout the '60s the name Oselli became synonymous with two

The boost is delivered in two stages, controlled by a "granny switch" neatly mounted to the fascia just to the right of the steering column. In its lower position the engine is producing in the region of 150 to 155 brake horsepower, and it thus follows that performance is similar to that of a 2.9i-equipped XR4x4; only the lower level of bottom end torque gives the game away there. With the rocker switch flicked over to its high position, the entire two hundred-odd horses will course their way out.

The standard unturbocharged car has reasonable performance. When the lower boost setting is selected on The Graduate the acceleration becomes lively, and when the higher setting is selected it becomes positively electrifying; our table details the precise differences between the various grades of available power.

On its lower setting, the car has a wonderful air of "point and squirt" about it, and the driver is able to make full use of the machine's power and torque virtually regardless of weather conditions; the combination of firm damping, excellently smooth power delivery and wonderful levels of traction combine to make the car a thoroughly enjoyable driving machine. Flick the switch and you are ready to go and have serious high-speed fun.

The traction, the handling, the tractability are all completely unimpaired by introducing the additional horsepower — these are, if anything, actually enhanced. Oselli have produced an extremely user-friendly XR4x4 with very lively performance. The heavy duty clutch which is a part of the standard package is, on first acquaintance, very heavy. However, after the first mile or so the driver becomes used to it and is able to use it smoothly and progressively, and it is only when the driver gets into another, non-modified XR4x4 that the weight of The Graduate's pedal action is thrown back into sharp perspective.

Whereas on lower boost the car is very much a point and squirt device, when the switch has been thrown over to its

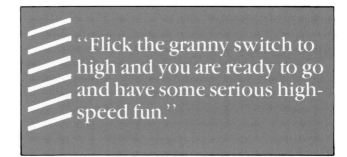

"Flick the granny switch to high and you are ready to go and have some serious high-speed fun."

serious setting the car becomes much more businesslike and starts to flex serious muscles. The car can still be thrown, almost with abandon, into a bend and it will come out on the far side unscathed, but the difference will immediately be felt in terms of the time between leaving one bend and reaching the next — the time scale can be markedly reduced.

The XR4x4 comes complete with anti-lock braking as a standard feature, and so deceptive is the level of

PERFORMANCE

	SIERRA 2.0 XR4x4 (STANDARD TRIM)	OSELLI GRADUATE (LOW BOOST)	OSELLI GRADUATE (HIGH BOOST)
0-60	9.7 seconds	6.8 seconds	6.1 seconds
0-100	19.1 seconds	16.1 seconds	14.7 seconds
50-70 (5th)	7.6 seconds	5.1 seconds	4.5 seconds
Maximum Speed	119 m.p.h.	130 m.p.h.	135+ m.p.h.
Fuel Economy	28.3 m.p.g.	26.9 m.p.g. overall	26.9 m.p.g. overall

marques of car, the Mini and the MG, and even today the various race teams and owners clubs devoted to those cars still consider that the Oxford company is the perfect place to have their cars prepared and repaired.

As the '70s dawned it became apparent that whilst there was still a lot of Mini and MG tuning work to go around, the products of Ford were beginning to come to the fore in not only competition but also fast road work, and so in 1972 a major research and development programme was undertaken to see how far Oselli could go with the products behind the famous blue oval. The answer was a long way; in the eighteen years since that programme was instigated Oselli have done just about everything possible to all manner of Ford cars, and their range of tuning equipment and services for Ford engines is formidable.

As time went on then so the range of

machining equipment and manufacturing facilities grew to match the volume of work, and the number of staff grew also. The only thing which didn't grow was their premises; the small facility just off the Swindon Road a half mile from Oxford city centre was reaching bursting point and clearly something had to be done. In November 1988 a site adjacent to their lifelong home was cleared by bulldozers, and the footings were put in place for a brand new purpose-designed building which opened in 1990. Now at last the company has enough room to house the equipment and facilities which it craved throughout the later '70s and into the '80s.

A substantial frontage, with the impressively-stocked retail shop, is the first sight which presents itself to the customer drawing through the gates. Here the considerable range of products by companies such as Weber, Spax, Magard, Jetex, Kent,

Koni and countless others can be bought over the counter, from staff who speak the required language of tuning. But that shop is merely the tip of the iceberg, for concealed from view behind it is a large stores area, and behind that what has to be the most impressive machine shop which *Performance Ford* has ever seen. Because Oselli are established engine remanufacturers, and a highly regarded member of that industry's trade body, they are capable of carrying out just about any machining and remanufacturing process that could ever be asked of them; whilst we were looking around, we spotted everything from a newly rebuilt 230 b.h.p. Essex V6 right through to a 1928 Aston Martin cylinder head (in for repairs to cracks between the chambers) in the workshops.

Before getting as far as the machine shop all engines are thoroughly stripped and cleaned, and every job, no matter how small or how

FIRST CLASS HONOURS

/ / / / / / / / /

performance which may be experienced in The Graduate that it is this which can be the first serious warning of overcooking things on a bend; the handling will be flat and neutral, there will be no warnings from the steering wheel and there will be no screaming noises from beneath the

bonnet, but if the brake pedal starts to click, then things are in danger of getting out of hand ...

Only when attempting to break basic laws of physics will the car start to display anything other than impeccable manners; although the chassis modifications are more than up to the work in hand, and if anything even exceed the revised power output of the engine, Oselli are engineers and not outright magicians — they have managed to push the pockets of resistance out further than those of the standard car, but not so far as they rewrite Newton's Theory of Relativity, or indeed the principles of gravity. Try too hard to make the sheer mass of a ton and a quarter

of car change direction too quickly, too abruptly, and it will start to bite back for your sheer impertinence.

Biting back will start with the onset of progressive understeer, a phenomenon so gradual that the corners of the car all but write a postcard to the driver. Only the most insensitive would ignore such a warning, and if he or she is so indifferent to the wealth of information which feeds through from the road through the steering wheel and through the base of the (optional) Recaro seats, then he or she deserves everything which comes their way. We were cornering at indecently high speeds (even by the already high standards set by the XR4x4) when we started to get the warnings, and so did the sensible thing and started to ease back a shade. Only an idiot would actually get into trouble in this car, so communicative is its chassis.

And just in case there is an oaf behind the wheel, Oselli have taken the precaution of replacing the front disc brakes with Tar · Ox items which prove themselves resistant to fade at far higher rates of useage than the standard system would be able to tolerate.

Oselli have put together a mightily impressive package, one which we found ourselves unable to resist taking out at every opportunity, in spite of the abysmal weather which was ravaging the country during our tenure of the car. Their conversion is vice-free, and considering the amount of work which goes into it and the nett result of their labours, do so for a very reasonable sum; the list price of the complete package of engine modifications, suspension uprates and braking system enhancements is £6,687. For an additional £500 the power can be stepped up still further to 224 dyno-proven brake horsepower.

For those with 2.0i XR4x4 models who wish to improve the power output but do not require such a radical conversion, Oselli are able to offer a more modest 175 b.h.p. conversion (the basic turbocharger installation plus the same big-bore stainless steel exhaust system as that featuring on The Graduate, which makes lovely but totally unobtrusive noises) for £2,320. A full information pack is available to serious enquirers; contact Oselli Engineering on 0865 248100. You will not be disappointed! ●

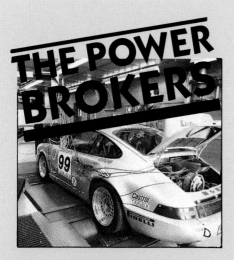

THE POWER BROKERS

substantial, is allocated a work card which allows its progress to be monitored through each phase of its time at Oxford. Once completed, the engines are either shipped back to their owners on crates shrink-wrapped for protection, or are installed into the customer's car. Every car which leave Oselli's premises does so with a computer

print out of its dyno readings.

Which brings us neatly to the dyno cell. In a fully soundproofed room towards the back of the building is a state-of-the-art four-wheel drive rolling road with the ability to handle up to 750 brake horsepower at the wheels. This is able to handle just about any vehicle, is climate controlled for stability of readings, and can be used for anything from a power run on a Mini 850 right through to a full scale final tune on a Group A Cosworth race car — the machine will work with front, rear and four-wheel drive machines.

As well as regular engine rebuild work Oselli are geared to producing one-offs, and have the very latest in machining equipment on site in their workshops — and are also geared to research and development work with full flow-bench facilities. Amongst their clients are a jolly well known company who specialise in building world-beating endurance

racers, and various other big-name équipes who race Porsches, Ferraris, and other esoterica. The company also have a totally confidential engine research and development facility, tucked away on the upper floor of their Oxford headquarters.

As well as engine work, Oselli's expertise in chassis development is also increasingly popular; they are able to supply tailored handling packs for all popular production models, prestige performance cars, and restored classics.

A full range of publications has been produced by Oselli, with dedicated tuning manuals for all of the popular Ford engines. For details of these, and for a comprehensive brochure which details the company's areas of activity (and also for a copy of their special dyno-tuning rolling road facility), contact Oselli Engineering, Department P.F., Ferry Hinksey Road, Oxford OX2 0BY. Telephone: 0865 248100. ●

FASTER FIESTAS

Jeremy Nicholson samples a modified XR2, borne out of racing experience in the Fiesta Credit championship, but translated into a useable fast road package.

Now, when faced with a performance conversion, as these things are usually called, I ask myself three questions: What have they done to it? Does it work? Will it keep on working? Last year I came across a gentleman who builds racing engines for a living and who has put together one of the nicest, most practical fast road conversions I have ever come across, and the price is reasonable, too.

Mario Di Capite owns a garage with rolling road alongside the A127 just outside Wickford in Essex. As from the beginning of the year, however, he also runs a Formula Vauxhall Lotus team with a promising young driver named Mark Albon.

Mario has worked for a number of people in the racing game, and being based in Essex he had to work for Ford

The XR2 of Paul Stevens. The engine is based upon the powerplants which were used in the Fiesta Challenge.

66 Racing improves the breed,'' or so the saying goes. In my experience this may relate to the work of a handful of major manufacturers, but nothing could be further from the truth for the average "special".

In my time I have driven a fair number of home-botched cars under the description "tuned" and found that racing certainly didn't improve them. On the contrary; they made a noise like a dumper with a hole in the exhaust, had a bottom end power level which wouldn't pull the skin off a damp rice pudding, and a power band the width of an estate agent's tie. Combine this with oiling plugs, overheating in traffic and twenty-minute starting rituals and you start to imagine why I wince when people start to tell me about their particular road rocket.

at one time or another. In fact he used to build engines for Ford's Research and Development operation at Dunton in Essex and then started his own garage business, spending his time on various exotica and building engines for various racers. One of these was long-time-friend Michael Helm's XR2 Fiesta which contested the Ford Credit series until last year.

The work he did on Michael's car, along with the number of his customers who wanted to improve the performance of their XR Ford road cars, led him to experiment with a few tweaks for the normally aspirated CVH engine and he came up with a "fast road" package specially designed for the XR2.

Although it is outclassed in performance by cars such as the Peugeot 205 GTi, the XR2 is a great little machine for the money and the chassis is capable of taking considerably more power than the carburated CVH engine produces in standard form.

Two of Mario's regular customers, Keith Barnard from Harlow and his mate Paul Stevens, a car bodywork specialist from Chingford, both owned XR2s and each

"They wanted a bit more life from the engine without spending the earth."

decided they wanted a bit more life from the engine without spending the earth. Mario decided against upping the capacity for this reason and opted instead for the archetypal "head job", comprising judicious gas flowing and polishing to complement the basis of the conversion, which was to be a couple of 40mm Dellortos. Mario reckons these carbs are currently the best of the bunch when it comes to overall performance and cost. Using these cars as research and development vehicles he spent hours on the rolling road trying out various settings and using the feedback from Keith and Paul he set out to make the conversion as civilised as possible, bearing in mind we are talking about somewhere in the region of a 30% power increase without altering the engine's capacity.

These words should be engraved on the heart of anyone who thinks they can build fast engines — "tuning is all about balance". If the carbs don't have the correct airflow through them the effect will be worse than with the standard set-up. So the next step was to change the cam. "I wanted one with a

high lift, but without a very long duration, as I wanted the engine to be civilised enough for road use and it had to idle smoothly," explained Mario. "The cam I went for in the end was the Piper HR270." To get rid of the exhaust gases a Janspeed manifold and system replaced the standard item.

Eventually the whole package started to come together. The head replaced, static timing was set and the car is run up on the rolling road. For many this would be the end of the process. For Mario it is only the beginning. "When we first ran the car on the rolling road using the recommended settings it only produced the same power as a standard engine and it ran a lot worse. I wasn't really surprised, you cannot make a better

Mike Helm's XR2 Fiesta racer at Snetterton. This car was one of the inspirations for the road-going machines which Mario Di Capite has produced.

engine just by bolting pieces on, but I was amused by the fact that the engine wasn't producing any more power than standard. I fitted a vernier adjustable cam sprocket and made small adjustments to the valve timing, by moving it less than half a tooth, maybe a quarter, I found another 30 b.h.p."

The basic conversion was extended and modified as Keith used the car and small improvements came to light. In addition to the two DHLA 40mm Dellortos and their manifolds there is now an electric fuel pump, a pressure regulator, ITG filters, the vernier adjustable cam sprocket and all the necessary cam followers and springs, the cam and all the gaskets. Then there

is about £200 worth of gas flowing and machining work. Add this lot together and you start to realise why even a comparatively mild job like this can cost a few bob. All up the cost of the conversion works out at around £1,300 including V.A.T.

The road-going package takes advantage of much of the knowledge Mario gained while working for saloon car racer John Mowatt and later at Dunton. The lack of restriction on a road car engine allows him to overcome problems which face competitors in the Fiesta racing series. For example, the hydraulic tappets used in the Fiesta Credit racers tend to pump up at high revs, spoiling the valve timing and robbing the engine of power. This was one of the areas which Mario could not do much about because of the racing ►

FASTER FIESTAS

A reliable package of twin Dellortos, Piper HR270 camshaft, Janspeed manifold and system and a careful build-up have resulted in a tractable engine which is ideally suited to the XR2 chassis.

regulations but which has been sorted out on the road car.

So how does it go? "Very well," is the answer to that one. The car starts on the button and soon settles into a regular idle. There are a couple of niggles which are immediately apparent, and spoil the overall impression of the car unnecessarily, because they are the only ones I could find. The electric fuel pump is clearly audible and this becomes a little annoying in traffic. Mario has found another pump to use, which is quieter, but Keith reckons the noise doesn't bother him. He also claims to ignore the significant amount of induction noise which is present. This is probably because the combination of noises becomes more of a blessing than a nuisance when you find a piece of

open road, but as most cars spend more of their time in traffic than they do being blasted across the Pennines I would still opt for a little more soundproofing.

Once out on the open road the quality of the engine work really starts to shine through. There is no loss of tractability in the mid range, while revving the engine out produces a glorious mixture of sounds and hurtles the car past dawdling traffic. The standard XR2 is pretty much overgeared, so the extra power matches well to the ratios and playing on the lever to keep the engine above 4000 r.p.m. means you can cover ground pretty rapidly, embarrassing a number of cars which would appear to be faster on paper.

Although I did not get a chance to try

for a top speed reading I would estimate that the little Fiesta could get within spitting distance of 120 m.p.h., with a 0-60 m.p.h. time in the mid seven second bracket.

However, the area where the Di Capite conversion really scores is in the 70-90 m.p.h. speed range, where the standard car is really running out of steam. The converted car just keeps on coming and wants to rev well into the red. For this reason I would suggest it would be well to invest in an electronic rev limiter, such as the Micro Dynamics one, as you cannot always rely on watching the tachometer. According to Keith the fuel consumption is practically unaltered in everyday use and the car has been as good as gold.

The XR2 has good traction characteristics in standard form and is well up to handling the increased power, being reluctant to spin its wheels even in the wet — although it

> "The lack of restriction on a road car engine allows Mario Di Capite to overcome problems which face race car constructors."

will if you insist. The power figure is 105 b.h.p. at the wheels, equivalent to 130 b.h.p. at the flywheel.

It is always a difficult decision, whether to alter the car you own or sell it and buy a faster one. Mostly the answer relies upon the sort of money you have available and the sort of car you need — you won't make an RS 200 out of a Fiesta Popular however much you spend. Mario Di Capite's engine work is about as good as you are going to get from a standard capacity, normally aspirated, CVH engine without losing "roadability". If you have an XR2 or 3 with good bodywork and you don't want to take the risk of changing your car, this kind of conversion makes a lot of sense, and a lot of fun. ●

Mario Di Capite Engineering (Department P.F.), Unit 10, Adams Business Centre, Cranes Farm Road, Basildon, Essex. Telephone: 0268 280862.

When rally star Mark Lovell turns his attentions to a road-going XR2i, the resulting package ought to be interesting. It is; the car has become the XR2i which Ford ought to have been selling from the very beginning ...

By Dennis Foy.

LOVELLY
LITTLE MOVER

Despite the fact that he is this year driving a Golf 4x4 in the Shell British Open Rally Championships, Mark Lovell is still considered by so many to have a name synonymous with Ford. This is hardly surprising, especially when his career is reviewed in fast forward mode; in 1981 he started stage rallying in a Mk I Escort, and by the end of that year had won his way through to the finals of the T.V. Times/Castrol Rally Challenge. His showing in that competition was enough to bring him to the attention of John Taylor (the former European Rallycross Champion) who took him under his wing and channelled Lovell's obvious talents in the right direction.

By 1983 the tall, rangy native of Axbridge in Somerset was riding high, having won five rounds of the Ford Escort Turbo Championship (enough to take the title), and having finished a very creditable 23rd overall on the Lombard R.A.C. Rally.

By 1985 he was behind the wheel of a Works Nissan on the Shell National trail, and another trophy was his. A year later he was inside the cosy cockpit of the sensational RS 200 (C 200 HKJ was his regular machine) and by the end of the season, despite not having a single win, he had accumulated enough points from high placings to guarantee him the Shell Oils British Open Rally Championship. This was a double entry in the record books for Lovell, he not only being the youngest driver ever to win that particular series, but also his being the only driver ever to win the National and the Open titles in consecutive years. He was 26 by the time he took the Open trophy home to its place on his mantlepiece.

Although he is running the VW Works entry in the British series this year, Mark is also to be found behind the wheel of a Cosworth — as this issue goes on sale he will be out in Malaysia in a Ford Works car, hopefully maintaining his successful association with the blue oval. But there is another link with Ford which is not, perhaps, quite as obvious, for when he is not actively participating in competitive rally driving (or in development and test sessions), Mark is to be found in Weston-Super-Mare, Avon, running P. & P. Performance Engineering — hence the link with this rather tough-looking XR2i.

P. & P. Engineering is a division of Passey & Porter, a substantially sized Ford dealership which was established in 1965 and which has three members of the Lovell family (Mark included) on its board of directors. Keen to make their RS and sports model clientèle aware of how special Passey & Porter feel that they deserve to be, Mark has recently masterminded a new facility expressly designed for that section of their customer base. Featuring dedicated personnel working within a self-contained building adjacent to the main dealership, RS, XR and Sport model drivers will be able to relax in their own waiting area, reading magazines which reflect their interests, and watching appropriately entertaining motorsport videos.

But the plans do not stop there, for Mark also plans a series of special-edition cars — of which this XR2i is the first.

According to not only his own experiences but also those of existing and potential clients, there are a number of inherent flaws with the XR2i when it is viewed as a serious sporting machine. The first is that with only 110 brake horsepower — and sometimes not quite that — the car is not quite powerful enough to keep up with the competition. The other is that its handling is not as precise as it might be. So he set out to find remedies for both.

LOVELY LITTLE MOVER

fuelling and ignition timing to suit the requirements of the enhanced breathing arrangement. Then there are cures for the inherent faults which the use of EEC-IV on small engines brings with it, such as mid-throttle hesitation, the rapid return-to-zero of the ignition timing on the overrun, and the excessive leanness at idle sped. By using their modified management system, Power have been able to iron out these "bugs" and appreciably enhance the driveability of the engine. Finally, the car is treated to higher grade spark plugs (NGK V-Groove items) and to a sumpful of Shell Gemini. A new oil filter is also included in the package.

Once the modifications have been completed the car is put back on the rollers and a final power reading is taken; this is guaranteed to be at least 125 b.h.p., and is often slightly over that; the figure for this specific example worked out to a hundred and twenty seven brake horsepower, with gains right through the power range. We have included a print-out for this particular car which shows the two sets of figures.

Having tried the car with its new-found levels of motivation, Mark was even more concerned about the chassis behaviour, and set to (along with the supremo of his team at P. & P. Performance) seeking a remedy for the twitchiness which he detected.

It was soon determined that most of the problems were being brought about by the rear of the car attempting to steer the nose, and so it was decided to take the radical step of not only altering the springs and damper combination, but also to change the wheel and tyre geometry. There is no provision for such changes in the standard package as it comes from Ford, and so it is necessary to "cut and shut" the existing hardware so that such a provision can be made — and that in turn involved building a jig to ensure total accuracy.

> "I suspect that this is the sort of package which the enthusiasts within Ford's design and engineering departments would like to have offered, had they been unfettered by the accountants ..."

Both camber and toe-in have been changed, with the nett effect of dialling out the steering effect of the rear wheels. To make the most of the revised geometry, the rear axle package was completed by adding a 20mm diameter rear anti-roll bar (affixed to the car whilst it is on the alignment jig, to ensure its fidelity to the wheel angles) and then installing totally new springs and dampers. The springs are rising-rate items which are ultimately 26% stiffer than those they replace, whilst the dampers are purpose-valved items which increase compression resistance by ten per cent, but which offer a 26% increase in extension resistance. With springs and dampers in place, the car sits 20mm nearer to the ground at its rear.

At the front of the car a similar degree of care and attention has gone into revising its standard settings. The original springs have been retained, but now are controlled by a set of slightly firmer dampers which feature equal uprates on both extension and compression. New track control arms have been fitted to the foot of either front strut, which give

◄ Because of their considerable knowledge of supercharger installations, Power Engineering of Uxbridge have been recruited to the Volkswagen Golf rally team headed by Mark — the car he drives is a Group A variant of the G60 Synchro — and when he discovered that they were in the advanced stages of developing a new tuning package (to go along with their existing Power Pack for the carburated versions of the CVH engine) for the XR2i, they seemed the logical people to handle that side of the intended package.

Their first move was, as always, to put the development car on the rollers of their state-of-the-art dyno, where they found that the engine was all but delivering what it was supposed to do; their power graph yielded a flywheel figure of 109 b.h.p. at 5,775 r.p.m. Ford claim that peak power is 110 b.h.p. at six thousand revs exactly, but the dyno showed that at that point in the engine's speed range power had already started to fall away — a situation which led Power to believe that there was a degree of airflow restriction inherent within the car's standard intake arrangement.

The package which they evolved for the car started with their own-designed SX428 camshaft, which offers improved valve timing. This is driven by a Vernier pulley which allows ultra-fine adjustment — it is a widely known fact that no two engines are ever identical in their timing requirements, and so each engine is set up individually, with the drivegear being adjusted until peak power figures are achieved. To allow the engine to rev more freely at the top end of its power band, Motorsport-grade lifters are used, and dual high-lift valve springs are fitted to each of the eight stems. The camshaft takes care of one aspect of the engine's breathing but there still remains the problem of airflow through to the engine from the atmosphere — Bill Blydenstein discovered this some time ago and offers extensively reworked airboxes, Power Engineering prefer to use a K&N filter element, and Mark Lovell prefers to modify the original airbox as he felt that the K&N generated unacceptable levels of noise.

The third part of the Power Pack (as the system is known) is to override the standard EEC-IV management system to offer a number of improvements. The first is to modify

LOVELY LITTLE MOVER

50-70 in fourth would normally take a little over seven seconds, but L79 managed that burst in a shade under six. The improved upper-reaches breathing also yields a bonus of seven miles an hour on the car's maximum speed.

The combination of a wide-ranging, flexible and powerful engine with a chassis able to display all of the neutrality of a United Nations Peacekeeping Force sounds like a formula close to small-car heaven. So what didn't we like about the package?

Basically, nothing that couldn't be attended to — or more accurately things that should have been attended to in the latter stages of the XR2i's development at Ford, prior to its release onto the market. The noise levels which are generated by the engine gave us cause for concern when we first tested the XR2i on its launch, and matters there are unchanged eighteen months into production; the raucous din within the cabin when the car is being worked hard are frankly unacceptable for a car costing more than eleven thousand pounds. A good aftermarket soundproofing kit seems to be the only solution, as Ford themselves seem indifferent to the problem. The other things we do not like about the car are its seats and its steering rack.

The seats when new are reasonably supportive, but conversations with owners of higher mileage examples of the car elicit the information that they lose their lateral support, and allow the occupant to slide sidewards. Perhaps Ford ought to do what they suggested they were going to do, and start to offer Recaro front seat options for the model? As for the steering rack, this requires some four and a quarter turns from lock to lock, which makes parking something of a pain — and makes the negotiation of traffic islands at low speeds unnecessarily awkward, as the driver has to battle with great armfuls of lock if a tidy line is to be achieved. The faster-acting rack from the RS Turbo Fiesta would be a far more appropriate fitment for the XR2i. This again was something which Ford led us to understand would be integrated into the XR2i package by now, but obviously has not been.

None of those three niggles is in any way the responsibility of P. & P. Performance Engineering, but rather of Ford Motor Company.

In putting their package together, P. & P. have produced a pleasing car, one which takes the XR2i to the levels of performance which it ought to have enjoyed from Day One. What is more, they have taken a major initiative concerning the way in which it can be bought and paid for. The prices are extremely competitive, especially when the gains are taken into account; the engine package costs £585 plus V.A.T., whilst the handling pack is priced at £610 plus V.A.T. Buy the two together and there is a package price of £1,125 plus tax. Appreciating that not everybody will have the ready cash to match their desire to have such alterations made to their cars, P. & P. have formulated a 36-month payment plan, which brings the costs within the reach of any owner; the engine modifications work out at £6 per week, and the handling pack £7 a week. The payment plan can be applied to equal success to either brand new cars being bought from Passey & Porter, or to a car already in the client's possession — and if both engine and handling packs are combined on the payment scheme, the cost drops to a mere £12 per week. The wheels and tyres are not a part of the basic scheme of things, because of the number of different permutations which are available, and so P. & P. Performance suggest that these items be discussed with them.

P. & P. Performance Engineering are at Department P.F., Winterstoke Road, Weston Super Mare, Avon BS23 3YE. Telephone: 0934 628291. ●

SPECIFICATIONS

ENGINE TYPE
Transverse SOHC (CVH) four cylinder
BORE x STROKE
80mm x 79.5mm
SIZE
1596cc
BHP @ RPM
127 @ 6,160
TORQUE LB/FT @ RPM
132 @ 4,000
FUEL SYSTEM
Ford EEC-IV engine management system with Power Engineering override module, modified airbox.
DRIVEN WHEELS
Front
TRANSMISSION
Five speed manual transaxle
SUSPENSION, FRONT
MacPherson struts (uprated) with modified L-bar lower links to add castor, revised tracking, standard anti-roll bar
SUSPENSION, REAR
Torsion beam rear axle with modified trailing arms, 20mm anti-roll bar, 26% uprated rising rate springs, altered damper rates
BRAKING SYSTEM
Ventilated front discs, rear drums, optional electronic anti-locking
WEIGHT
1,960 lbs
POWER/WEIGHT RATIO
145 b.h.p./ton
WHEELBASE
96.3"
LENGTH
147.5"
WIDTH
73"
HEIGHT
51.4"
TEST MILEAGE
1,220 miles
MANUFACTURER'S MPG
28.5 (standard XR2i)
TEST MPG
29.7
PRICE AS TESTED
£11,320 plus £585 + V.A.T. engine Power Pack, £610 + V.A.T. handling uprate (package price £1,125 + V.A.T.), plus wheels and tyres, and any special-order Ford items
INSURANCE GROUP
Special quotation
MANUFACTURER
Ford Motor Company (standard car)
Modifications carried out by P. & P. Performance Engineering, Weston Super Mare, Avon

0.75° of additional negative camber, and the tracking has been altered to give additional toe-in as an aid to straight-line stability. To finish off what is obviously a very complex set of alterations to the suspension system, P. & P. have fitted a set of 14″ x 7″ Hi-Tech six-spoke cast aluminium alloy rims fitted with 185/50 tyres. Although these work nicely to set the car apart visually and to enhance steering sharpness, Mark Lovell is at pains to point out that they are not essential to the success of the package — the revisions to the suspension were based on testing carried out with the car on its standard 13″ x 5½″ wheels with 185/60 tyres.

So much for what they have done. What counts most is; was it worthwhile? In a word, yes.

The car is a delight to drive, and is the machine which Ford ought to have put on sale in the first place; I suspect that this is the sort of package which the enthusiasts within Ford's design and engineering departments would like to have offered, had they been unfettered by the accountants and the marketing people. The car is able to corner with a pleasing fluidity of movement at speeds comfortably in excess of those attainable by a standard example. Body roll is wonderfully under control, and the car is so well balanced in mid-bend, so totally neutral with neither understeer nor oversteer regardless of the amount of throttle, that this particular Fiesta is in an entirely different league from any standard example. Ask the driver of the 16 valve Golf (a car noted for its chassis precision) who conceded his attempt to keep up with me on a cross-country run recently. He could hang on along the straights — fair enough, he had got a few extra horses beneath his bonnet, and a similar power/weight ratio — but he just couldn't take the curves as confidently as I was able to do.

Where I was also able to score was in the way that the power is delivered from beneath the pristine white (apart from the dead flies ...) bonnet of the Fester. With 118 lb/ft

of torque, the Golf owner wasn't badly off; with 132 lb/ft I was positively rich. What is more, the torque curve is more of a plateau on the XR2i, mirroring that of the standard car but raising it by a constant 15% or so right along the way. Peak torque is developed at 4,000 r.p.m., but two thousand revs either side of that there is still more than ninety per cent of the maximum being developed. Which means that it is hard to be caught off the power band. Throw in the fact that the revised engine is still developing serious, useable horsepower on the wrong side of 6,750 r.p.m., and you may start to get some idea of why the picture takes on such a rosy glow.

Pottering around town, getting caught up in the usual traffic jams or searching out a slot in the perpetually over-subscribed car parks, there is nothing to give the uninformed driver the impression that this car is any different from any other XR2i. The seats, the controls, the fittings, all are unchanged. Pedal weighting is just as it is in any other Fiesta, and the steering action feels quite allright;

the revised geometry brings with it a sharper self-centering action, and the turn-in is no heavier than it would be in a standard example. Because the way in which the engine develops its torque is unchanged — there is more of it, but it is not in the least bit ''peaky'' — that also adds to the in-town illusion that this is just an ordinary Fiesta.

Yet get it out on a motorway and the differences come into sharp perspective. The standard car is a little prone to sidewind twitchiness, but not L79; the changes made to the suspension system endow the machine with a nonchalant indifference to crosswind direction or strength. The little white car simply tracks along its intended path unaffected by the forces of nature or the bow-waves generated by juggernauts. Lane changing is equally undramatic, thanks to the way in which the altered front wheel angles have taken out the straight-ahead woolliness which so often affects front wheel drive cars using rack-and-pinion steering. A slight tug on the wheel in the appropriate direction is all that is required to move from one lane to another cleanly and precisely.

When describing the engine modifications I mentioned the engine's new-found power levels in the upper reaches of its speed range, and these too aid motorway driving; if the driver is using an intermediate gear there is no longer the need to make an upshift at the 5,500 r.p.m. point because there is still a good 1,500 slice of power band to play with in this particular car.

That same facility aids country road driving, too. Attempts to press on hard in a standard XR2i are usually hampered by the need to shift up and down the 'box in an attempt to avoid the power vacuum beyond 5,750 revs, but in this car that extra burst to seven thousand can be used instead of the clutch pedal. The perfect remedy for unnerved chassis balance when the county council throws an unexpectedly long sweeping bend at a driver without any warning.

Those extra horses also make themselves useful when it comes to acceleration, again by reducing the frequency of time-sapping gearshifts. The 0-60 time is clipped to a very respectable 7.6 seconds (a standard car takes nine ...) and there are similar gains to be made on the in-gear times;

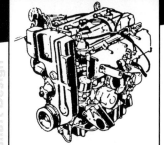

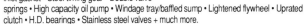

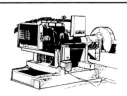

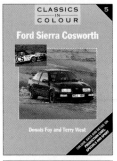

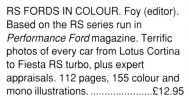

ON TOP OF THE MOUNTAIN

Paul Cooper's XR4i is no ordinary restoration special ...

By Dennis Foy.

There comes a point in every restoration where the owner walks in, takes a look at the massive mountain of parts lying in the middle of the garage floor, and convinces him- or herself that the project is doomed. The next move is usually to put together a small ad in a bid to get rid of everything as an unfinished project; only the most dedicated will see beyond the hurdles which lie ahead, and pursue the process to its (hopefully sweet, rather than bitter) end. Paul Cooper is one of the latter.

At the beginning of this year, his Caspian Blue XR4i was at the "mountain of parts" stage, right in the middle of an absolute rebuild which had been caused by a moment's inattention on the part of a Vauxhall Midi van driver on August 23rd 1990. Paul had acquired the car some two years earlier, after a good deal of searching for an XR4i which combined both an affordable price and an acceptable condition in one; as anybody who has ever tried to purchase one of these machines will attest, for every good example there are another nine which do not bear close inspection — and the prices being asked rarely relate to condition, age or mileage.

Basically sound and with just under sixty two thousand miles on the clock, Paul's acquisition was fundamentally good and by the time that he had invested in a new sports exhaust system, spent a few months flushing and replenishing the engine lubrication system, and replacing many of the ignition components, he was happy with his car. Apart from preventative maintenance (such as having the fuel injection system checked and overhauled by a local garage), the car ran beautifully, and Paul was a happy man.

Then came the incident with the Vauxhall van. Paul was sitting happily at a red traffic light, waiting for the change to green, when he noticed a van bearing down behind him at rather high speed with smoke pouring from its lock-up tyres. With nowhere to go but into the flow of traffic crossing his path, he could do no more than to let the Midi remodel the rear panel of his pride and joy. At first glance the damage was not too serious; the van had scrubbed off a good deal of its speed, and Paul's action in letting off the hand brake was sufficient to ease the impact slightly. Then it was realised that as well as denting the tailgate and the back panel between the lights, the impact had also creased the floorpan in the boot, around the spare wheel well. Appropriate professional advice from a selection of sources all concurred that a selective panel replacement was a less than ideal solution because once the car was back on the road a degree of rear frame and floorpan twisting would be inevitable, as the behaviour patterns of the new metalwork would be incompatible with those of the original six year old panels surrounding them.

After a number of conversations with local bodyshops and with Paul's insurers, it was agreed that the only sensible solution was to reshell the car. A great idea — but something of a non-starter, because new shells for these cars were non-existent. He could have as many Cosworth shells as he liked, but "Six Lite" XR4i shells have not been available through the Ford network for some time, as every dealer he approached (which included Trimoco of Dunstable, normally an excellent source for such hardware) attested.

Then he picked up a back issue of *Performance Ford* — the very first issue, in fact — and spotted a ➤

ON TOP OF THE MOUNTAIN

Although the body damage looked nominal (inset), the floorpan had been buckled. After some consultation with bodyshops and with his insurers, a complete reshell was decided upon.

◀ photograph which reminded him of Andy Rouse's years with the XR4i. On a long shot, he found the number of RouseSport in Coventry, and rang to see if anybody there had the slightest idea of where he might be able to obtain a new shell for the 4i. The lady who answered the telephone was very helpful and promised to call him back if, after enquiring of her colleagues, anybody could come up with a lead. Ten minutes later the telephone rang at Paul's Newcastle, Staffordshire, home, and on the other end was Andy Rouse himself, seeking further information about the project. It transpired that his company still had one new, slightly modified, XR4i bodyshell sitting in the back of the workshop, and it was now possibly surplus to requirements. Would Paul like to pop down to RouseSport H.Q. and take a look at it?

The shell proved to have never been used for active competition work, but had served to form a basis for building roll cages; there were strategic pads on each corner of the

floorpan, and the ends of the fascia roll had been cut away, but in all other respects it was in perfect shape. The shell was a true XR4i six-lite item, and being a motorsport-specification item was a "tin top" with no provision for a sunroof. The deal was struck, and within a few days the shell was in its new home in Staffordshire.

Paul's first move was to remove the pads onto which the roll cages had been built, and to completely clean it down to bare metal inside and out. A coating of primer was then applied to form a measure of protection. The shell was then despatched for painting (a new pair of doorskins and new tailgate had been procured, but the bonnet from the original car would be reused) and work continued on stripping out everything, but *everything,* from the old shell. The single biggest problem area was the wiring loom; the complexity of this task was minimised by carefully labelling each and every connector with a handwritten baggage tag.

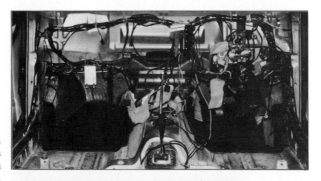

Wiring loom removal. Subsequent reinstallation was aided by the use of luggage tags detailing the purpose and position of each and every connector.

The entire driveline of the "old" car was unbolted, but left suspended on a variety of blocks and axle stands, and then on New Year's Day 1991 the damaged bodyshell was lifted neatly off the running gear, and disposed of. By this point the car had accumulated some ninety thousand miles of running, and so Paul decided that the time was appropriate to overhaul the 2.8 litre V6 engine; as it was already out of the car half of the work was already done. The heads were professionally reworked to

> "The body arrived home, freshly painted, towards the end of February, and by the end of the same day the running gear was located."

incorporate triple-angle valve seats, and to open up their ports slightly; these were matched to their manifolds at the same time.

A Kent camshaft, the V6T21 giving lift of .395″, 284° duration and 114° overlap, was chosen and installed in the block, and then the complete assembly was rebuilt with dual springs and fresh followers; Paul wanted to enhance mid-range torque, but without compromising the impressive low-range torque which makes the 2.8i such a pleasant engine to use, hence the choice of camshaft. The engine rebuild was completed as soon as possible, as he did not wish to create any unnecessary delays once the new bodyshell came back from the sprayshop.

The body arrived home towards the end of February, and by the end of the same day as the shell had returned the running gear was located with strategic bolts tightened so that nothing would fall off again. A month later work had progressed to the point where it was simply a matter of filling the braking system with fresh fluid (Teves Blue Racing Fluid, chosen for its low rate of hygroscopy and its long working life) and by the Easter weekend the car was mechanically complete and ready to a run-up to temperature. Paul took advantage of the situation to drive the car out of the garage, turn it around and reverse it back in; this would make reinstallation of the trim appreciably easier.

The glazing was carefully removed from the old shell when it was being stripped out, and this was affixed to the new body with equal care; a friend who works for an auto glazing company looked after that particular task, as the bonding operation is very much a specialist process. The rear side windows, which are etched with a unique pattern of lines, are particularly difficult to obtain, and Paul had no desire to start having to try and locate a set ...

The DoT certificate of roadworthiness (an MoT ticket, to most of us ...) had expired whilst the car was undergoing its transplant surgery, and so the car was booked in, and examined in detail by a local station. It passed first time, with no problems or reservations. A few days later the Man From The Ministry came along to check over the car (standard practice with rebuilds) and passed the car off as roadworthy, enabling Paul to pop down to the local Post Office and invest a hundred pounds in a tax disc.

The car went into his local garage (the same one which had overhauled his injection system earlier in the car's history) for a full engine tune-up, and from there went on to Turbo Systems, who had already been contracted to make a few changes to the suspension system.

Paul had been exploring different means of improving the car's handling for some time, and almost everywhere that he went to, the suggestion was to see if Cosworth Sierra springs, dampers and anti-roll bars could be affixed. However, Paul was most specific in his desire not to build a Cosworth replica, but rather to enhance the virtues of the XR4i. In the early days of ownership he had obtained a rear beam location kit from Brooklyn Motorsport, which dramatically reduces the amount of movement within the rear location rubber bushes. This on its own had already improved matters, but to get the car to handle more precisely still a package of fresh springs and dampers was formulated.

The damper units are the excellent (in terms of both performance and value for money) Monroe GasMatic items, and these are teamed with fresh springs offering both lower ride height and higher poundage; the front sets are now 10″ free height, 145 lb items (the originals were 14.5″ and 112 lb), whilst the rears are 10.25″, 325 lb items, rather than the original 11.5″, 250 lb pieces. The ▶

THE XR4i SIERRA

The car was produced between the spring of 1983 (following on a few months behind the mainstream range of new Sierras) and March 1985, and was intended from the very outset to be a fast five-seat saloon rather than a sports coupé. All design work on the car was executed at Ford's Merkenich plant, the team responsible being encouraged by Bob Lutz (then Ford of Europe Chairman) to be as extrovert as they felt possible. Part of their interpretation was to eschew the usual three or five door bodyshells, in favour of a special "six lite", or four-pillar, shell — this was specially tooled up for the car and has never been used on any other Sierra derivative in Europe; the Merkur XR4Ti shared the shell, but in Europe no other car was seen with a six lite side window arrangement.

dealers, rather than on the Cologne production line. 14″ x 5½″ "pepperpot" aluminium wheels were standard issue, with 195/60R14 tyres, usually from Uniroyal.

The packaging for the car was essentially in the mould of the Grand Tourer (XR had, after all, taken over from GT in Fordspeak) with the top line light and bumper arrangement from the Ghia Sierra being joined by full length plastic lower body cladding, and that biplane rear spoiler. Claimed cd figure for the car was 0.32, rather than the 0.34 claimed for the rest of the range. On the inside a set of Scheel sports front seats (trimmed in a then-trendy checked fabric) were used, and there was much red pinstriping to be seen around the hub of the

At the time of conception, Ford had no plans whatsoever for a motorsport derivative of the Sierra, and so the Cologne V6 was chosen as motive power; the original development was done around the 2.3 litre version of that engine, but once it became apparent that there was inadequate power coming from the flywheel of that engine the decision was taken to replace it with the Capri 2.8i's powerplant. This gave an increase in power output of 36 brake horsepower, taking it up to 150 b.h.p. Backing up the engine was a five speed transmission (the then-new T9 unit) and at the rear of the car the centre section of the independent rear suspension was a 7″ crownwheel differential unit. Interestingly, presumably because it was never intended to be anything other than a road car, a limited slip differential was only available for the car after a great deal of hassling at your local dealership; this item was almost invariably fitted at the

two-spoke sporty steering wheel, the instrument binnacle, and the top of the gearknob. A fuel computer also featured as standard equipment — but power steering (which improved the turning ratio from 4.3:1 to 3.6:1), power windows, a sunroof, tinted glass and central locking were all optional extras. By the standards of the day the car was expensive in basic form at £9,170 — and buying a loaded one would push the price to the topside of £10,300.

In all some 25,600 examples were registered, with the initial year's 18,300 production run accounting for the vast majority. The car was replaced in 1985 by the XR4x4, which gave the benefit of four wheel drive for a price which was still in the same ballpark as that of the XR4i — by that time the two wheel drive car was retailing at £10,400 — albeit with most of the former exras being absorbed into the base price. ●

ON TOP OF THE MOUNTAIN

◀ new springs are linear-wound, which improves the manufacturing consistency.

A front anti-roll bar from a Cosworth was employed to aid the spring interaction, this being 2mm greater in diameter than the original item. The original XR4i rear anti-roll bar was retained, but new Motorsport-grade bushes were used throughout the suspension system, along with Motorsport track control arms. The result is a car which has dramatically reduced roll characteristics, a sharp steering turn-in, and no loss in ride quality. The XR4i also looks better than standard, by virtue of its lowered ride height.

In all other respects, Paul's XR is totally standard; although he shuns the idea of showing the car in concours d'elegance, he is most particular about wishing to retain the authenticity of his (relatively rare) Ford. The engine modifications (including the free-flow exhaust system from G.D.S., which endows the car with a lovely deep burbling note) ensure that power levels are slightly higher without having sacrificed driveability, and the suspension changes have added much to the driving pleasure of the car without taking away practicality, it will still carry a full complement of passengers and luggage without bottoming out.

Had he wanted to produce a Cosworth lookalike, Paul Cooper could have done so with considerably less difficulty than he has experienced putting his XR4i back on the road in its present order. The bodyshell would have been easy to obtain (these are available through all Rallye Sport dealerships for under £2,000 in race specification) and he would have also been able to put together a package of Cosworth suspension components with less trouble than he had to take putting together the arrangement found beneath the his Caspian Blue 4i. But he didn't want to build a Cosworth lookalike; the XROC member wanted to retain the special blend of components which made him seek out an XR4i in the first place.

Having briefly sampled the car, I am in a position to underwrite Paul's faith in his decision; this is an extremely pleasant car to drive, with the under-stressed V6 doing just what it ought in the way of providing forward motion, the suspension system enabling the car to corner sharply and precisely, and the braking system being about as good as they come. The car is also capacious, and distinctive — two of the features which had attracted Paul to the package in the first place.

Our photographs prove that the rewards are there if you face the mountain of parts, take a deep breath, and carry on with the task ahead ... ●

TWO TIMING

The second generation of Fiesta XR2 has received the radical Panique Styling Systems treatment.

Call it the evolution process. A couple of years ago Paul Newton owned a Mk II Escort which was, he felt, crying out for a little help in the styling department. Accordingly, he used his spare time and the facilities of his father's boatyard to devise a complete set of new panels for the car. Then he became a victim of the economic recession hitting his home town of Barrow in Furness, and decided that

if he could offer replicas of his own car's panels to other Escort owners, then he might stand a chance of getting a small business off the ground. It was a better option than being a redundant draughtsman, late of V.S.E.L. shipbuilders.

This proved moderately successful, but things really started to take off when he added a second car to his range of panels; this was the Mk I

Fiesta which featured on our April 1991 front cover. Then the inevitable happened, when potential clients started to enquire whether or not the new kit could also be appended to the second generation of Fiesta. "It won't," said Paul, "but we are working on it ..."

This is the fruit of those labours, a complete styling package attached to the Mk II Fiesta XR2. Although essentially like that earlier package of panels, the complete nose section has had to be reworked to allow it to fit neatly onto the revised body panels introduced by Ford when the Fiesta was given a fresh lease of life in 1983. In essence the second generation of Fiesta had new inner and outer front wings (the former to allow the free use of the five speed transaxle, the latter to de-emphasise the angular appearance of the bodyshell) along with new lamp units — the front trafficators were relocated outboard of the headlamps — and correspondingly curvy moulded bumper units. Despite the fact that little of the main structure of

The new rear spoiler differs considerably from the first generation, being altogether more subtle; the original (see inset) was deemed too angular for the curvier shape of the second-generation car.

DENNIS FOY

the car behind its bulkhead was changed, there were still sufficient detail structure alterations to cause Panique (as the company has become known) a substantial amount of work revising their original panelwork.

The introduction of a second Fiesta kit also gave Panique the opportunity to amend the design of the rear spoiler, an aspect of the original package with which they had never been altogether happy. We'll come back to that later. First it might be an idea to outline what was involved in reworking the original set of panels. As might reasonably be expected, the first move in the game was to purchase a tidy example of Mk II Fiesta upon which to work. Given that the majority of interest to date has been from XR2 owners, this seemed a logical place to start, and so a middle-aged XR2 was purchased locally.

The rear wing extensions fitted readily onto the later bodyshell once the original Ford trim strips had been removed, and these were quickly ►

TWO TIMING

integrated with a variation on the original rear bumper moulding. At the front the story was more complicated, mainly due to the way in which the trafficators on the new bodyshell wrap around the leading wing edges. This modification entailed appending a set of the first-generation panels, modifying them in situ, and then springing fresh moulds from the finished products. For the combined front bumper and spoiler moulding, Panique started with the standard Ford moulding, widening it to suit the extra width of the wings with which it would meet on its outer edges, and from those beginning trying a whole variety of different treatments before settling on one which gave the desired visual effect. Although sympathetic to the Ford item it actually differs considerably, being blessed with extra swages and provision for a pair of under-bumper driving lamps. The result is a car the front elevation of which is still recognisably XR2, but which is sufficiently different to

make it stand out from the herd; in this respect it follows the philosophy of Dimma, whose styling kit for the Peugeot 205 GTi achieves a similar end.

The side skirting of the Mk I kit is carried straight over to the Mk II; this is unsurprising when one realises that Paul intended the panels to suit both models of Fiesta when they were first designed. Rather neat detail touches on the front and rear mouldings are the way in which the original trim inserts designed by Ford have been integrated into the Panique mouldings; on their demonstrator these have been finished in electric blue, which contrasts nicely against the car's black paintwork and which ties in with the silver and blue graphic set applied to the car.

Which leaves only the rear spoiler. The original Fiesta spoiler was a tall, angular item of the style first seen some years ago on the Plymouth Superbird. As anybody who has ever worked with glassfibre will tell, such designs are fraught with danger, in that they are inherently weak structures once finished and affixed to the car. Besides this, the curvier body styling of the Mk II Fiesta was against the adoption of such a

striking spoiler design; something a little less angular would be more desirable.

The finished product — again the result of much experimentation in moulding foam and glassfibre, filler and battening strips — is a much lower-key item which seats neatly towards the lower edge of the rear screen, and which is based around sets of curves far more sympathetic to the later bodyshell. So successful is this as a piece of styling that it has been adopted for both sets of panels.

As with the earlier Fiesta the revised set of wings call for a set of suitably wider wheels and tyres, with their inset and offset carefully predetermined so that handling is not adversely affected. On the demonstrator these are Compomotive split-rim items, but in view of the serious delays which affected supplies of these particular items, Panique are looking into offering a variety of options from various manufacturers. On the demonstrator the front pair of wheels measure 15″ x 7½″, as also do the rears; Panique are looking into the possibilities of a slightly narrower seven inch rim for the front axle, with a similar sized rear rim as well. This will allow a more suitable 195/50/15 tyre rather than the slightly oversized 205/50 items which feature on the demonstrator.

As well as their own panels — which come complete with full fitting and finishing instructions and a full telephone trouble-solving service — the kit for the Mk II also includes a pair of bonnet vents. Rather than use the RS Cosworth Sierra items which had ventilated the compartment lid of the Mk I car, they have wisely decided to instead offer the Mk III Fiesta RS Turbo items; these are supplied ready-modified to drop readily into holes cut by the purchaser, these holes being marked out from a template which comes as a part of the package of fitting instructions.

As well as supplying complete boxfuls of ready-to-fit components which enable the purchaser to convert his or her car into a Panique Fiesta, the company is also able to undertake to fit their high quality glassfibre laminated panels to a customer's car. For full details of their products and services, contact Panique Styling Systems (P.F.), 22 Strathnaver Avenue, Barrow in Furness, Cumbria LA14 3DG. Telephone: 0229 472633 or 472655.

The revised front spoiler is based around the Ford moulding, but differs considerably in width and depth. It integrates extra swaging and has a pair of driving lamps integrated below the bumper line.

SIERRA XR4x4

DAMPENED OUT AND SHARPENED UP:
Evaluating the driving enhancement module newly available from Detection Techniques

arvin the Paranoid Android was not a terribly pleasant piece of hardware to live with. Also known as EEC-IV, Marvin's rôle is to control the fuel and ignition programming of our Sierra XR4x4, the idea being that it optimises the delivery of each and thus maintains the engine in its most fuel efficient state at all times. As a part of its complex programming the device effectively shuts down the fuel supply and zeroes the ignition timing each time the throttle is trailed — a sound ecological move in that there is no wastage of petrol.

However, the downside to this particular characteristic is that the engine is given to fluffing slightly when throttle is reapplied; in on-off-on-off throttle conditions, such as when driving in fast moving town traffic or when exploiting the potential of some of our less well occupied twisting country lanes, this can become a pain, making progress unnaturally jerky. Compounding this trait is the overall leanness of the fuel mixture, which again reduces the driveability of what is otherwise a very satisfying car.

Detection Techniques have turned their attention to this problem in response to requests from a number

of clients belonging to both themselves and their substantial network of agents; because EEC-IV is used virtually across the range of Ford cars the problem is obviously too big to ignore.

EEC-IV is a very complex piece of computer, designed originally to perform fuel economy miracles on the range of excessively thirsty V8 engines in use in Ford's North American range; effectively two computers in one, the device has as a part of its repertoire the ability to

shut down half of the eight cylinders in certain situations — a trick which is simple for such a powerful microprocessor to perform. It does, however, serve to illustrate the considerable abilities of the device. It is reckoned that only eleven or twelve per cent of its capacity is used in European applications — which may indicate a much greater reliance on it in time to come. It is also widely acknowledged that Ford's various attempts to make it inaccessible to outside modifiers have been, as a general rule, very successful — this is at least in part attributable to the unique and dedicated "language" which has been adopted by Ford's talented electronics experts.

What they didn't count on was the equal talent available inside the modest and unprepossessing Buckingham headquarters of Detection Techniques. By using the monitor port which Ford have thoughtfully provided on the back of the EEC-IV, and by using a tremendously impressive amount of very specialised computer programming knowledge, D.T. have been able to create a module which attaches neatly to the Ford microprocessor unit, interfacing via an "interpreter" another, far more

OUR CARS SPECIAL

easily programmed computer unit.

About the size of a ten-packet of cigarettes, the module can be programmed to exorcise the inherent traits of EEC-IV; as there are a

an average of 24.7 miles to each gallon of low octane lead-free fuel and we half expected this to suffer as a result of the additional fuel which would be provided by the new module. However, a close monitoring

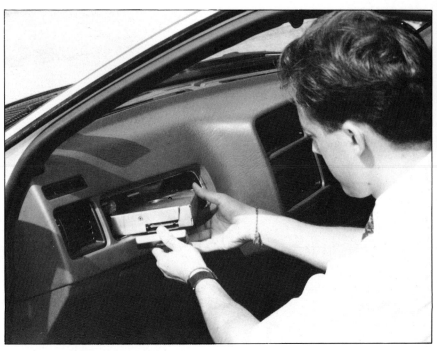

number of different series of the Ford unit, there are different programmes for the Detection Techniques modules which are easily tailored to specific applications. It takes but a few moments to install the additional module, and its diminuitive size means that the Ford microprocessor's installation is unaffected; the complete revised assembly simply slides back into place, and concealed beneath its moulded cover.

If there is no trace of a modification visually, the new module certainly makes its presence known when the car is driven. The fluffiness which previously bedevilled the car has gone completely, as also has the overrun ''shunting'' which was another trait when decelerating from high engine revs in a low gear. Rapid progress through twisting bends is now far less uncomfortable, and the car is subjectively quicker under such circumstances because power recall is now an instantaneous thing. We had one cause for concern immediately before having the new module fitted, and that was any adverse effect it might have on the XR4x4's fuel economy; a check on mileage over a two thousand mile period of mixed driving had shown

of the next couple of thousand miles worth of mixed driving has dispelled our fears because the figure has remained between 24.5 and 25 miles to the gallon.

And yes, the car continues to run on lead-free fuel. In fact, the promise from Detection Techniques is that the module enhances the driveability of any EEC-IV controlled car regardless of whether it is set to run on low or high octane fuel, and with or without lead. They do not claim any gain in performance from their module, simply offering improved tractability because of its more consistent fuel and ignition cycles, the excesses of the standard Ford microprocessor being neatly dampened out.

The XR4x4 is certainly more pleasing to drive since we had the module fitted; if you would like to improve the tractability of your EEC-IV controlled car (which is effectively all current models of EFi Ford from mid 1989 onwards), contact Detection Techniques at Department P.F., Buckingham Industrial Estate, Buckingham MK18 1XJ (telephone 0280 816781), or any of the Superchips agencies who grace our advertising pages. ●

XR3i ARRIVES

First test of the first XR with twin-cam power

By Dennis Foy

DENNIS FOY

T he burning question is, have Ford shot themselves in the foot with this car? After driving the new XR3i on demanding, twisting, altogether enjoyable roads in the South of France the issue is not whether the car is good enough, but rather how sales of the RS 2000-16v will be able to hold up in the teeth of such sharp competition. In a nutshell, the new 130 brake horsepower XR3i, with its 1.8 litre, dual-camshaft, sixteen valve engine really is a cracker of a car.

The new engine has been a long time coming — and having now had the opportunity to sample it in a selection of XR3is, the conclusion is that its arrival was not a moment too soon. Revving freely and sweetly right to its seven thousand revs redline, it delivers its power in a way which is pleasingly deceptive; whereas with the earlier CVH engine the driver knew that he or she was making the powerplant work hard for its living, the lucky chap or chapette behind the wheel of the newest car to bear the XR legend is able to feel only that each and every one of the horses is offering its services voluntarily.

What is more, they are green horses; each and every exhaust pulse of gases — which are already lead-free — passes through a three-way catalytic converter before exiting the modest matt-black tailpipe of the car.

XR3i ARRIVES

FORD PHOTOGRAPHIC UNIT

◄ and, in our test example, a rather rubbery shift gate which showed an initial reluctance to engage any gears. However, after a little persuasion, first slotted into place, and the pleasingly well balanced clutch bit progressively as the car pulled away. In the hubbub around the airport the car was as tame and under control as a 1.3 Escort L. The ergonomics of the car are good, so good that even in the unfamiliar left-hand drive format that we were trying, the car's controls still took no special effort to locate and use, despite their partial reversal of position. If it wasn't for the stupid positioning of the switches for the front and rear screen heaters, the control arrangement would be beyond reproach.

The chance to start exploiting the potential of the car wasn't too long in coming; the twisting roads in the hills above Nice served perfectly as an evaluation route. Because the RS 2000-16v's suspension arrangement — itself the object of much praise amongst road testers of all persuasions — had been plundered almost wholesale to provide a suiable undercarriage for the new XR3i, it was no surprise to discover that the car was able to deal more than

ESCORT XR3i CABRIOLET

Previously confined to a maximum of 108 horsepower, the Cabriolet Escort is now available with both 105 and 130 b.h.p. variants of the Zeta engine, in both cases matched to the MTX-75 transaxle.

One of the worries we expressed was that the open-topped car would twist and shake a little too much for comfort when treated to a healthy extra chunk of muscle, and sampling the 130 version of the car justified our concern; whilst there is little scuttle shake from the car when on even roads and with the hood erected, pointing the car onto less-than-smooth mountain roads after the hood had been stowed away it was possible to watch the screen twist. Having said that, the car was still acceptably quiet in terms of squeaks and groans from the panels, even when pressing on in a businesslike manner.

In view of the amount of flexing which a Cabriolet variant of a monocoque design car inevitably must have, it came as no surprise to discover that the car was not quite as happy to follow the intended line when being pushed hard, but even so the car did not wander unnervingly — it simply skipped a little here and there when encountering a mid-bend pothole or lump on the road surface. The same package of suspension uprates and the excellent power steering rack have found their way across to the Karmann-built convertible Escort, and these combine to control what in the previous Escort would certainly have been considered excessive amounts of power. The car is quiet and refined, with precious little buffeting even when cruising at 160 k.p.h. on the French autoroute with the roof down and the winter sun warming the backs of our necks. I suspect that most Cabriolet purchasers will be quite content with the 105 b.h.p. engine — the car's marketplace is far more for those who wish to pose than for those who wish to pose a threat to society — but anybody wishing to acquire a 130 b.h.p. variant of the car will be pleased with its balance, poise and overall level of performance.

DENNIS FOY

The original XR3i was one of Ford's success stories, with sales accounting for some fourteen or fifteen per cent of Escort sales virtually from its creation almost a decade ago. It had, however, started to decline in the later years of the Mk IV Escort, no doubt because its dynamics and overall packaging were being eclipsed by other contenders in the same marketplace such as the Astra GT/E, Golf GTi, Peugeot 309 GTi, and a whole host of Japanese contenders. The faithful still bought XR3i models, but those more concerned with performance, handling and levels of trim and equipment were being tempted away from the Ford badge and towards other marques. When the time came to close the chapter on the Mk IV Escort range, the percentage of sales for which the XR3i accounted had slipped by several points — and it thus had already become apparent that when the equivalent model in the forthcoming Escort V range was announced, it would have to be something a little more special than its predecessor.

In a bid to hold onto at least some of the Ford owners whose XR3is were coming up for replacement when the new model of Escort was going on sale the company produced the 1.6S, a package which was essentially the engine and transaxle of the old XR3i dropped into a new Escort three-door hatchback body, and matched to a sporty set of springs and dampers. Meanwhile, work was going on in a big way behind the scenes, readying the *real* replacement model — the one you see on these pages.

Beneath the bonnet of the new car beats a Zeta engine, a powerplant which was originally destined to make its début in the new Escort and Orion model range which was launched in October 1990 at the British Motor Show. But things went awry with the timing, and it is only now, almost eighteen months later, that the two parts of the CE-14 development programme have meshed together as originally intended.

In a bid to gain insurance acceptance, the new engine is being made available in two different power outputs; XR3i buyers will be able to specify either 105 or 130 brake horsepower variants of the car. By doing this, Ford hope to be able to soften the blow of obtaining insurance — the hope is that the lower-powered car will be classified a little lower in the new listings which are at present being put together by British insurance companies. True to form, our first fling was with the one-thirty version of the car; we'd come back to the hundred and five model later in the day, once we had established just how satisfactory the rest of the package was …

Whilst still considered by some to be a little "dumpy", the overall styling of the new Escort has steadily gained acceptance, and in XR3i form with its extensive colour coding and spoilers, and a smart set of five spoke aluminium wheels shod in sixty-profile tyres it looks suitably sporty. For the purposes of the press evaluation programme, we had a choice of but one colour — black. Apparently when production examples start to filter through to showrooms (which ought to be any time now) the potential customer will have a far more comprehensive range of shades to select from; I suspect that Radiant Red will be the most favoured, followed by the lovely new metallic blue which is becoming available.

FORD PHOTOGRAPHIC UNIT

New seats, still made on the moulded plastic frame principle but featuring a much sportier level of design, are the first impression which greets the newcomer to the car. Providing a worthwhile bucket effect, with masses of lateral support on their squabs, the new seats follow the trend set by sports seat manufacturers such as Sparco in that they have wraparound "wings" at shoulder height; the effect is of sitting in the seat, and a good deal of sidewards support for the driver's torso is a welcome development.

Ford have made great play throughout their various presentations to the press of the fact that the Zeta engine has been designed for instantaneous starting, thanks to a totally new design of sequentially-controlled (via the ubiquitous EEC-IV engine management system) fuel injector rail. Sure enough, one twist of the key was sufficient to bring the 1796cc engine bursting into life. It immediately settles down to a smooth almost imperceptible tickover — it could be mistaken for a BMW unit in that respect.

In the XR3i (and in one or two other applications — more about that later) the engine is teamed with the MTX-75 transaxle, which is the front wheel drive version of the MT-75 inline gearbox. This has a final drive ratio of 3.82:1, an identical set of ratios to that found in the RS 2000-16v, ➤

PERFORMANCE

	0-62 MPH	MAX. SPEED	PRICE
XR3i — 130	9.3 secs	126 m.p.h.	£14,995
XR3i — 105	10.5 secs	117 m.p.h.	£14,295
Cabriolet — 130	9.3 secs	124 m.p.h.	£17,820
Cabriolet — 105	10.5 secs	117 m.p.h.	£16,420

Manufacturer's data: P.F. test figures not yet available.

adequately with virtually every bend into which it was aimed. The spring and damper rates vary slightly from those on the RS 2000-16v, but only slightly; the lighter weight of the Zeta engine when compared with the RS's 2.0 litre unit accounts for the alterations.

Also taken straight from the current brand leader in the Escort family is the wonderful power assisted steering rack. This is of variable rate, which means that whilst full assistance is provided at low speeds, the amount of aid given to the driver gradually disappears as road speeds increase. Excellent feedback to the thickish plastic rim of the XR3i's new three spoke steering wheel is a hallmark of the system. Likewise, the road wheel geometry rates of the RS model have cascaded down the range, and are to be found when measuring up the XR3i — hence steering turn-in pressures are identical in both models, and torque steer is all but eliminated.

At the rear of the car is to be found an anti-roll bar, and this enhances chassis sharpness by a pleasing amount, when the car is compared with, say, the late (and not much lamented) 1.6S. On particularly tight bends it is possible to get the inside rear wheel going light (a total break in tyre-to-road contact is achievable), but this does not detract from the sharpness of the cornering power; it simply proves that the torsion beam is doing its job. Body roll is there, but nicely under control — rising rate springing action is an effect of the rear beam.

The only thing which detracted from an otherwise excellent chassis was the choice of tyres on our initial test examples. These were Uniroyal 340s, a model of tyre which has already been rendered virtually obsolete by the

newer 440 model developed by Uniroyal over the last couple of years. The 340s would start to "sing" earlier than might reasonably be expected, and could be made to squeal like something off the soundtrack of an episode of Magnum P.I., or any other American detective series. Production models will be coming through with the usual choice of sixty-series tyres from makes such as Firestone, Goodyear and Pirelli, and also with the (favoured by S.V.E.) Michelin MXV, and apparently none of these other makes are anything like as prone to emulating the entrants in a movie car chase.

Those same tyres were, we suspect, equally responsible for the occasional "chirrup" when braking; the car did, on occasion, bring in its quick-responding anti-lock braking system a little too readily. Again, this is a problem which we were assured does not occur when a more modern tyre is used on the car. When asked why the XR3i was running on tyres which are a generation out of date, we were told that "the German engineers like them" ... Perhaps they have relatives in Hanover who were able to offer a good deal on a clearance lot of tyres!

The new one-thirty engine is a very impressive piece of hardware, with a smooth, even, power delivery right across its range. The unit has a pair of pleasantly sporting camshafts which endow it with a sense of urgency in the upper reaches of its speed range, and even in the territory beyond six thousand revs there is a meaningful and useable amount of power being delivered. There is a reasonable amount of noise coming from beneath the bonnet — Ford have deliberately engineered in an appreciable amount of induction roar, together with a sporting exhaust note — but this never becomes obtrusive or tuneless; the impression is that it sounds like it does because it is *supposed* to sound like that.

So what of the other, less powerful, variant?

Because it gives away twenty five brake horsepower, we expected the 105PS version of the engine to feel quite flat by comparison with its more powerful stablemate — and were thus very pleasantly surprised to discover that the ➤

SPECIFICATIONS

ENGINE TYPE
Transverse four cylinder, belt-driven dual overhead camshafts, four valves per cylinder
BORE x STROKE
80.6mm x 88mm
BHP @ RPM
130 @ 6,250 (105 @ 5,500 option)
TORQUE LB/FT @ RPM
120 @ 4,500 (113 @ 4,000 option)
FUEL SYSTEM
Ford EEC-IV electronic sequential injection
DRIVEN WHEELS
Front
TRANSMISSION
5-speed manual (3.23:1/2.136:1/1.484:1/1.114:1/0.854:1, 3.82:1 final drive
SUSPENSION, FRONT
Independent, MacPherson struts, L-shaped lower links, 16mm diameter anti-roll bar
SUSPENSION, REAR
Torsion beam axle, MacPherson struts, semi-trailing arms, 20mm diameter anti-roll bar
BRAKING SYSTEM
Ventilated 260mm front discs, 270mm solid rear discs, dual circuit, full servo assistance, optional Teves anti-lock braking
WHEELS AND TYRES
Aluminium alloy 14" x 6" wheels, 185/60/VR/14 tyres
WEIGHT
1,225 lbs
POWER/WEIGHT RATIO
119 b.h.p./ton (96 b.h.p./ton option)
WHEELBASE
99.4"
LENGTH
159"
WIDTH
66.6"
HEIGHT
55"
MANUFACTURER'S MPG
T.B.A.
INSURANCE GROUP
T.B.A.

XR3i ARRIVES

THE OTHER OPTIONS

As well as the new XR3i, the Zeta DOHC unit is being offered in a variety of other cars within the Escort and Orion family group. Both three and five door LX models of Escort, and the four door Orion LX gain the 105 engine (but with the older B5 transaxle, not the MTX-75), as also does the LX estate car. Ghia variants of Escort five door and estate gain a similar package of 105 Zeta and B5 gearbox, and the Ghia Orion also benefits from the new engine in 105 form.

The most exciting of the other new developments, though, is the 130 b.h.p. Ghia Si. This has the MTX transaxle, and combines the suspension package of the XR3i (with appropriate minor changes to the rear spring and damper rates, in order to compensate for the additional rear overhang) in the urbane Orion bodyshell. Trim is to Ghia specification, and a set of five spoke aluminium wheels are a part of the £14,100 package. We are expecting a test example in the near future, and will report on it at the earliest opportunity.

milder engine is, in fact, still able to deliver the sensations expected of a twin-cam, sixteen valve powerplant. True, it does start to feel a little flatter and more breathless at higher engine speeds, and at six thousand revs it was possible to feel the restrictions made by the catalytic converter, but in all other respects the engine is as sweet as a cup of tea with three spoonsful of Tate & Lyle in it.

In all other respects, the 105 b.h.p. XR3i is identical to its more powerful sibling — the same MTX-75 transaxle, the same suspension and braking system, the same trim and equipment, all aspects of the car are common to either engine. The only difference to be found is on the engine cam cover, where the power output is detailed in two inch high lettering.

The package is a pleasing one, with little to criticise. Its power delivery is smooth and progressive in either format, and both variants share a chassis which is every bit as good as that of the RS 2000-16v. The car can accelerate briskly, can stop quickly and foursquare (a slightly spongy pedal on anti-lock equipped cars fails to detract from the effectiveness of the brakes), and the car is well equipped. At just a fiver short of fifteen thousand pounds for the 130 version and £14,245 for the 105 b.h.p. version, it is no longer quite the bargain which the older XR3i was (at the point of going out of production the Mk IV's XR3i variant sold for £11,700), but then the newcomer is an awful lot more of a driver's car; the difference in price is more than adequately compensated for the first time that the car is aimed into a sequence of bends with a vengeance.

There will always be those who prefer to buy the RS version, and so the (deliberately) limited supplies of RS 2000-16v ought to still be able to find good homes. However, for £1,500 less, it is now possible to buy a car which offers most of what the RS 2000 can give, and with an altogether more pleasing engine into the bargain. And that £1,500 can compensate for the astronomical rises in insurance costs which are about to hit us here in Britain. ●

FIESTA BACK ON THE BOIL

Road testing the new 16 valve XR2i – and having some fun in the hills into the bargain ...

By Dennis Foy

The first thing which struck us about this car was its colour. A fabulously deep shade of metallic blue, the hue suited the car perfectly, offsetting the 14" x 6" five spoke aluminium alloy wheels. The second thing which struck us about it was just how lively the 105PS engine is when dropped into the compact Fiesta bodyshell. That, and the rattle from the exhaust system which caused a series of concerned expressions from onlookers during our tenure of the car ...

On first impressions the newest XR2i is not greatly different from its CVH-powered predecessor. But there is more to the car than simply a fresh engine which gives a broadly similar power output to the unit it has replaced. In addition to the new Zeta 1.8 twin overhead camshaft engine there have been a number of fine tuning detail changes made to the suspension system, with spring and damper rates being altered, along with the geometry angles. The steering rack, which is unassisted, is of the variable-input type which Ford developed some time ago in order to improve straight line stability without increasing the amount of input needed from the driver at parking speeds.

There is also now an anti-roll bar fitted to the rear of the car, and the twin-tube dampers of yore have been replaced by gas-filled units. These combine with the existing front anti-roll bar to endow the diminutive package with a level of grip and poise which is appreciably greater than might be expected of a car of this size.

On the way back from the photographic session (which was in deepest Derbyshire) we were blessed with a stretch of road which we know and love, the Cat & Fiddle Pass. Normally during the week this is densely populated with heavily laden trucks wending their way between Stockport and Buxton or vice-versa, but on this particular day him upstairs must have been smiling upon us (either that or everybody had found a transport café and stopped for lunch), because the road was almost deserted. This gave us a rare chance to run the little machine hard on some demanding bends, and to persuade it to show its mettle.

It did not disappoint.

Pushing hard on the roads through the Pass, the front pair of Pirelli P-700 Zero tyres occasionally scrabbled to gain traction, but for the most part they were able to bite deep onto the tarmac and transmit the power into forward motion in a most effective manner. Over enthusiasm, for which read going into a bend just that two miles an hour faster than is prudent, is met by a sudden lightening of the front wheels, but pile on the power and the car will drag itself back into shape and follow the intended line, albeit a touch raggedly. Touch the brakes at that point and you are searching out the number of the nearest bodyshop, because the car would lock up and slide. Unless, of course, you have had the foresight to order your new XR2i with anti-lock braking, in which case you might just get away with mounting the kerb or kissing a tree lightly, depending upon the immediate environment.

This is definitely one of those cars where the dividend for getting the braking over in a straight line is tidier handling; braking deep into the bend will have the nose running wide, with a resultant need to compensate for understeer before the apex of the bend is reached. To get away with such a manœuvre you will need a lot of room, and unnerve all occupants of the car, yourself included. Instead, get the braking over with the wheels still going straight ahead, get into the appropriate gear to suit road speed, and go for a "slow in, fast out" technique. The car will pay you back by responding neutrally. The revisions to the rear axle have gone a long way towards eliminating the rear-steer effect of which a number of XR2i drivers have complained, with the nett result that the car handles cleanly and sharply when treated with a light touch.

The torque spread of the engine is such that if the

FIESTA BACK ON THE BOIL

◄ driver miscalculates and is in one gear too high, there is sufficient power available to pull the car through tidily – even at 1,500 r.p.m. the Zeta 105 is producing 101 lb/ft, and by 2,500 it is producing 110 lb/ft. The peak torque of 112 lb/ft is achieved at 4,000 revs per minute.

It is the torque spread, rather than the nett flywheel horsepower, which makes this such a pleasant car to drive – the free-revving Zeta gives up its power willingly, although at 6,000 r.p.m., where the horsepower peak of 105 is reached, the engine falls off its powerband quite acutely. There is little or no point in pursuing the other thousand revs which are

available beyond that point because there is no power left to come.

Because the MTX-75 will not fit into the Fiesta floorpan the car comes with the familiar B5 transaxle, which means that existing Fiesta owners will have no need to get used to countering a rubbery shift pattern and the occasional wrong upshift. The range of ratios is good, although there is a hole between second and third, and the well chosen final drive gearing allows the driver to eke every last ounce of available performance from the car without too much difficulty.

That run on the Pass highlighted one problem area

which more, erm, enthusiastic drivers might find disconcerting. By the eighth or ninth sequential bend – and bear in mind speed on the straights was getting quite high – the brakes started to show signs of fading. We didn't push the car to the point of seeing how far we could go before we ran out of brakes completely, but were aware that it was taking increasing distances to achieve a similar rate of detardation. This is a side effect of the decision to retain drums, rather than fitting discs to the rear of the car. A set of M171 pads ought to compensate for the high level of heat which saps braking power.

On normal, regular roads rather than on demanding passes through the Peak District the brakes behaved superbly, arresting progress quickly and foursquare without any tendency towards weaving or darting. Nor does the nose weave and dart when accelerating hard, despite the absence of any kind of slip-limiting differential; the L-arm bottom links used by Ford on the Fiesta are good in the first place, and by the time that they have been treated to uprated "bobbins" and are aided by a substantial anti-roll bar, they become very good at controlling torque steer; when one brakes traction the other continues to track true. This applies equally, whether the road surface is wet or dry.

> *"Go for a 'slow in, fast out' technique; the car will pay you back by responding neutrally."*

At parking speeds the steering of the XR2i is ridiculously heavy, but this lightens once the car is on the move, and becomes pleasingly positive when cornering; turn in is precise and the castor action well-set to ensure a rapid return to the straight ahead.

Despite having aerodynamics like a housebrick (any gains made by having the sharply raked windscreen will have been cancelled by the slab-like front bumper/spoiler moulding), the car can manage to reach beyond 115 m.p.h., and at such speeds the car was feeling sure-footed, with lots of downforce holding the front wheels in firm contact with the test track surface. We achieved an overall 33.42 miles to every gallon of unleaded fuel, too, so that aerodynamics cannot be *that* bad.

Resistance to crosswinds is surprisingly good for such a small car, again presumably because of the downforces generated by the protruding bumper and the little over-screen rear spoiler. The bow-waves of trucks will cause a mild deviation from the straight ahead, but this is never so much that it becomes disconcerting, and the car seems impervious to all but the strongest of sidewinds on exposed sections of motorway.

One unforeseen side effect of the aerodynamics of

the XR2i which we noticed on several occasions when travelling with the windows open and the sunroof on tilt was that the exhaust fumes were being drawn back into the car. This seemed to happen at a speed of about 50 to 60 m.p.h., and was made obvious by the fact that [a] the inside of the car started to smell of rotten eggs (the sulphurous emissions of catalytic cars always smell like that ...), and [b] on two occasions there were no other cars in sight. Until we became convinced that it was the Fiesta which was generating the smell, we were blaming the nearest Volvo for it!

At all other times the XR2i's cabin is a pleasant enough space to spend time. Interior noise levels are not unreasonably high – the engine lets you know that it is working for its living thanks to the tailored-in induction and exhaust roar, but it never becomes intrusive; when in full cry the Zeta makes wonderful, proper twin cam noises. Wind noise levels are commendably low with the windows closed, even when the sunroof is tilted open. The car gives its occupants the impression of being in a larger machine thanks to its large glass area and low waistline, and the driver ergonomics are to Ford's usual standards.

The front seats, taken straight from the XR3i, are of the style favoured by Sparco, in that they wrap around the shoulders, and offer more width across the back than the Recaros favoured for the other new Fiesta, the RS1800. A leather-rimmed steering wheel with three spokes is standard issue, and the gearknob is similarly covered. Plenty of stowage for odds and sods (although nowhere specifically tailored for cassettes) is provided, and the standard stereo system is the Ford 2006. This latter item is a good piece of hardware, having Ford's excellent RDS auto-tuning system, auto-reverse tape deck, Dolby NRS and so forth, but is let down by the tiny speakers of the Fiesta. These are unable to handle much of a dynamic range, with the result that tapes carrying a broad sound spectrum end up being interrupted by "cannon fire". We can foresee a lot of Fiesta owners installing more substantial speakers into their cars.

The level of equipment to the XR2i is reasonable, without being too extravagant; the sunroof is of the tilt or remove type (which means that open-roof driving must be pre-planned, because it cannot be slid open whilst the car is in motion). It is similarly advisable to ensure that the mirrors are perfectly aligned before setting out on a journey, because their remote levers are manually operated, and rather clumsy in actuation. A quartet of additional driving lamps, the five spoke cast aluminium alloy wheels and a rear wash/wipe facility join tinted glass and central locking as standard features, but the Hotscreen and ABS are optional extras at £144 and £481 respectively. Which means that the price of a fully loaded XR2i like the one you see on these pages is a substantial £12,158 plus the usual delivery charges, number plates and such. However, the way that the market is at present it ought to be feasible to put one on the road for under eleven thousand pounds once the initial rush of orders has died away.

On balance we rather like the XR2i, but feel that the equipment levels are a little on the mean side and that build quality still leaves room for improvement; a rattling exhaust system and a not terribly impressive paint finish should not be a feature of a new Ford in the '90s. ●

FORD PHOTOGRAPHIC UNIT

SO WHICH ONE?

Are Ford being economical with the truth? Both of the new Fiestas, the XR2i and the RS1800, share a common driveline which starts with the all-new Zeta engine, rolls on to the B5 transaxle, thence to uprated suspension settings, disc/drum braking, and similar aluminium wheels with 185/60 x 14 Pirelli P700-Zero tyres. The difference between the two models (which are priced almost £1,200 apart) is accounted for by the fact that the RS1800 claims an additional 25 brake horsepower over its sibling.

Whilst both of the Zeta engines are of the same 1796cc capacity, that in the RS1800 is rated at 130PS, whilst the XR2i is given the detuned 105PS version. Yet trying the cars out back to back seems to contradict the fact that the RS1800 has almost a quarter as much power again as the XR2i. The difference in overall performance between the two cars – especially where it most counts, on twisting country lanes – is virtually indistinguishable, with both cars displaying a similar levels of urgency as they attack the task in hand. On motorways the additional top-end power of the 130 unit makes itself apparent, but only when the car is being stretched.

Given a free choice between the two models we would plump for the XR2i every time, feeling that its overall balance is better, and more suited to the rôle it plays. It isn't that the RS1800 is a bad car – simply that in our opinion the XR2i is better. Furthermore, we would always have the option to upgrade the 105PS engine to 130 specification for less than the £1,200 difference in price ...

Afterword

So what does the future hold for the XR brand of Ford?

Plans for the immediate future are for a further revitalisation of the Fiesta XR2i — it has already gained a new engine, the 105bhp version of the new Zeta dual camshaft, sixteen-valve powerplant which is also to be found in the XR3i. Whilst this technically means that the power output of the Fiesta has dropped by five brake horsepower, in real terms it results in a still livelier car with improvements to both cabin comfort and fuel economy. It will also be relatively simple to upgrade the power level to that of the other Zeta 1.8 engine — the additional 25 brake horses of that powerplant are achieved by a different pair of camshafts, a bigger-bore throttle body, and changes to the engine management system and its ancillaries.

Early in 1993 there are further improvements scheduled for the XR2i, when it gains the new power steering system which is being developed at the time of writing. A variation on that already found in the XR3i Escort, the power assistance system will finally bring to an end the parking hassles which beset XR2i owners.

As for the XR3i, whilst this is at present badged with the same plaques regardless of power output, the word is that Ford will be changing that in the very near future so that the specific power outputs are detailed outside the car. Then there are the 4x4 variations on the theme which are still to come… These will coincide with a facelift to the entire Escort range for the 1993 model year, intended to align the model range more closely with the Sierra replacement which is due in the spring of 1993.

The XR3i makes use of the all-new MTX-75 transaxle, a transverse application of the same technology already to be found in most of the inline-engined Ford car range. When developing the transaxle, Ford's design engineers also made provision for an additional power take-off which will allow the rear wheels to receive a share of the available power. This car will differ from the 4x4 Sierra in that the driveline bias will be towards the front wheels, in much the same manner as the Lancia Delta Integrale. The XR3i 4x4, which will use the 130bhp Zeta engine as the standard powerplant, promises to be a stimulating car to drive.

It is also looking increasingly likely that there will be an XR version of the new Sierra replacement when that range sweeps in with the spring of 1993: there will be mundane Sierras and there will be a Cosworth-powered version, so the chances of the XR tag being carried over to the newcomer are very high. As with the existing XR4x4, it is likely that the car will be a sporty performer with acceleration and top speed abilities somewhere in between those of the mainstream models and the 220bhp RS Cosworth model. Also high are the chances of that car taking a few months longer than the rest of the range to put in an appearance…

The two model ranges in the Ford family which are unlikely ever to feature XR derivatives are the Orion and the Scorpio/Granada: in both cases, the use of the XR label is considered inappropriate by Ford. This is understandable, since both cars are aimed at a more serious, less sporting saloon-minded market.

I cannot honestly subscribe to Ford's corporate theory on that, but what I can subscribe to is the theory that there will always be a place in the hearts of Europe's drivers for cars which offer the package of fun, affordability and driveability that the XR models represent. We have all learned to recognise what that is, even if we don't know what the letters XR stand for!